WHORES

Why and How I Came
To Fight the Establishment

WITHDRAWAL

Also by Larry Klayman

Fatal Neglect

WHORES

WHY AND HOW I CAME
TO FIGHT THE ESTABLISHMENT

LARRY KLAYMAN

FOUNDER OF JUDICIAL WATCH
AND FREEDOM WATCH

New Chapter
Publisher

 Published by New Chapter Publisher

WHORES
WHY AND HOW I CAME TO FIGHT THE ESTABLISHMENT

ISBN 978-0-9792012-2-6

For information, address and editorial inquiries, please contact

New Chapter Publisher
1765 Ringling Blvd, Ste. 300
Sarasota, FL 34236

Library of Congress Cataloging-in-Publication Data has been applied for.

FIRST EDITION

Cover and layout by Shaw Creative, www.shawcreativegroup.com

printed in the United States

This book is dedicated:

To my grandparents,
Isadore and Freda Klayman and Yetta Goldberg,
who tried to teach me the meaning of honesty
and hard work, and whose unwavering belief in God,
goodness and family influenced me greatly.

My inspiration to carry on in their memory
is reinforced by my children Isabelle, named
after Isadore, and Lance, named after me.
In the Jewish tradition, I was named
after my other grandfather, Louis,
who died before I was born.

To Alice Alyse,
the "American Ballerina,"
who set me free from the recent past
and showed me the future.

To my mother, Shirley Klayman,
who died of Alzheimer's last year.

To my father, Herman Klayman,
for his enduring optimism.

And last, but not least, to
Laura Termini for her faith
and passionate love of life.

The main reason Larry Klayman is exasperating to many people across the political spectrum is that he ignores the rules of partisan combat that define Washington. Many political observers have come to realize that Klayman is impossible to sway, because he seeks no Establishment credentials, and has none to protect.

—National Journal, June 29, 2002

ACKNOWLEDGMENTS

I would like to thank Piero Rivolta for having the courage to publish this book, as well as his fine staff, including Chris Angermann, who was of tremendous help in editing the final edition, and Sonia Velasco and Vanessa Houston who also assisted in the project.

I want to thank my good friend, Pino Cignarella, for being an inspiration. Also, I am appreciative to Judith Regan for having initially had the vision to support this book and to Mike Ruby who did initial editing of the manuscript.

A very special thanks goes to Louise Benson, who has been like a mother to me.

None of my experiences would have been possible without the support of my clients and the American people, as well as my staff and the regional directors, previously at Judicial Watch and now Freedom Watch, including Russ Verney, Sandra Cobas, Mike Pendletonand John Vincent, as well as my secretary, Kristen Pons.

Finally, I want to thank all the federal judges and lawyers who pushed me to the point of becoming a legal revolutionary.

Contents

Foreword

I decided in the 1970s to leave my country of origin, Italy, and the thriving city of Milano, where I had a beautiful home and business, only for one reason: to find a place where I would have the freedom to prove myself and not have to deal with government interference, political pressure and other similar nonsense. I used to joke with my new American friends, calling myself a 20th-century pilgrim. Like the original Mayflower passengers, I even arrived from Europe in my own sailboat.

I knew many parts of the world quite well, having worked in a number of countries to keep my business in Italy going, but my wife and I decided that our new country could only be the United States. And so we moved here. Although it was a difficult new beginning, we liked it and decided to become Americans.

After a career of building and designing cars, operating a horse farm, and sailing thousands of miles around the world, I all but started over by designing and constructing large-scale real estate projects, building sailboats and motoryachts, and spending my free time promoting a classical music festival.

In 2007, I started a small publishing company called New Chapter Publisher. Part of the decision was personal—my busy, sometimes chaotic life had been dotted with decisions dictated by the joy of trying something new, and I have always tried to fulfill my original passion, which is writing poetry and poetic novels. I had already produced a few books with different publishers, but it became clear to me that there was a need for a publishing corporation that is committed to authors and their books. If you want to examine how recurring and unchanging aspects of the human condition manifest themselves in particular historical periods, you and your publisher better be in it together for the long haul.

For me, one of the important aspects of humanity is its desire for freedom, but I have always believed that freedom is not only a right, but a duty—a duty that includes respecting your obligations, contributing to the well-being of society and, eventually, trying to be an amabassador of love. The world of today speaks of freedom of speech, but in the meantime, because politically correct people control the flow of information, we are exposed only to their version of the facts. I see a lot of similarities to the Dark Ages of medieval times, when churches and the aristocracy tried to impose a way of life and system of beliefs. However, I am still convinced that a new renaissance can occur here in the United States, although it would be very different from what we are experiencing now.

For this reason, New Chapter Publisher and I have agreed to publish *Whores*, a book that passionately argues for much-needed change in our legal and political systems. While we may not share all of Mr. Klayman's views, we want people to know what he has to say and give them the opportunity to make up their own minds.

In these trying times, we need to encourage candid and creative thought for the good of the nation, since much of the country, in the aftermath of September 11, seems to be in a mood to simply follow the partisan and populist policies of its confused leaders as abetted by the media. I believe that *Whores* is the kind of cutting-edge book that will wake people up, provoke important thought and dialogue.

Whores was supposed to be published by HarperCollins, a large publishing company that ultimately refused to do so because of its potentially controversial content. Even *The New York Times* criticized this decision. Today we see so many people eager to judge and dismiss opinions that don't square with their ideological beliefs in the newspapers, on radio and television, and on the Internet.

We don't judge, we publish. You be your own judge.

— *Piero Rivolta*
New Chapter Publisher
July 2009

Prologue

In the fall of 2008, Googling my name—which I do from time to time to see what is "out there"—I came upon an advertisement on Towerbooks.com selling my book *Whores*. I later checked Amazon.com and Borders.com only to find the same advertisement, announcing a publication date of December 30, 2008, just a few months away. I was surprised because HarperCollins had put the book on hold after the Judith Regan fiasco over the O.J. Simpson biography. With glee, thinking that Harper had finally seen the light, I notified friends that my book was coming out. I even added a link for book sales to Freedom Watch's Internet site, www.freedomwatchusa.org, so our supporters could buy a copy. Indeed, many of them did so and I was pleased.

But when I did not hear from Harper and wrote to see when the book tour would happen, and the media appearances would be scheduled, I received a letter indicating that the book had been cancelled. Incredulous, I e-mailed Harper's head lawyer and demanded an explanation, but was stiff-armed—basically told to buzz off. I then threatened legal action, but got no positive response. I could only guess that Rupert Murdoch, the owner of HarperCollins, had killed the book ex post facto, as had happened with the book by the former governor of Hong Kong, Chris Patten, as widely reported in the media at the time. Given my criticism of his network, Fox News, and my pending lawsuit against him for illegally firing *New York Post* reporter Jared Stern, I figured he had something to do with pulling the plug. At the time, Fox News also had a suit being tried before federal judge Denny Chin, and my criticism of the judge in a book published by a sister company of Fox might not sit well with him. In any case, Murdoch and Harper had apparently decided that *Whores* was too hot to handle.

But what made matters worse was that Harper had used the publicity my name would generate to fraudulently sell the book. The buyers had not even been informed of the subterfuge, nor had their money been returned to them.

I will sue Harper and Murdoch at a time and place of my choosing, as they have damaged my reputation and defrauded the public.

For more than two years, my book has existed in limbo and as a ghostly entry on Internet websites. But now, thanks to New Chapter Publisher, *Whores* will finally see the light of day and reveal not only the corrupt behavior of the Washington establishment, but the sleaziness of my own former publisher, now the largest, most powerful media tycoon on the planet.

— *Larry Klayman*
Los Angeles, California
May 2009

How the faithful city
   has become a whore!
   She that was full of justice,
   righteousness lodged in her—
   but now murderers!
Your silver has become dross,
   your wine is mixed with water.
Your princes are rebels
   and companions of thieves.
Everyone loves a bribe
   and runs after gifts.
They do not defend the orphan,
   and the widow's cause does not
   come before them.

Therefore says the Sovereign, the Lord of hosts,
   the Mighty one of Israel:
Ah, I will pour out my wrath on my enemies,
   and avenge myself on my foes!
I will turn my hand against you;
   I will smelt away your dross as with lye
   and remove all your alloy.
And I will restore your judges as at the first,
   and your counselors as at the beginning.
Afterward you shall be called
   the city of righteousness,
   the faithful city.

—Isaiah 1:21-26

Introduction

When I lived and worked in Washington, D.C., there was an area around 14th Street known for its lively trade of the world's oldest profession. Hookers all but lined the sidewalks and openly solicited business throughout the day and night. In time, it got a lot of people upset. There were even newspaper editorials and speeches by politicians decrying the decay in morality in our nation's capital. As the chorus of outrage swelled, the city fathers decided to take action. In a widely publicized raid, the cops rounded up all the whores and herded them across the 14th Street bridge in Virginia. That action spoke volumes about the American way of dealing with problems by relocating them, and it didn't work. The ladies of the night like disobedient cats turned around and sashayed right back over the bridge. Before long, it was business as usual—the whores will always find a way to come back.

I have never engaged the services of a prostitute, but I have encountered a lot of whores during my career—people and interests that will sell out their nation, if not their family, for money, power and fame. Unfortunately, such people exist at the highest level of all three branches of our government, as well as in the media, which all too often enables their whorish behavior. If the last three administrations in Washington have demonstrated nothing else, it is that without an independent, outside force checking the worst tendencies and abuses, our government may be "by the people," but it certainly isn't "for the people."

I have always been the outsider ready to take on the insiders—those appointed to public office or, worse, the people elected to public office who violated the trust their fellow citizens had vested in them. The experience of several years working at the U.S. Department of Justice as a young attorney actually reinforced my belief that an assault on political corruption and dishonesty had to originate from outside the government. My chronological peers—the baby boomers—were coming into power, the elites of their generation, and too many of them were proving to be a national embarrassment. What was needed, I increasingly thought, was a private attorney general.

In 1994, I founded Judicial Watch, the nonprofit, equal-opportunity watchdog group that became what I envisioned—and much more. We took on the Clintons over their fund-raising scandals. We broke the "Chinagate" affair, centered in the U.S. Commerce Department, wide open. On the other side of the aisle, we battled House Speaker Newt Gingrich and sued the vice president of the United States, Dick Cheney, to gain access to information on his energy task force that rightly belonged in the public domain. By being the aggressive outsider, Judicial Watch found itself at the center of American political life—an unofficial brake on abuse by the three branches of government. Through it all, I nurtured, coddled, disciplined and developed what I came to think of as my baby into a major force for honesty and good.

In the process, I became a public figure and a darling of the conservative movement—the adopted son flattered by all the attention and a bit dazzled by it, too. The attention was a mixed blessing. It took a painful toll on my marriage and, in the spring of 2003, my wife Stephanie and I decided to separate. The decision was difficult; we had two young children—Isabelle, age 5, and Lance, age 3—and I loved them dearly. There were other factors, of course, but from Stephanie's perspective, the major issue probably concerned the constraints imposed by the security required to guard a public figure's family. It was too much for her to handle. We were constantly threatened, and the kids even had to have security detail take them to school. There were many days when Stephanie would not even talk to me. We had grown far apart and hadn't had a substantive conversation in years. We no longer had anything but the children in common.

Over the next three years, my life took some strange turns. In a sense, you could say I was wandering in the wilderness. After the separation, I moved back to Florida, where I'd lived earlier. The Sunshine State was my home, and I often dreamed that someday I might run for office there. In fact, I did run, as a Republican for the open U.S. Senate seat in 2004, in a strange odyssey that taught me more about politics than I ever knew, or even wanted to know. An old friend and political consultant, Scott Reed, had enthusiastically believed I could win, but Scott was wrong: I couldn't win, not given the twists and turns on the Florida campaign trail—a journey of exhilaration and betrayal that I will describe in some detail later in this book. When it finally ended for me in the late summer of 2004, I no longer was dazzled; I was simply dazed, a fighter who suddenly realized that his "friends"—in my case, many of those good conservatives who had once helped me—had disappeared, in part because they didn't want to cross a White House that was central to their prestige and fund-raising efforts. I was down, but I knew that I'd come back. There was still a flicker of that old spark inside of me.

Still, it seemed as if I'd lost my way. I returned to private practice, first with the firm of Walker & Haverfield in Cleveland, Stephanie's hometown and the city where she settled with the children after the divorce. They were good people at Walker & Haverfield, which I joined as a partner in charge of international trade and regulation in the litigation section, but they hadn't counted on what they eventually must have regarded as a crusader in their midst. It was the summer of 2005, and there was big judicial news coming out of Washington with the nomination of John G. Roberts, Jr. to the U.S. Supreme Court—first to replace the retiring Associate Justice Sandra Day O'Connor, then to become chief justice after William Rehnquist's death. Because of my national profile, I got calls for comment and analysis from the local media, which I provided. This was, I thought, one of the reasons W&H wanted me on board. But partners of the firm who had lived in Cleveland all their lives clearly felt eclipsed whenever they saw my face on television. Still, nothing explicit was said and they were polite enough initially to remain silent.

However, when I started to propose the sort of work Judicial Watch did, particularly defending those with legitimate grievances against government power, they began to get nervous. I had brought a couple of pending cases with me, which raised some eyebrows, but what really soured my relationship with Walker & Haverfield was a hysterical e-mail from managing partner Ralph Cascarilla on New Year's Eve 2005, demanding to know whether I intended to sue the president of the United States.

In fact, I was thinking about doing just that on behalf of a former congressional aide, Scott Tooley, who was convinced that he was on a terrorist watch list and that the government was keeping track of him by using illegal wiretaps and tracking devices. Scott and I had discussed his situation and the possibility that it could be a landmark lawsuit. But how could Walker & Haverfield know about that? Had they been monitoring my e-mail?

It was the last straw for me. We parted company officially on February 1, 2006, and I filed a federal lawsuit on Scott Tooley's behalf 16 days later. In many ways, I felt as if I had escaped from behind an iron curtain and rediscovered what it meant to have the freedom to be myself again. I felt reborn and stronger than before.

The Tooley case, which continues to this day, went directly to abuses of power—this time, by an administration that colored itself conservative but too often behaved as if the Constitution is an inconvenience to be sidestepped or even ignored. It's no wonder the Republicans experienced a resounding defeat in the 2008 elections, pushing the country to the far left under the new Obama regime as a reaction to years of Bush-Cheney bungling, economic incompetence and arrogance. Bush and Cheney did more to pave the way for Obama's push toward socialism than Marx, Lenin, Stalin and Mao Tse-tung could have ever dreamed or hoped for.

So-called conservatives distrust government to deal with social problems, but they seem to think anything goes when it comes to the military and police powers; liberals, of course, tend to be the polar opposites. What I realized once again is that each issue has to be evaluated in the context of certain basic truths and principles laid down in the Constitution. It isn't a matter of left or right, Democrat or Republican. The country was in severe crisis, with fundamental privacy rights threatened and rampant political corruption. I was ready to pick up the mantle of crusader again, and I knew exactly where I needed to begin.

Judicial Watch was in trouble, and I partly blamed myself because I had hired and left in charge a man whose actions had put it in jeopardy. Tom Fitton, Judicial Watch's president, had misrepresented his background to me and, over the two-plus years since I had departed to run for the Senate, sent out false and misleading fund-raising letters, misused donor money and disparaged me. When I left, Judicial Watch was resting on financial bedrock; in little more than two years, Fitton and his friends had chiseled away that foundation to the point where its continued existence was at issue.

But when it came to taking legal action, I hesitated to pull the trigger. I had once sued my very own mother on a matter of principle involving the health and safety of one of my grandparents. I had sued members of my own political party on matters of principle as well. Judicial Watch was more than an organization— it was a living and breathing thing; it was my baby. Could I really sue my own child? It took a chance meeting and subsequent friendship to stiffen my spine and push me to set things straight.

In late 2005, Alice Alyse walked into Houston's restaurant in Coral Gables, Florida, with a female friend. I was there having dinner at the bar, and as I got up to leave, I told them that I'd offer my seat to two beautiful women. They both smiled and Alice's friend, Michelle, took my chair. For some reason, I felt that I had to stay. Alice sat down at my left and—I don't know why—I just knew she was a dancer. I asked her whether she was and she said yes. "Are you a ballerina?" Again her answer was yes. She said that she had been starring in "Movin' Out," the hit Broadway show based on Billy Joel's music, but had been injured and was recuperating in Miami, where she owned a condominium on Biscayne Bay.

A few days later, we met over dinner. The story she told me that evening filled me with anger about what had happened to this world-class actress and ballerina. Alice had been sexually harassed by the production manager of the national touring company and felt her career was in danger. She was right about that. Soon, her world would be turned upside down by powerful producers who ignored her charges of sexual harassment and then dismissed her because she would not agree to release them from liability as a precondition to returning to the show. A few months later, I filed a huge lawsuit on her behalf against choreographer Twyla Tharp and the billionaire owners behind "Movin' Out." But shortly before I did, this exceptional woman sat me down and read me the riot act.

"I've only known you a few months," I recall her saying serioiusly, "but based on what I have seen, I think you've lost some of your confidence." Some of my concerns about Judicial Watch had become familiar to Alice because I had confided in her. Now, she was telling me that I had to stop talking and act, that I had to take on Judicial Watch in court. "You've got to be fearless, Larry," she said. "I admire you, and you've got to be Larry Klayman, not only for yourself but for me." Alice and I had become good friends. I knew that she trusted me with her life and because of this, her words that day rang true far beyond saving Judicial Watch.

Two weeks later, on April 13, 2006, I brought suit in federal court against the organization I had created, nurtured and loved over a decade of hard work on the public's behalf.

In the meantime, I had started another watch-dog organization: Freedom Watch.

For much of my career I have been dealing with American politics from an outsider's perspective, but my experience in running for the U.S. Senate taught me that the other side of the looking glass is even worse than I had imagined. There remains much to be done in cleaning up our tarnished and corrupt political system. Ronald Reagan's dream of a shining city on the hill is still just that, a dream. The Washington establishment's power, furthered by an often complicit elitist press, must be reined in if this country is to survive. As for me, I'm not through yet. My work this year has refocused my energies on what is really important—including much greater transparency in government. To borrow from President Reagan, I intend to be part of the solution, not part of the problem—and I intend to do it by staying true to the principles of honesty and integrity that have been part of my DNA from my earliest days growing up in Philadelphia. As I learned then, you can't run away from a fight. To the contrary: You've got to take on the bad guys.

1

RAISED TO FIGHT

I was born on July 20, 1951, 25 years to the day from when my father, Herman, was born. Like his father, Isadore, who was smuggled out of Ukraine by my great-grandfather shortly after the Bolsheviks seized power in 1917, my dad became a meat packer. As a young boy, during summers and holidays, I proudly worked in his slaughterhouse in Philadelphia, first pulling fat from the entrails of hogs in a sweltering side room by the killing room floor, later throwing loins onto conveyor belts and, finally, becoming a full-fledged "teenage" butcher.

During lunchtime breaks, Isadore would take me to Horn & Hardart's restaurant on Cottman Avenue and tell me how he spoke to God and sought his guidance every day. Many years earlier, when my father was overseas during World War II, Isadore had suffered one of many nervous breakdowns. Unlike other butchers in South Philadelphia, he refused to circumvent President Roosevelt's meat quotas and would not sell his products on the black market. While his friends and competitors became rich, my grandfather did not. Instead, the pressures of the times ate away at him; he drank, smoked and had nervous breakdowns. My grandfather told me that as he lay in bed, with the doctors predicting that he would not live until morning, God spoke to him and said, "Izzy, I want you to live and start a big pork packing plant." So my grandfather lived and, from that day forward, stopped smoking and drinking. And he imparted his faith to his grandson.

Isadore was born Jewish. But when he passed through Ellis Island on his way to America, the immigration officers asked him his birthday. Not knowing— young Ukrainians were rarely told the date of their birth—he answered, "Give me Christmas; if it's good enough for Christ, it's good enough for me!" My grandfather told me that he believed Christ was the son of God. He saw no inconsistency between Judaism and the Christian faith. At one time, he had

1

wanted to be a rabbi, but after that talk with God, he said, he decided to devote his life to pork, despite the fact that it wasn't kosher, although he never ate it himself.

His father, my great-grandfather, was a gambler, who lost all his money and hung himself in a closet, rather than face his family. Isadore was the one who found him and cut him down. Still, Isadore could not break the family gambling tradition. He played cards, went to the track and generally lost whatever he wagered. This scared my grandmother, Freda, who had found her way to America from Ukraine via Argentina. She would assiduously remove money from Isadore's wallet to save for her family's future. She too was the salt of the earth, and she had a sense of humor to go with it. Having lived through tough times with Isadore, Freda was the rock of the Klayman family, working side by side with her husband.

My other grandmother, Yetta, came from Poland. Her husband, Louis, a Lithuanian immigrant and a socialist, died when she was 40; the two of them had only one child, my mother, Shirley. Yetta clung to my mother and came to live with her when my mother married my dad. When I was very young, I often dreamed of the Wicked Witch of the West from "The Wizard of Oz." I would awaken and go screaming from my room and crawl into my grandmother's bed. It was Yetta who raised me. She was a dress saleswoman on Chestnut Street. Inwardly religious, she never wore her faith on her sleeve. Like Isadore and Freda, family and honesty were everything to her.

My grandparents imparted their values to my parents, who never quite seemed to rise to the occasion. Perhaps it was the pressure of the post-World War II era, perhaps it was their rocky marriage; I never knew for certain. What I did know, or sensed, was that my guiding stars would always be my grandparents, even if living up to their high standards was difficult. I still think of them each and every day. Isadore, Freda and Yetta were hardened by the tragic events that beset their generation, but they never lost sight of their humanity.

My first few years were spent in Northeast Philadelphia, but my parents moved to Greenhill Farms in Overbrook Park when I was three. While not quite as rough and tumble as downtown Philly, it was tough enough. I went to Lamberton Elementary School, where I was often picked on by bullies. Waiting for me when I got off the bus, they would throw my books in dog doo, then beat the crap out of me. I can still remember the name of the ringleader, little

Johnnie Weisswasser. Seeing me bruised and bloodied on several occasions, my dad finally warned me: "Son, come home beaten up one more time and I'll beat you up when you get here!" I got the message: Learn to fight or perish. So the meatpacker's son got boxing lessons from his dad and learned the art of self-defense. And the bullies learned their lesson and left me alone.

When I was eight, we moved up in class to Main Line, a trendy and nouveau riche suburb of Philadelphia, where the kids were a lot softer, and for a while there, I seemed to morph into my old nemesis, Johnnie Weisswasser—not so much a bully, though, just the toughest kid in school.

Still, there was another side of me. My mother told me that if too much change was returned when she bought something from a vending machine, I would cry until she put the excess coins back into the machine. I was Mr. Honest, but I also had more than my fair share of neuroses. I needed certainty and order in my young life. I refused to play with toys that had springs because I knew that the springs would ultimately break. I would only wear solid-colored shirts; the commotion of plaids or stripes was unsettling. I once asked my dad to cut off all the fringe on my Davy Crockett outfit, because I found the fluttering unnerving.

Perhaps it was this fixation on rocklike certainty and the need for solid rules that made the law so appealing. Or maybe it was the influence of my Uncle Mike, the husband of my father's sister, Aunt Gloria, who, from my early years, pushed me in that direction. The wise guy of the family, Uncle Mike would always say, "Become a lawyer, it's a license to steal!" I would later think of it as a license to change the world.

I was a teenager for most of America's involvement in Vietnam. I always supported the war, but I never really thought about why. Most of my friends were against it, and I guess that in retrospect, you could say they were liberals. Their Jewish parents certainly were. But from the days of Johnnie Weisswasser, I had learned that you don't give in to bullies. Watching President Johnson talk about the war on television, I saw the Communist Vietnamese as bullies and instinctively sided with our government against them. After all, my grandparents had fled communism. I trusted our government then, particularly after President Kennedy had "saved us" during the Cuban missile crisis. At the time, I did not know how our government had actually sold out both the Cuban and American people by cutting an under-the-table deal to leave the Communist dictator Fidel Castro in power.

While many of my liberal friends went to the University of Pennsylvania, an Ivy League campus filled with long-haired, pot-smoking antiwar radicals, I took a different route. With my conservative bent, I was lucky to be accepted at Duke University, a genteel Southern school with a golf course and warm weather. But my early days on Duke's North Carolina campus were not easy. I was the only Jewish kid in the freshman house and my Christian brothers—most of whom had never met a Jew—nicknamed me "Seemy," short for "The Semite." When I was rushed by a Christian fraternity, and the upperclassmen learned of my background, they told me to go to Zeta Beta Tau, a Jewish fraternity across the quad. I refused, not wanting to be part of any exclusive group. The scene at Duke bothered me a lot, and I asked my dad to let me transfer to Yale, where there were no fraternities. He said no and told me to deal with it—again, not to give in to the bullies, whether they were fighting with fists or playing mind games.

It was ironic that I was subjected to anti-Semitism because my mind was pretty open in religious matters. When I was in Hebrew school as a young boy, I would challenge the teachers for not talking about Christ, a Jew: "If he wasn't the son of God," I said, "then why did the whole world come to believe in him?" Aghast at my brashness and nonconformity, my angry instructors responded with stony silence and poor grades.

During my junior year, I left Duke for a semester abroad—a program sponsored by Vanderbilt University in Aix-en-Provence. The French excursion fit nicely into Western European studies as part of my political science major, but I had never been very good at the language; in high school, the girls made fun of me when I spoke French. I kept at it, however, because I refused to admit to any shortcomings and simply give in. This became a recurrent theme in my life: The things that threw me at first I later mastered. I simply hated to fail at anything. By the time I graduated from Duke, with honors, I was fluent in French and had become heavily influenced by French literature, especially Moliere, Rousseau and Voltaire.

I also took many courses on religion at Duke. Considering the discrimination I experienced as a freshman, I figured I better learn about my Jewish roots. Nevertheless, throughout this period, I had many Christian friends and a Catholic girlfriend, and gravitated to the "other" religion. I took courses in the Old and New Testaments, Renaissance art and Christianity, all the time wearing a Star of David around my neck. I was the kosher pork packer's grandson.

4

During the 1968 presidential campaign, Richard Nixon had promised to end the fighting in Vietnam. But the war raged on while I was at Duke. Nixon promised again during his 1972 reelection campaign, when I cast my first ballot for president by voting for him. During my college years, I never really thought about the possibility of being drafted; I didn't struggle with what I would do if it happened because I knew I would go if called up. My lottery number was 120, well under the previous year's limit; it was likely that I would get drafted. But Nixon ended the draft in 1973, the year I graduated with plans to go on to law school.

But God had other things in mind for me. Despite having graduated sixth in my class in high school and with honors in college, I never was very good at taking standardized multiple-choice tests. During the Law School Admission Test (LSAT), I basically choked. My poor score did not qualify for a top-tier institution, so I decided to take a year off and work in Washington, D.C., despite having been accepted at the prestigious London School of Economics in its European Studies program. Perhaps it was a harbinger of my future professional legal career that on the day I graduated from Duke as an underclassman, standing on the main quad with me receiving his Duke degree in law was one Kenneth W. Starr. I did not know Starr at Duke, but our paths certainly crossed again years later during the Clinton years.

In Washington, I found a job working as an aide to Republican U.S. Senator Richard Schweiker of Pennsylvania, a liberal who opposed our continued involvement in Vietnam. Schweiker also was a harsh early critic of Nixon's conduct in Watergate, a third-rate burglary of the Democratic National Committee that, thanks to the president's cover-up and deceit, turned into what at the time was the biggest scandal in modern American history. As the office gofer—I would take the senator his coffee, make deliveries and open and sign his constituent mail with an "auto-pen"—I was working just down the hallway from a young staff lawyer on the joint congressional committee investigating Watergate. Her name was Hillary Clinton. She and I also were destined to cross paths again.

Schweiker was generally an honest and decent man, but I was sickened at having to sign form letters to constituents. There were sometimes as many as six versions, reflecting a range of positions from left to right, on any one subject— the war, abortion, Watergate and more. It was quite an offensive awakening for me about the backstage realities of politics. So was the time I opened an envelope to find a large campaign check from Rockwell International, which was quickly snatched from my hands by my mail-room supervisor. I hoped it wouldn't go into the senator's coffers, because even then, I knew that corporate contributions were improper.

Enough of the U.S. Senate, I thought, vowing then never to become a politician. Resetting my sights on law school, I did just fine on my second go at the LSAT and gained admission to Emory University School of Law in Atlanta. Later, while I was still in law school, Senator Schweiker had a miraculous conversion, became a conservative and ran in primaries in 1976 as Ronald Reagan's first pick for vice president. I found the ideological flexibil-ity breathtaking, but at that point I can't say that I was really surprised.

2

A CAREER'S
UNCERTAIN BEGINNING

During law school I focused on my goal of becoming an international lawyer to the exclusion of all else. Reverting to my high school days, I worked night and day. I had little social life, and my comrades joked that I lived in the law library. I took things, then as now, too seriously. I graduated with a respectable B average, but my guess is that loosening up a bit would have yielded better grades.

When I left Emory, I was offered a job as a clerk to the administrative law judge of the U.S. International Trade Commission in Washington, D.C. I declined and instead moved to Miami to be with my grandparents Isadore and Freda, who had retired there. I wanted to learn how to try cases—a prerequisite, I thought, for all attorneys. The largest trial law firm in Florida, Blackwell & Walker, offered me a position and I took it. Blackwell & Walker was mostly a blue-blood collection of conservative WASPS. I was the Jewish associate, one of three "tokens" that also included a young Cuban and a woman. I relished working with the best trial lawyers in Miami, but by my second year, I was beginning to yearn for what I thought were the big leagues—the nation's capital.

During a summer vacation, I traveled to Washington, appeared cold turkey at the office of John Shenefield, the assistant attorney general for antitrust in the U.S. Department of Justice, and asked for a job. Antitrust was then a hot area of practice for international lawyers. Shenefield's assistant, Douglas Coulton, met with me and a week later offered me a position. It was tough leaving my grandparents, whom I loved, and Miami, which I thought was the city of the future, but I had larger aspirations. The Justice Department was prestigious, and snagging a job there as a young lawyer was a bit like being accepted at Harvard Law School as a student. I felt that it would make me a crusader for justice. And it would launch my career and allow me, after a few years, to land a big job with a law firm specializing in international law.

But over the next couple of years at Justice, things didn't work out that way. In my first job working for the consumer affairs section of the antitrust division, which represented various government agencies such as the Food and Drug Administration, the Federal Trade Commission and the Consumer Product Safety Commission, I saw laziness and a lack of discipline among the attorneys. It was a far cry from the professionalism I had experienced at Blackwell & Walker in Miami. I had the audacity to make my views known and to suggest some changes. The response from my supervisors was classic bureaucratese: This is the way we do things here in government. As my complaints continued, my chief eventually retaliated, delaying my promotion and telling me that I should lighten up and take things a little easier. Perhaps he thought that my work ethic was setting a bad example.

What was even more troubling, however, was an experience I had on one of the section's cases. It involved a manufacturer of childrens' sleepwear in North Carolina. The company's product had been seized by the Consumer Product Safety Commission and placed under government bond in a private warehouse. The problem with the pajamas was that they contained a flame retardant, TRIS, which initially had been approved and mandated by the commission, but was later found to be a carcinogen. As a result, they were destined to be destroyed by court order. However, after I had the pajamas seized, the company, through its owner, had them shipped to Venezuela, in flagrant violation of the bond they had had to post. Not only was this illegal, it was an attack on the kids of Venezuela. Were they any less deserving of safe pajamas than their American counterparts?

My assistant chief, John Fleder, the one truly diligent supervisor in the section, pressed to have the company's owner indicted, but his boss, Patrick Glynn, pressured by higher-ups at Justice, refused. It turned out that the company's owner was a close friend of the U.S. attorney in Greensboro, and the department yielded to the political lobbying and influence of its chief lawyer in the region. As a compromise, only the company itself, a bankrupt shell at that point, was charged.

What an outrage! A company owner violates a court order, breaks bond, ships cancer-causing pajamas to Venezuela where children will be subjected to a high risk of terminal illness, and the Justice Department takes no meaningful action, except to proceed against a faceless and bankrupt corporate shell. This was not the Justice Department I had signed on with, this was the Injustice Department!

Regrettably, that case was not the only example of favoritism I experienced at Justice. I learned that those on the right side of the political fence were frequently not prosecuted and those on the wrong side got nailed. It upset me enough to ask for a transfer—and I got one, to the section of Justice prosecuting the mammoth telephone monopoly AT&T. It was quite a change: Here were dedicated young lawyers who believed that competition needed to be created in the telecommunications industry. Still, the bad taste of the TRIS episode and other similar cases never faded, and I left Justice after two years for a small, highly specialized, boutique international trade law firm in Washington.

My experience at the Justice Department, considered by many as perhaps the most noble and professional agency in the executive branch, had been eye opening. It showed me that, rather than being the friend of the people, the government was often their enemy. The laziness, lack of discipline, waste, intellectual dishonesty and political corruption left a stench and I wanted to never be a part of it again.

When I left in February of 1981, Ronald Reagan had just been elected president, following the long and humiliating Iran hostage crisis. He had campaigned in part on his views of a more limited—and efficient—role for government in American life (Reagan liked to joke that the most frightening words in the English language were "Hi, I am from the government and I am here to help you!"), and his arrival in Washington was a welcome breath of fresh air for the nation. I also viewed his election as a conservative antidote to the big problems I had experienced and witnessed at the Justice Department.

Reagan replaced a president who was a terrible disappointment, if not a national disaster. While I was in law school at Emory, I actually had worked as a volunteer to help elect Jimmy Carter in 1976, thinking that this seemingly honest peanut farmer and former Georgia governor would be right for the nation after the cesspool of the Nixon years. But Carter miserably failed the country. His foreign policy was feckless and naïve, culminating in our humiliation at the hands of the Iranians; and his nearly ruinous stewardship of the economy, with double-digit inflation and sky-high interest rates, took years to reverse. In fact, the Carter administration, with its regulatory bumbling and intrusions in the private sector, significantly strengthened my conservative politics. With Reagan in charge, I thought that things might improve a bit but, given the ingrained bureaucracy, I wasn't holding my breath. For me the time was just right to leave Justice for the private sector.

I signed on as a senior associate at a small and prestigious international trade law firm on K Street. Even though the firm turned out a good work product, and nearly always won its cases, the firm's partners also proved to be weak and ethically compromised.

The firm generally practiced before government administrative agencies that regulated the flow of imports into the United States. When U.S. industries filed complaints against the foreign exporters and American importers of such goods, arguing that their practices were anticompetitive and illegal, these government agencies determined whether tariffs, quotas or other trade restraints should be imposed. But the agencies needed help: They were highly dependent on the information they received in questionnaires filled out by the lawyers representing the foreign exporters and American importers.

In one particular case, our firm was provided information by its exporter and importer clients, which our lawyers used to fill out the questionnaires. The government agencies, relying on the information, which lawyers call "material," decided not to impose trade sanctions. Later, however, the information proved to be false. When that came to light, I did an analysis and determined that even the correct information would not have dramatically altered the result: In other words, the government agencies almost certainly would have made the same decision based on the correct information.

I strenuously argued with the partners to do the right thing and push our clients to correct their questionnaires. It is a criminal offense under the U.S. Code to make false statements to the government, and I believed strongly then, as I do now, that a lawyer has an ethical duty, as the government's first line of defense, to make sure that the truth prevailed. But the partners wouldn't budge. The firm was collecting massive legal fees to defend its clients, and the partners chose not to revisit the issue.

I left the firm shortly afterward, realizing that I would need to practice on my own if I wanted to control my destiny and avoid the ethical traps I had encountered thus far. But I still had some unfinished business with the firm. Even after my departure, I asked the firm to follow through and correct the errors in the questionnaires. When the partners continued to stonewall, I asked for an advisory opinion from the Office of Professional Responsibility of the District of Columbia bar. To my chagrin, in a strained opinion that did not square with the law in many other states, the D.C. bar found that the firm was under no obligation to force its clients to correct the administrative record; nor was the firm required to reveal the correct information to the government agencies involved. Instead, the firm's only obligation was to quit its representation of the clients, which of course it never did.

That the bar had effectively let the law firm off the hook revolted me. It was yet another example of the inability of, or lack of desire by, attorneys to police themselves. I was determined to do things differently. The Law Office of Larry E. Klayman, as my new private practice was called, would raise the bar (no pun intended) for the legal profession.

Around this time, I got married. I had traveled to Brussels shortly after I joined the international law firm to participate in a three-month internship in what was then known as the Competition Directorate of the Commission of the European Communities. On my first day, listening to an English translation of a Greek parliamentarian in one of the great halls of the Berlaymont building, I met Cesira D'Aniello, a 24-year-old intern from Rome. We had a whirlwind romance and got married in the spring of 1982 in a small church, almost 2,000 years old, overlooking Rome's Palatine Hill. Cesira returned to Washington with me. Her father, Guido, a former director general of the Italian Ministry of Education, later traveled frequently to the United States, and we went to Rome several times a year. I learned Italian by listening to Cesira and her dad, and my changed circumstances also created an opportunity to develop an Italian and European client base at my new firm. Cesira and her father worked with me, and I will always owe them more than simple love for their dedication and support.

One of my first cases was similar to the one that had caused me to leave my prior firm. I represented an Italian company accused of unfair trade practices in the importation of merchandise into the United States. It began as a typical Italian family affair: With Cesira's half-sister, Ludovica, and brother-in-law, Gianluigi, in tow, Cesira, Guido and I traveled to the company's factory. The meeting with the owner went well. A small, powerfully built man, he ran a plant as clean and modern as any in the United States.

I all but moved into his office and, with the help of Danila, his attractive female assistant for exports, toiled away responding to U.S. government questionnaires. One day, as I listened to Danila explain to the owner what data she was providing to me, it became clear that all was not kosher. I heard him say, "Gioca con questo," or "Play with this." Alarm bells sounded in my head and I immediately confronted him, demanding to know whether the data I was receiving was accurate. He shot back, "Are you my lawyer, or the lawyer of the devil?" I pressed on, despite my financial dependence on him as one of my first clients. I needed to know whether the information was correct, if I were going to live by my rules of conduct.

The next day, the owner, still angry at my questioning his data, took me on a mountain hike in the Italian Alps. Stopping at a steep cliff, he told me to look down. Then he jokingly said that I would wind up at the bottom of the ravine if I did not win his case. It seemed to me that he meant it only half in jest. With a strained laugh, I told him that to win the case I needed accurate data and that he would have to provide it. There was no alternative.

He later came through, but not without difficulty, and we were successful. Yet, he always resented me for my persistence. It seemed that this was the first time he had ever won anything honestly in his whole life. After paying grudgingly for my services, he never again used me as legal counsel. I had paid a price for insisting on the truth and acting as my own Inspector General, my own office of professional responsibility, but I felt good about myself. I was different.

But keeping my clients honest, and fighting my own profession, were not my only challenges as a young lawyer. The influence of politics and money on decision making by government regulators and judges became all too apparent as my legal career progressed.

At the age of 31, and with a law firm composed of only one other associate besides myself, I had to use creative means to compete against the Washington mega-firms for business. In making my sales pitch, I would tell prospective clients that we were a small boutique operation and, as such, they would gain my personal attention. The big firms, I said, probably would assign their work to a mere associate. But what frequently clinched the deal was when I compared us to the Israeli Air Force during the 1967 Middle East War. "We take out their planes while they are still on the ground," I told clients—a reference to the aggressive style I used in fighting the government in trade and other regulatory cases, as well as in private litigants in business-related matters.

An "attack dog" litigation style was intended to combat big corporate and labor interests that used campaign contributions and other political means to buy influence with government regulators. In the private sector, prestigious multinational companies whose cases were assigned to federal judges could not make campaign contributions as a means to have an effect on decision making, but the influence money can buy with politicians who can advance a judge's career ambitions is frequently enough to get the desired result. And in state court, where judges are usually elected rather than appointed, law firms and the bar can generally donate to a judge's campaign directly, thereby affecting potential decision making.

In short, I made it clear to the prospective clients that a strong, aggressive, dedicated lawyer named Klayman was needed to offset the influence that big interests frequently used to pervert the findings of government agencies and the courts.

To have maximum effect, however, an aggressive approach against the powers that be alone was not enough. The government official or judge who was subject to making decisions based on politics or money would need to be held accountable to level the playing field. Generally, government officials and judges are personally immune from legal actions questioning their decision making, but I found creative means to pierce this protective shield. If a government official, for instance, blatantly exceeded his authority under statutory law or an agency's regulations, or violated U.S. or state constitutions, he could be subject, in theory, to a cause of action against him personally. Threats of legal action or, if the threats didn't work, the actual filing of lawsuits against government personnel, were thus a means to coax them to do the right thing and make decisions on the merits.

And my approach worked. In my early years of practice on my own, I quickly developed a reputation for being a hard-nosed, no-nonsense litigator who could not be bought. While government officials did not like my style, they respected it; and the Law Office of Larry E. Klayman developed a reputation for winning cases that was second to none. I was a type of economic civil rights lawyer, who successfully represented the underdog on a shoestring budget, with little manpower, and no money or inclination to stuff favors into the pockets of politicians and judges.

But my style also ruffled feathers and provoked retaliation. As I confronted corrupt and incompetent judges whose decision making favored the vested

13

interests, this retaliation became acute over time, causing me to lose even more faith in my own profession. One case, in particular, changed the entire course of my legal career.

─ 3 ─

JUDICIAL WATCH IS BORN

My client was a Taiwanese manufacturer of bathroom accessories and its U.S. importers. The company was accused by a powerful American manufacturer, Baldwin Hardware Corporation, of having ripped off its design patents and trademarks for products such as towel racks, soap dishes and the like. The problem with Baldwin's case, which it first brought to the U.S. International Trade Commission (ITC), was that for functional shapes, or for designs that had become commonplace in the industry, no intellectual property protection is given. And, for this simple reason, Baldwin lost at the ITC.

But the company did not stop there. With its vastly superior financial resources and high-priced, big-firm lawyers, it continued to push its claims and filed suit in federal court in Los Angeles. The case was assigned to Judge William D. Keller, a Reagan appointee who was reportedly close friends with former Attorney General Edwin Meese.

When the case was first assigned to Judge Keller I did not think twice. I'd had cases in Los Angeles federal court in the past, but never before him. I was comforted that at least he appeared to be an ideological "soulmate," having been picked for the federal bench by my favorite modern-day president. But during my first status conference before his court, where the parties and the judge met to lay the ground rules for the case, I observed a strange demeanor. Judge Keller had a penchant for pontificating from the bench—that is, talking endlessly about subjects that had nothing to do with anything other than his own concept of politics and the world. I almost felt as if the poor guy must have a wife who didn't listen to him at home.

The more troubling behavior I observed that day, however, centered on his attacks on lawyers representing minorities, such as Mexican-Americans

15

and blacks, in police brutality cases. Watching him conduct status conferences on a number of other cases in order to get a better feel for his court, I saw Judge Keller chastising, berating, mocking and sometimes even penalizing these minorities with monetary fines and other legal sanctions. This made me feel more than uneasy, given that I was representing a foreign company and its owner, their U.S. importer and major customers, among whom were Asians, Jews and gays. But the judge's conduct toward other minorities was not immediately leveled against my clients, so I filed the experience away in the back of my mind for future reference.

After about a year of preparation, the case finally came to trial at the height of the Rodney King riots in Los Angeles. When I arrived at the federal courthouse, police sharpshooters were in place on tops of buildings and in the streets of downtown Los Angeles, as rioters were looting stores and generally wreaking havoc. I was staying at Hotel Myako in Little Japan Town, just a few blocks away. The scene, which was literally a war zone, seemed analogous to my impending legal war with a judge who not only proved to be a bigot and a drunkard, but certifiably crazy.

On the opening day of trial, my Taiwanese client, Frank Su of Franksu Enterprises, Ltd., was unable to attend, having just had surgery in Taipei for a severe hernia. He was scheduled to arrive the next day. The client's attendance was not required on the first day, since opening arguments before the court and other preliminary matters could be handled by the lawyers and the judge. But this did not stop Judge Keller from denouncing Frank Su for not being there, suggesting that somehow he was being disrespectful of his court. The judge also suggested that my client had lied about his hernia operation as an excuse to come late.

After Frank Su arrived and the trial progressed, the judge grew more and more erratic. He would refer to me as "Mr. Schmuckler," a derivation of the word "schmuck," which in Yiddish literally means penis, and generally refers to a clumsy, stupid oaf. He also would make fun of and screamed at the Chinese interpreter who was translating for Frank Su. With regard to the Jewish and gay importers, they were referred to as "Mr. Carter and his ilk," and "you people." For good measure, Keller even added the proverbial anti-Semitic giveaway, "Some of my best friends are Jews."

While Keller cast aspersions on my clients, he frequently complimented Baldwin's people, praising their appearance and demeanor. As the judge would leave the bench after each of the early days of trial, he would sneer in the direction of my clients and me like the villain from some Hollywood horror movie. With his tall, hunched frame, in his black robes Judge Keller looked more like an oversized crazed vulture than a federal law enforcement official.

Finally, I couldn't take it anymore. It was apparent that my clients were not going to get a fair trial, and I asked them to authorize me to move to disqualify Judge Keller. They agreed. I had never before moved to disqualify a judge; it is extremely difficult, because other judges will generally rally around their colleague and not remove the offender if he refuses to recuse himself. But I was secure in my belief that this step needed to be taken, if for no other reason than to create a record for an eventual appeal.

On the fourth day of trial, I made my move. In rising to speak, I trembled a bit and tried to be as diplomatic and polite as possible in laying out my reasons for disqualification. I told Keller that while he was a judge with integrity, it may be difficult for him to see that he had prejudged the case. I then listed the remarks he had made in support of my argument. In response, Judge Keller just stared at me and walked off the bench with a parting sneer, exiting through the door to his chambers.

When we returned for trial the next day, he refused to disqualify himself and accused me of improper behavior instead. In a harsh tone, he threatened to try me for my impudence at the end of the case. He charged me with making improper objections during the opening days of the trial, talking over him, misstating facts, and other alleged disrespectful behavior. As with the civil rights lawyers in the police brutality cases I had watched, he added that I may have to pay with sanctions for my acts. I stood silently, in shock and frankly frightened, as I endured his tirade.

But I was a tough guy and had confronted bullies before. I was not going to back down with Judge Keller. Throughout the course of the trial, each time he made a bigoted remark, I stood up, objected, and noted the latest outrage on the record for appeal. In retaliation, Judge Keller continued to threaten me with sanctions, which he promised to mete out at the end of the case. On several occasions, he even threatened to throw me in jail for criminal contempt during the conduct of the trial.

Some days, Judge Keller had us wait in the courtroom for hours before he appeared, other days he did not show up at all. There were also times when it was obvious that he was drunk on the bench.

On Fridays, to punish me for my impertinence, he ordered me to research inane and irrelevant legal issues for his "enlightenment" and barred me from returning to Washington to meet with my small office staff. Since my law firm, by then called Klayman & Associates, consisted of only three lawyers and a secretary, and since I had one of the two other lawyers with me in Los Angeles trying the case, this put a significant financial hardship on me, especially since Frank Su was in arrears in paying his legal fees and costs. In effect, I was being held hostage at legal gunpoint by a Looney Tunes judge who knew exactly what he was doing; he was bent on destroying my law firm and me, not to mention my clients, by turning a simple case into a full-fledged mega-litigation dripping with prejudice and bias. It was nothing less than an inquisition. What was originally scheduled to last only five days turned into a grueling seven-week trial.

By the end, I was emotionally spent. Frank Su's unpaid legal fees and costs continued to mount. And since I was stuck in Los Angeles with my associate, I was prevented from working on other paying cases. The firm and I were on the verge of bankruptcy. It came as no surprise that Judge Keller ruled in favor of Baldwin and, as he had promised, asked me to stand up at the close of the case for his mini-trial of my behavior. Without allowing me to speak, he meted out the sanctions—a $20,000 fine and banishment from his court forever. To top it off, I would have to attach a copy of his eventual written orders, which he said he would issue soon, to any future request to appear before another judge in federal court in Los Angeles. At the end of this travesty of justice, I demanded to place my comments on the record. Grudgingly, he relented and sat there grimacing as I laid out my case for the appellate court.

Badly shaken, I referred to my background as the grandson of Ukrainian, Polish and Lithuanian Jewish immigrants. I talked about the sense of right and wrong they had instilled in me and how they, despite being minorities, were entitled to the respect of their fellow Americans. The whole scene produced a deep emotional outpouring on my part that in some ways caused me to pontificate like Judge Keller. But I tried to stay relevant. At the close of my speech, in which I defended each and every aspect of my behavior and explained why I had to stand up to the court, Judge Keller just got up with his characteristic sneer and left.

I was sure that I had acted properly, but I left the courtroom in a daze, knowing I had just experienced a watershed in my legal career. I had no idea if the firm and I would survive financially. I also knew that every legal adversary in the future would try to use Judge Keller's sanction orders against me to discredit my legal representation. But even with all of this adversity, or maybe because of it, I relished the road ahead. I had not buckled. I was a fighter, and with God's help, I wasn't about to give up!

This was not a happy period in my life. In addition to the traumatic experience with Judge Keller, Cesira and I had recently divorced. We had a deep admiration and respect for one another, but our differing politics and concepts of how to live were causes of constant friction. Paradoxically, to remain close, we had to go our separate ways. During the trial, I called her frequently in Brussels, where she had returned to work for the European Union, and the consolation she provided helped me persevere. Fortunately, we had no children.

Financially the trial had brought me to my knees, and upon my return to Washington, I was forced to borrow $100,000 to keep the practice afloat. This imposed a huge emotional and monetary strain, but it needed to be done if I planned to take the appeal and carry on with my other paying cases. As for Frank Su, he returned to Taiwan, totally disgusted with the American legal system. Perhaps as a result, he never paid me the hundreds of thousands of dollars he and his company owed. I'd put my head on the train tracks to protect Frank and his heritage, and he left me in the lurch. It hurt.

A few weeks after my return to Washington, a friend from California sent me an article in the *Los Angeles Daily Journal* about a Jewish civil rights lawyer, Stephen Yagman, who had just been sanctioned by Judge Keller. Yagman apparently had difficulties with other federal judges in Los Angeles as well, and the court was now considering disbarring him from future representation. The acts that provoked this proceeding were comments Yagman made publicly about Judge Keller. He called him a drunk and an anti-Semite, and pointed out how he had sanctioned the last six Jewish lawyers who had appeared before him. For this, Yagman was being prosecuted in a secretive Star Chamber proceeding by the disciplinary committee of the court. His lawyer was Ramsey Clark, former attorney general during President Johnson's administration. Clark at least had succeeded in bringing the matter under public scrutiny. Feeling that my own experience was confirmed, I picked up the phone and called Yagman's attorney.

Ramsey Clark had a well-earned reputation for being a maverick. While I had never met or spoken with him before, I admired his independence, even though his extremely liberal politics were far different from my own. During our conversation, he impressed me with his candor. After explaining my similar experience with Judge Keller and offering to appear as a corroborating witness in Yagman's trial, I asked him if he had sought the help of the Anti-Defamation League (ADL) in pressing his client's case. He replied that it would be a waste of time. The judges of the federal courthouse in Los Angeles had attended fund-raising events for the ADL, and the public-interest protector of Jewish interests would take no action in his or my defense. Out of fairness, Clark said, his own chances of getting legal assistance were small because he had represented Palestinian terrorists; the ADL was not his biggest fan. He did not dissuade me from trying, only cautioned me that in his view it would be a futile exercise.

At the time, the ADL had a high profile. It was embroiled in a public battle with Louis Farrakhan and the Nation of Islam. Farrakhan was giving speeches calling the Jews Christ killers and referring to Judaism as a "gutter religion." The ADL was running huge ads against him in many major newspapers and raking in money hand over fist through its fund-raising efforts.

To appeal the Keller sanctions orders and Frank Su's case, I needed to get a copy of the court transcript of the proceedings that would document all of the bigoted remarks and bizarre behavior of the judge. But I could not afford to purchase it. Because of the seven-week behemoth of a trial, the clerk's office estimated that it would cost many thousands of dollars. So I decided to contact the ADL not only to seek its support in asking the court to waive the costs, but to join me in my appeals.

As Ramsey had predicted, my letter to the ADL went unanswered. It was not until I wrote to the executive director, Abraham Foxman, himself and threatened to publicly raise the roof, that I got the ADL's attention. I told Foxman that while it was very lucrative for the ADL to raise money by denouncing Farrakhan, it was ignoring the interest of ordinary Jews who had been harmed by a crazy anti-Semitic judge. I pointed out what Ramsey had told me about the ADL's fund-raising activities with the federal bench in Los Angeles. As a topper, I asked Foxman if he would like to see publicity about the ADL's hypocrisy in the same newspapers that were running its ads against Farrakhan.

I finally got a response, but it was merely a weak letter supporting my request to obtain the transcript for free from the federal court. Foxman offered no direct help in my upcoming appeals, as I had also requested, and it was clear that he and his organization were not prepared to stick their necks out to defend ordinary Jews who could not raise the big bucks.

So I turned to another fellow Jew, U.S. Senator Arlen Specter of Pennsylvania, a Republican who sat on the powerful Judiciary Committee. As a former Pennsylvanian who had worked for his predecessor, U.S. Senator Dick Schweiker, I thought that Specter could help me to obtain the court transcript and even begin a congressional investigation of the Keller matter. I called his office to set up an appointment, but never got a response. Finally, in exasperation, I contacted Schweiker, who had retired from his post-Senate job in the insurance industry, and asked him to set up an appointment with Specter on my behalf. He succeeded.

I met Specter in a small conference room inside his office in the Hart Senate Office Building. He was joined by one of his senior staff, Richard Hertling, who was also a lawyer. After I thanked him for seeing me, Specter launched into a diatribe, criticizing me for setting up the appointment through Schweiker and claiming that he would have seen me in any event. I ignored his harangue and described to him what had happened in Judge Keller's court. I detailed his history of sanctioning Jewish lawyers and asked for Specter's assistance. In grave Nixonian tones, the senator expressed his deep concern and offered his help. He dictated a letter to Hertling on the spot, to be sent to the federal court to get the transcript for free and promised to look into the matter through the Judiciary Committee.

I was delighted. Finally, someone with clout was taking an interest. But as weeks passed, Specter never sent the letter to the federal court and did not initiate even a request for a Judiciary Committee inquiry. I called Hertling and asked why nothing had happened. He said that he did not know, but had sent the dictated letter in to "the boss" three times for a signature, and nothing came back. This was usually a sign, according to the aide, that the Senator had changed his mind.

Then, out of the blue, Specter announced that he was running for the presidency. Suddenly, it all made sense: The senator did not want to offend federal judges in Los Angeles and throughout the country, who indirectly could help his campaign. Nor did he want to be identified publicly with Jewish interests; that might work against him during the 1992 Republican primaries. So, in a repeat performance of my strategy with Foxman, I wrote the senator a letter, threatening him with bad publicity if he did not act. For good measure, I told him that if he could not take a strong stand on behalf of his own people, then how did he expect to be president of all the people? That got him to take action—sort of. He sent a letter to the federal court, but it was not the one he dictated. Instead, he mailed a watered-down version that cast doubt on the sincerity of my claims about Judge Keller and apologetically asked that I be provided with the transcript. I once again wrote to Specter asking for a tougher approach but never got a response. And, needless to say, he never sought to initiate a Judiciary Committee inquiry.

By sending his spineless letter, the senator was merely covering his political ass. In hypocrisy even exceeding the ADL's, Specter made biting criticism of the Christian evangelical right a centerpiece of his campaign. But what separated evangelicals from the senator is that they stood up for their proper interests; Specter simply slithered away like the coward he proved to be on that and other occasions in later years.

At the time, Specter was the head of the powerful Senate Judiciary Committee. His recent conversion—becoming a Democrat for political gain—is just his latest "sellout," and should increase his grip on power in this committee under President Obama's time in office. God help us all!

What could I do? I considered throwing in the towel, but I decided to soldier on and pursue my appeal in the Keller matter. I filed with the U.S. Court of Appeals for the Ninth Federal Circuit in San Francisco and asked the court to obtain the trial transcript. (Since Frank Su's case involved patents and trademarks, this was the appellate court that had jurisdiction, even though the case had been tried in Los Angeles.) But as I had suspected, the court was loath to prove one of its own a bigot and never ordered that the transcript be produced. Without it, I had no real proof of Judge Keller's conduct and lost the appeal. Indeed, in their written opinions, the appellate judges expressed resentment that I had the nerve to call Keller a bigot, even though I had attached to my briefs sworn declarations from the clients setting forth their recollections which substantiated the offending remarks.

Judges, I had learned over the years, hate to sit in judgment of their peers. To take remedial actrion, the judicial offense has to be so severe and the proof so overwhelming that they have no choice but to act. The experience with Keller was not the first time I reached the conclusion that federal judges, who are appointed for life, generally believe they are above the law. They know that they cannot be touched from the outside, so they are unwilling to subject themselves to the scrutiny of their peers.

My last recourse was to ask the disciplinary committee of the federal appellate court in California to review the matter. I lodged an ethics complaint against Judge Keller and, to my surprise, Chief Judge Alex Kosinksi of the Ninth Circuit Court of Appeals responded, stating that he would order up the transcript. But when he did so, the clerk's office told him that it had been lost. In a twist straight out of a John Grisham novel, the court reporter had died, so the court did not know how to proceed. To his credit, the chief judge ordered a new transcription, but large parts of the original tape recording of the trial were missing. When the transcript finally was recreated, there were huge gaps, and nearly all of the offending remarks were gone. The disciplinary committee, without a full and accurate transcript, never had sufficient direct evidence to proceed, and the matter was closed.

But it was not closed for me. I had experienced a lot of egregious misconduct in my relatively short legal career—I had been practicing for about 15 years by then—but this case was the straw that broke the camel's back. When I was finally out of the financial hole Judge Keller had dug for me, I vowed to take some steps to reform the judiciary and the legal system. I did not yet know how I would proceed; I only knew that something needed to be done. The system of justice envisioned by our founding fathers was broken, and it needed to be fixed. What I had experienced not only cost me dearly financially, it had also resulted in a huge emotional catharsis. I knew then that, when the time was right, I would do something about it.

Over the next two years, my outrage did not subside. With each new experience before the government and the courts, my impression of our political and legal systems grew worse. I thought about quitting the legal profession altogether, but quitting is not my nature.

By the summer of 1994, I was better prepared to move. Thanks to a large contingency fee in a case I settled concerning insurance fraud, I now had the financial wherewithal to do something to try to change things. Bill and Hillary Clinton were in office, two lawyers who, in their first two years as president and first lady, were setting a terrible example for the nation. Not only was there an ongoing investigation of an alleged fraudulent land deal named Whitewater underway, the Clintons were busy paying for their legal representation in the case by panhandling dollars from the American people. Never before in the history of the country had a chief executive and his wife openly solicited funds, outside of campaign contributions, directly from the people, and much of the press was up in arms, since it created a loophole to the federal antibribery laws. Anyone seeking to influence the President and buy a favor could drive through this Clinton-created exception.

The thought that the president and first lady were effectively shaking down the public for money was repulsive. They seemed to be the "Bonnie and Clyde of American politics," even more crooked than the dishonest lawyers and judges I had come across in my early professional years. They were, I thought, the poster children for the need for change. The time was right to act on my ethical beliefs.

I remember the exact moment when my thoughts about what to do finally jelled. I was walking down M Street in Georgetown one Saturday past a Sports Authority store. Stephanie Luck, then my girlfriend, was at my side. It came to me out of the blue. I would start a public interest group and name it "Judicial Watch." We would use all the tools of the legal profession, including civil lawsuits, to become a private attorney general. In effect, I could be what I knew from first-hand experience the government's Justice Department could never be—a true legal advocate for the people. Judicial Watch would "watch" the judiciary, and use the judiciary to watch the other two branches of government—the executive and the legislative. And I would become to the cause of cleaning up government and legal corruption what Ralph Nader had become to the cause of consumer protection. I had found my calling.

4

THE GREAT
CHINAGATE SCANDAL

When I filed the appropriate corporate papers for Judicial Watch as a public interest foundation on July 29, 1994, I already knew what my first case would be. I would take on the president and first lady over their illegal solicitation of defense funds. In combating abuses of power, why not start at the top? After all, it cost no more to sue a president than to bring a personal injury case for someone slipping on a banana peel.

Shortly after its incorporation, Judicial Watch sued the president's legal defense fund, To be able to go after this illegal solicitation of money by the Clintons, I had to conjure up a unique legal theory; otherwise, a public interest group would not have standing to challenge the conduct. I used the Federal Advisory Committee Act as a vehicle, arguing that the legal defense fund was receiving advice from the trustees on legal means to raise the money. Indeed, it had asked for a legal opinion on the conduct from the so-called Office of Government Ethics (OGE), in order to provide cover for the trustees' derrières. The OGE, which is controlled by the White House as an executive branch agency, nicely complied and rubber-stamped the activity. However, under the act, full accountability needed to be provided to the public when a president was receiving advice from persons outside of the government. When the legal defense fund refused to respond to my requests for information and documentation about its activities, I filed suit, arguing that the fund, pursuant to the law, would have to be shut down.

The results of this case were mixed; the court held that the alleged illegal activity did not fall within the scope of the Federal Advisory Committee Act because the act of soliciting money did not constitute an advisory function. But publicity and subsequent events ultimately created a groundswell of further

25

scrutiny and criticism. The end of the Clintons' first legal defense fund came with the discovery that it was being used to launder hundreds of thousands of dollars in Communist Chinese cash into the president's and first lady's bank accounts. What was most important about the case was that it was a harbinger of things to come concerning China and its successful attempts to buy inside favors from the Clinton administration. In my view, the story is one of treason, plain and simple. (Is it a coincidence that Hillary Clinton's first trip, as secretary of state under the Obama administration, was to travel to China?)

This much broader and more sinister story began when, on a flight back to Washington from Los Angeles in September 1994, I browsed through an airline copy of the latest *Business Week*. There, in the Washington news section of the magazine, was a story entitled, "Clinton Cozies Up to Business." I took a special interest in the article because it was about Commerce Department Secretary Ron Brown and his foreign trade missions.

As an international trade lawyer, I had developed more than a strong appreciation for the political and institutional corruption swirling in and around the Commerce Department, where money and favors were historically doled out as corporate welfare to businesses that routinely lined the pockets of the political party in power. Indeed, whether Democrat or Republican, each new administration usually places its chief fund-raiser in the Secretary of Commerce slot, so he can continue to harvest the corporate and labor union money trees while in office. Before Brown, during the first Bush administration, the Commerce secretary was Robert A. Mosbacher, the elder President Bush's main fund-raising jockey. In the son's ad-ministration, President George W. Bush named his best friend, Don Evans, a Texas tycoon and fund-raiser, to the Commerce post during his first term. So the department has always been a repository for potential corruption, no matter which political party is in control of the White House.

In appointing Ron Brown, an African American, Bill Clinton had taken Commerce to a new level of potential abuse. From his days as the Reverend Jesse Jackson's campaign manager during Jackson's first presidential race, to his just-concluded stewardship as chairman of the Democratic National Committee (DNC), Brown had a reputation for being a political fund-raiser par excellence.

So when I read in *Business Week* that Brown was taking heads of companies on trade missions and helping them do business, alarm bells sounded. The alarm bells grew to sirens when I read further that Bernard Schwartz, the chief of Loral Corporation, a large high-tech defense and satellite company, was bragging that he paid $100,000 to the DNC and then participated in a trade mission to China. As a former antitrust lawyer, not to mention founder, chairman and general counsel of Judicial Watch, a freshly minted government ethics watchdog group, I was offended on two fronts. First, of course, money was obviously buying favors. But second, these acts also created competitive distortions in the marketplace. If a large company could get the government to take it on a trade mission and help it do business overseas based on political campaign contributions, where would this leave the smaller competitor who could not afford to ante up the cash? It was fundamentally unfair.

I was also outraged as a conservative with libertarian leanings who believed that government should stay out of the way in allowing companies and firms to do business on their own. This was a job for Judicial Watch! I kidded with friends and colleagues that all I needed was a Lycra body suit with the logo "JW" on my chest.

When I returned to Washington, I pondered how to get to the bottom of the scam. Using the Freedom of Information Act (FOIA), a legal mechanism for U.S. citizens and noncitizens alike to request documents from the federal government, I asked the Commerce Department to produce any and all documents about recent Clinton administration trade missions to China, Russia, India, South Africa and a host of other countries. The FOIA requests gave the department 20 days to produce the documents, as it was legally required to do. What I was most interested to learn was not only the names of the companies whose representatives went on trade missions, but especially those that were not chosen, and the reasons why. This would shed light on what was apparently a corrupt and anticompetitive selection process. According to Washington media heavyweights such as Bill Safire of *The New York Times*, Robert Novak of the *Chicago Sun-Times,* and even Watergate reporter Bob Woodward of *The Washington Post*, what I would later find—and not find—would spark perhaps the biggest government scandal since Watergate itself.

Instead of having the documents delivered on the 20th day, I got a mysterious call from a woman identifying herself as Melissa Moss, a Commerce Department official. I had never heard of her. Rather than receiving all the documents, which would take years to produce, Moss asked if I would settle for just the lists of corporate participants? No, I said, Judicial Watch wanted all of the documents. I offered to give the department a modest extension of time to produce them. The conversation grew testy and Moss refused to budge. Finally, she slammed down the phone, hardly a professional response. Shortly afterward, I got a call from another Commerce employee, a lower-level person assigned the job of processing my FOIA petition. She was apologetic about Moss's behavior, but said that she was powerless to act to fulfill my document requests, suggesting that something out of the ordinary was occurring. Indeed, shortly after that conversation, I got a letter from Moss claiming, falsely, that I had agreed to accept only the list of participants to the trade missions and would forgo getting the other documents. Outraged, I did some investigation of Moss's background and learned that she had worked directly for Ron Brown as his main fund-raiser at the DNC and was rumored to have had an affair with President Clinton himself. Now, two and two were beginning to equal four.

But rather than wrestle with the department over what seemed to me a likely cover-up, I decided instead to file suit in the U.S. District Court for the District of Columbia. Based on my many years of experience both inside and outside of government, I had learned that it did not pay to dawdle. You had to act forcefully and quickly in these types of situations. Besides, a failure to get before the court swiftly could result in the illegal destruction by Moss and others inside the department of the very documents I was seeking. The case was assigned through the court's random system to Judge Royce C. Lamberth, a Reagan appointee. He was familiar to me: Lamberth was the same judge who had the Clinton Legal Defense Fund case assigned to him.

Worried that the documents would be destroyed, I promptly followed up with a motion asking Lamberth for an early status conference. It was apparent that he was a no-nonsense judge: the court quickly ordered up the production of all of the requested documents unless a valid FOIA exemption—akin to privileged information—could be claimed. But as I predicted at the time to a group of Judicial Watch volunteers who met in the evening at my law office, the department produced very few documents. Given the wide breadth of my FOIA requests and the volume of documents the trade mission selection process would likely have generated, the slim pickings smacked of obstruction of justice. Most telling, there was not one document from inside Secretary Brown's office among them. This was important since Brown had been waging a public relations campaign, claiming that Bill Clinton was the "trade president" and that his Commerce Department's trade mission policy was the centerpiece of the White House's efforts.

Lacking vital documents, I again sought a status conference and Lamberth granted my request. Again, he acted fast. Lambasting the Justice Department lawyer, Bruce Hegyi, who represented Commerce, for not adequately responding to the requests, I asked the court to allow me to take discovery to try to uncover why an adequate response had not been made. Discovery—the process by which questions are asked orally or in writing, and documents can be demanded—is not standard operating procedure in an FOIA lawsuit, but Lamberth granted my request. In effect, he ordered up an investigation, under the supervision of the court, of why all the documents, especially those in Brown's office, were not produced for Judicial Watch.

During early depositions, I questioned the FOIA officers who were responsible for gathering and producing the paltry documents that were turned over to Judicial Watch. In deposition after deposition, I caught the FOIA officers lying about what they had done and contradicting sworn statements that they had signed to try avoid giving live testimony. At one deposition, Hegyi, not the sharpest knife in the legal drawer, acted like a pro-Clinton partisan hack and refused to produce documents the court had sought. I moved for sanctions, and Judge Lamberth, who grew to dislike Hegyi over time, granted my request. The case was turning ugly. Hegyi, on each occasion, would ask Lamberth to shut down discovery. At one hearing, Lamberth shot back by asking Hegyi exactly why he should stop the discovery process: "Every time Mr. Klayman turns over a rock," the judge said, "something else crawls out!"

But despite Lamberth's exasperation with Hegyi and his government client, and despite continued discovery, documents from Brown's inner office— documents that I believed would show seats on trade missions being sold for campaign contributions—were not forthcoming. The moment had arrived to request the deposition of Brown himself.

Hegyi predictably had Brown sign a sworn statement that, without saying so explicitly, gave the impression that no such documents existed. As he had attempted with lower level officials, the Justice Department lawyer hoped that Lamberth would accept this subterfuge and not order Brown's testimony. But Lamberth saw through the deceptive wording of the affidavit and blasted Hegyi before a packed courtroom of reporters for "trifling" with the court. Permission was granted to depose Brown.

Lamberth's order allowing for Brown's testimony was unprecedented in the annals of FOIA law. I would be able to question a cabinet secretary, who was required to appear before a public interest group to account for missing documents. I was indeed serving as a private prosecutor, and the court was giving me permission to do it.

I quickly issued and served the deposition notice requiring Brown to appear in Judicial Watch's offices on April 3, 1996. But just days before the deposition was scheduled to be taken, Hegyi asked the court for a continuance, claiming that Brown had to go out of the country on a trade mission to Croatia and Bosnia, new countries rising from the disintegration of the old Yugoslavia. The Balkans needed an economic revival and Brown, as the consummate politician's greaser and a master at grandstanding, wanted to play the role of capitalist helper. Because Hegyi presented the trade mission as a fait accompli, Lamberth had no choice but to grant a delay for Judicial Watch to obtain the secretary's testimony.

On the day I had specified for Brown's deposition, the plane carrying him and 34 American businessmen on the Balkan trade mission crashed and burned as it was attempting to land at Dubrovnik Airport along the Croatian coast.

I learned of the tragedy from a CBS reporter who called me while I was in a hotel room in Reno, Nevada, where I had traveled for a private case concerning an Italian-owned company my law firm was representing. I was sick and I felt knots in my stomach. While I believed Brown to be a crook, I certainly wished him no bodily harm. Now, it seemed likely that we would never learn the whole truth about his trade missions.

I called my brother Steven, a Hollywood producer and screenwriter, and asked him what he thought. His response was full of mordant humor: "The only one who will be happy about this is Bill Clinton. Moby Dick has just washed ashore." He was right. On a videotape later played on Rush Limbaugh's then television show, a smiling Clinton was caught on camera as he walked into the Washington National Cathedral for Brown's funeral. At the time, I did not fully appreciate why the President looked so pleased. I also attended one of the services held in Brown's honor, this one in a black Baptist church in Northeast Washington. I went not because I respected him in life, but because I was sad that his death would leave so many unanswered questions. I also wanted to see who would show up to mourn him. This could provide leads on others to depose in my case. And, whether I liked it or not, I had strangely become a part of the Brown legacy; in some way, I felt that I, too, needed to say farewell to him.

Without Brown, the search for the missing documents became harder. Discovery continued to uncover a pattern of lies and deceit, but the smoking gun—documents from inside the secretary's office—proved elusive. Nevertheless, other important papers were coming to light, such as a DNC brochure that advertised seats on trade missions and other perks for $100,000 in "soft money" campaign contributions, and a DNC donor list found in the files of one of Brown's top deputies. These documents created the strong inference that illegal campaign contributions were being solicited from Democratic donors in exchange for seats on a Clinton Commerce Department trade mission. But the first real break in the case came in the fall of 1996, when a Taiwanese reporter, a Ms. Lin, contacted me and asked for an appointment.

During our meeting, she asked me if I had ever heard of John Huang. I hadn't and asked her to explain his significance. She said that he had been a friend of the Clintons in Arkansas. Although he was a native of Taiwan and had hooked up with the Lippo Group, a huge banking empire owned by Mochtar and James Riady, a family of Chinese descent living in Indonesia, Huang was likely a Chinese intelligence agent. She added that he had been working at Commerce, but had recently moved to the DNC to do fund raising for the 1996 presidential campaign. According to Lin, there were also reports that Huang engaged in questionable fund raising at the DNC. The Taiwanese reporter asked if she could look through what at that point were boxes of Commerce documents that had been produced in discovery. I agreed.

In rummaging through the documents, Lin found evidence that Huang had helped to plan and implement Brown's trade missions, particularly the one to China. I gave her copies, but plotted how best to use them myself in the Lamberth lawsuit. It was apparent to me that the case was now about more than just taking bribes from corporations to go on trade missions. Incredibly, the Clintons, who, according to Lin, had placed Huang at the Commerce Department at the request of the Riadys, had inserted a possible Chinese Communist spy into the U.S. government.

5

THE DEPOSITION OF
JOHN HUANG

I decided to use the pretext of John Huang's involvement in the Brown trade missions as a way to have Lamberth order his deposition. I so moved in mid-October 1996—at the height of the presidential campaign—near the end of a status conference that dealt with a number of issues. As a last point, I slipped Huang's name in as someone I wanted to question and, predictably, Hegyi did not object, having already been shot down by the judge in his latest failed attempt to end discovery altogether. So little known was Huang at the time that when Lamberth issued his written order allowing for the deposition, he spelled his name "Wong."

Almost instantaneously, Huang's name became public. In columns written by Bill Safire of *The New York Times*, and in articles by other reporters at *The Wall Street Journal*, questions were raised about Huang's role at the department, his involvement with the Clintons and his fund raising on their behalf. The stories also raised questions about Huang's fund raising for the Democratic Party, which involved laundering illegal foreign money from overseas into the Clinton-Gore reelection campaign. Safire revealed that Huang had received more than 150 national security briefings by a CIA case officer while he was at Commerce, raising the specter that national security may have been compromised. As a result, Lamberth's order to depose Huang set off a feeding frenzy in the media just weeks before the presidential election.

It got even more pronounced when I attempted to have Huang served with a deposition subpoena and he ran. In status conferences that Lamberth himself was now calling on a daily basis, the judge would get updates on the attempts to find Huang. The U.S. marshal Lamberth had assigned to serve him reported that Huang had gone underground and cited as an example his attempt to find Huang at the DNC, where he was thought to be hiding. No one there was helpful to the court. But when the U.S. marshal entered the DNC's lobby, he reported to Lamberth, an Oriental man got up from a couch and scurried out the side door.

When Lamberth summoned officials of the DNC, including then-Chairman Don Fowler, to explain their involvement in what appeared to be obstruction of justice by thwarting his court's subpoena power, they at first refused to appear. But when the media glare became unbearable, the DNC general counsel, Joseph Sandler, finally showed up, only to charge that the burgeoning scandal was an anti-Chinese witch hunt and to imply that the U.S. marshal's report about an Oriental fleeing the DNC's lobby was racist. In response, in front of a full courtroom of reporters, Lamberth sarcastically asked: "Well, how many Orientals are there at the DNC who run from U.S. marshals?"

Also present at the status conferences was Huang's lawyer, John Keeney, Jr., who claimed that he did not know his client's whereabouts. (In later deposition testimony from Huang himself, this proved to be a lie.) Keeney and his sidekick, Ty Cobb, the grandson of the Hall of Fame baseball player of the same name, were from the law firm of Hogan & Hartson—coincidentally the legal alma mater of new U.S. Supreme Court Chief Justice John G. Roberts. Hogan & Hartson represented the government of China in trade matters, and the Clinton administration's national security adviser, Sandy Berger, was a partner of Keeney's and Cobb's before going to the White House. Chinese and Clinton administration involvement with Huang was evident for all to see. The press continued to have a field day.

The courtroom spectacle continued for several days when, late on a Friday, Lamberth—lacking any cooperation from the DNC—ordered it to disclose Huang's whereabouts. Over the weekend, I traveled to Philadelphia with my new wife, Stephanie, to visit my grandmother, Yetta, who still lived there. On my way home, listening to the radio news while driving south on Interstate 95, I heard the DNC had thrown in the towel and would now produce Huang.

At this point, the emergence of John Huang took on the proportions of a major scandal. Other journalists, including Bob Woodward, were writing front page stories uncovering new facts about Huang's apparently illegal fund-raising activities at the DNC, his CIA briefings at Commerce, where he had access to highly classified national security information, and his ties to Chinese intelligence through the Lippo Group and the Riadys. The fear was that Huang had passed on the information to his Chinese handlers, the Riadys and others.

Because we were only weeks away from the presidential election, the media scrutiny became especially intense. Senator Bob Dole, the Republican presidential candidate, was then about 15 percentage points down in the polls, and the Republican Congress was not faring much better. With the Huang scandal exploding, the polls started to improve for Dole and his party. While I had commenced the Brown investigation in 1995, well before the election, and never sought to influence the results of the upcoming vote, it was apparent to me at the time that the Huang scandal could affect the outcome on November 5, 1996. This was also not lost on Judge Lamberth and the media.

Huang's deposition was taken within a few days in Judicial Watch's offices. He entered the building through the parking garage and took the elevator up to our seventh floor office at 501 School Street in Southwest Washington. Outside were hundreds of press people from television, radio and print media. When I entered Judicial Watch's headquarters that morning, I was deluged by microphones and reporters asking me to comment. I tried to take it in stride, although in all my years as an attorney, I had never attracted so much attention or experienced such intense press scrutiny. This was a serious proceeding and I did not want to appear to be grandstanding.

Huang was escorted into the Judicial Watch conference room by his two lawyers, Keeney and Cobb. He came up to me and in soft tones introduced himself as John Huang. I was struck by his likeability and respectful demeanor. This was a real "professional," I thought, as slick as they come. And Huang did not disappoint. Throughout the deposition, he evaded one question after another, offered up little information and generally obstructed the entire process. But he did it effortlessly and with style. After nearly a day of testimony, little was gained. So I asked Lamberth for leave to continue the deposition. In a hearing before the court, Lamberth hinted that he would ultimately allow for limited additional testimony, but was careful not to look too partisan. At this point, the liberal pro-Clinton press was writing about him, too, characterizing the judge as a Republican conservative who was bent on giving the Democrats a hard time.

I videotaped the deposition of Huang and made it available to a number of television networks. On the news that evening, Huang's face became internationally infamous. ABC's "Nightline" devoted its entire show to him, pointing out that while federal prosecutors had backed off investigating Ron Brown after he died, Larry Klayman of Judicial Watch had not.

At the same time that I had begun my investigation of the Commerce trade missions, Brown had gotten involved in another growing scandal. This one concerned allegations that he had not fully reported his financial holdings in the federal disclosure statement that he had to fill out as a prerequisite to being confirmed as secretary of Commerce. Nolanda Hill, one of his reported extramarital girlfriends, and her communications company, in which Brown reportedly held an inte rest, were also implicated.

During this period, I too was becoming a national and international celebrity. "Who is this guy Larry Klayman?" the press was asking. Suddenly, I was getting invitations to do all the news shows, including Sunday morning public affairs television. Reporters were setting up appointments to visit Judicial Watch and to write profiles about me. But as the Clinton administration and the president's reelection campaign came under increased attack, and as polling began to show a decline in their lead over the Republicans, the Democrats began to panic and struck back.

First, seizing on the early statements of DNC general counsel Joseph Sandler before Judge Lamberth, the Democratic spinners were saying that the Huang controversy was just an attack against Asian Americans and Asians, part and parcel of Republican and conservative racism. This served the dual purpose of trying to blunt the impact of the scandal on the upcoming elections and persuading Asian Americans to vote Democratic. President Clinton joined in the chorus on his weekly Saturday radio address. Several liberal journalists criticized Clinton and the DNC for this cheap use of the race card, even noting that I had previously represented Chinese interests in my private law practice and had put my head on the train tracks for a Taiwanese businessman in the Keller matter. But that didn't stop the attacks from turning more direct and nastier. The Democratic Party and the Clinton administration unleashed their favorite reporters to write unflattering and vicious stories about me. As is often true in Washington, if you can't address the facts in the message, then destroy the messenger. And in these early days, I certainly got a full dose of what, in no small irony, the Clintons would later call the politics of personal destruction during the Lewinsky scandal.

The first set of attack dogs sent my way came from *The Washington Post*. *The Post*, no surprise here, was represented by the law firm of Williams & Connelly, the same lawyers who were representing the Clintons in the Whitewater and Paula Jones scandals. Reporters Paul Bluestein and Tony Loci, both of whom had been friendly when I was a mere international trade lawyer, contacted me to set up an appointment to write a profile. Naively, I invited them to visit Judicial Watch's offices and in a wide-ranging interview, told them my life's story. I even joked about Huang and the chair he sat in at Judicial Watch's conference table, calling it "the John Huang chair," as if he were an endowed college professor. Bluestein and Loci were letting me run off at the mouth, setting me up for the kill.

In a front-page profile hastily written and published in *The Post* a few days later, the two reporters massacred me. The gist of their story was that I was a two-bit international trade lawyer who saw an opportunity to use the Huang scandal as a way to hit the big time, and that all I had achieved and ever would achieve was embodied in this 15 minutes of fame. For good measure, they also wrote that I had been sanctioned by a number of judges, including Keller.

This was just round one for *The Washington Post*. In later years, the liberal pro-Clinton paper would dedicate an entire section to me in its business pages, publishing a column every two weeks entitled "The Klayman Chronicles," a spoof on "The Clinton Chronicles," the infamous video produced by conservative adversaries of the president. Every two weeks, the reporter for the column, David Segal, would call me late on a Friday for a comment, and he would smear me and my family the next Monday morning in his piece. The attacks did not cease, and Segal at one point even brought my infant daughter Isabelle into his reporting. Finally, having had enough, I sued both him and *The Post* for libel and shut them both up. The Chronicles ended, but Segal had left plenty of blood on the floor.

As for the Bluestein-Loci profile, an outrageous personal attack if ever there was one, I held back at the time, realizing that this was a unique period in history. If I was not prepared to take the proverbial heat in the kitchen, then I wouldn't be Larry Klayman and I never should have started Judicial Watch. When my anger subsided, I was actually flattered that these three *Post* reporters and their newspaper would devote so much ink to my growing notoriety. But as the Huang scandal continued to unfold, more pro-Clinton reporters found their way to my doorstep, and *The Washington Post* stories became the benchmark by which later stories were written and measured. Reporters, I learned, are generally lazy. Once a profile and related pieces are written, they are copied over and over again with little added value in the form of original new reporting. In subsequent years, many of my Judicial Watch clients would learn the same hard lesson.

Over time, and particularly during Chinagate, as it came to be known, I began to notice that most of the reporters in the liberal media who attacked me were Jewish. Since I am Jewish, this cut deeply at an emotional level. To let off some steam, I later wrote an article for the widely read Internet website, WorldNetDaily.com. Carefully choosing my words, I explained that while I am proud of my heritage, I also believe in Jesus Christ, as did my grandfather Isadore. I reasoned that this may help to explain the attacks. I went on to criticize the self-styled liberal Jewish intelligentsia, arguing that in one critical way, they had ceased being Jews: If they continued to back the Clintons, I maintained, they were not adhering to the ethical principles upon which Judaism was premised. I closed by comparing myself to Alan Keyes and other black conservatives, who were treated like "Uncle Toms" by most African-Americans. The article caused a stir. Not surprisingly, *The Washington Post's* media reporter and columnist, Howard Kurtz, who is Jewish himself, mocked me and made reference to my belief in Christ in one of his pieces.

The constant knifings by the elitist mainstream media actually emboldened me to press on. As Justice Clarence Thomas once said to me, "If you are afraid to get cut, then get out of Washington!" Years later, I realized that my concern for media hits was overblown. Rather than reducing the importance of Judicial Watch and me in the nation's eyes, these leftist reporters actually enhanced our reputation. In Washington, I learned that the more an antiestablishment public figure is attacked, the more he or she is ultimately perceived to be successful. Ralph Nader is a prime example.

By Election Day 1996, the Huang scandal had turned white-hot. Because of the negative publicity that included new reports that the Clinton administration had taken illegal donations from foreign sources in addition to China, the Democrats failed to win back the U.S. House of Representatives, as had been predicted just weeks earlier. The Republicans maintained control of the U.S. Senate. However, the controversy was not enough to save Bob Dole, whose lackluster campaign and tepid support, even among Republicans, cost him a genuine shot at the White House. Dole and running mate Jack Kemp were two political frogs, and not even the "kiss" of the John Huang affair could turn them into princes. Bill Clinton was easily reelected and the Clinton era, scandals and all, would continue for another four years. I joked at the time that Clinton's reelection would be good for "the scandal business" of the now famous Judicial Watch, but it was hardly good for the nation.

6

GROUCHO MARX, SOULMATE

Shortly after the elections, I received a prerecorded telephone message, left on my answering machine at home from Newt Gingrich, the Republican speaker of the House. In it, he boasted that Republican principles had won the day for the Republican-controlled House and, to assure that this would continue beyond the 1998 congressional elections, said that he needed donations to the party. I was struck by the arrogance of the message. Gingrich, who was himself under investigation at the time for alleged tax irregularities in his numerous political charities, was claiming credit for the Republican victory.

But Gingrich's 1994 Contract with America had flopped, for the most part, and the party was bereft of ideas in '96. I concluded, based on postelection polling, that the only thing that allowed Republicans to retain control of Congress was the John Huang scandal. I never pursued John Huang and Chinagate to help the Republican Party, but Gingrich's self-aggrandizing offended me nonetheless. In the back of my mind, I wondered whether Gingrich, or any other Republican leader, would ever call to congratulate me for having uncovered the Huang scandal, which continued to grow larger each day even after the election. That call, of course, never came.

What did come about a month after the election was a finding by a congressional special counsel that Gingrich had indeed violated tax laws and brought discredit on the House of Representatives. The finding was tantamount to ruling that Gingrich should be impeached for his behavior; it also presented me with an interesting ethical dilemma. I was clearly the up-and-coming darling of the conservative movement, invited to insider Washington parties, where I met and mixed with the movement's luminaries. But could I avert my eyes from wrongdoing by conservatives and others with whom I agreed politically?

I could not. I'd had the guts to take on the sitting president of the United States. Now, I felt, I had to stand up and take on the most powerful man in the U.S. House of Representatives, even at the risk of losing my new place as a prominent conservative.

I became the first conservative to call for Gingrich's resignation as speaker of the House. The invitations to parties ceased, a small price to pay for remaining true to my principles, and so did the speaking engagements. Grover Norquist, the anti-tax strategist, had asked me to give a talk at the Wednesday morning meeting he hosts for conservative leaders. Norquist, a strong Gingrich ally, promptly disinvited me. But I showed up anyway, demanded to speak and lectured Grover and his conservative yes men on the need for ethics and integrity in government. "If we conservatives feel bent on telling others how to lead their lives, in particular the Clintons, then we had better set the example," I pleaded. After I finished speaking there was a stony silence and I left the room never to return. It was at that point that I decided not to make any effort to rejoin "the conservative insiders club." To paraphrase the comedian Groucho Marx, I did not want to belong to any club that would have me as a member. This independence, unacknowledged by the liberal media during the Clinton administration, would serve Judicial Watch and me well in the years ahead.

As the bad press mounted for Gingrich, some other conservatives followed my lead in calling for his resignation. Gingrich finally was forced to step down as speaker of the House following the 1998 elections. Meanwhile, as the press began to dig in, the Huang scandal was turning into a bigger fiasco for the Democrats and the Clinton administration. One day, sitting in my office at Judicial Watch, I received a call out of the blue from Bob Woodward. He said that he would like to meet me near his home in Georgetown, at Billy Martin's Tavern on Wisconsin Avenue. Woodward wanted to compare notes on what we knew about the burgeoning Chinagate scandal. Given his legendary stature because of Watergate, and his prominent media role, I was anxious to meet with him. Woodward's interest could catapult Chinagate into the biggest scandal in American history, I thought, and create a groundswell of public support for accountability and justice.

A few days later I took a cab to Georgetown and met Woodward in the foyer of the tavern. In his flat Midwestern accent, he introduced himself and escorted me to the back of the restaurant, pointedly asking me to sit with my back to the entrance. I wondered whether Woodward's cloak-and-dagger theatrics meant that he wanted to tell me something really big, or whether he expected me to reveal a major exclusive to him. But as the conversation wore on over lunch, it became clear that he simply did not want to be spotted in my presence, given his standing as a liberal and my own as what his paper, *The Washington Post*, had crowned the biggest Clinton-hater in town. I chuckled at the notion that the great Woodward was apparently scared to be seen with me. After all, I was not Deep Throat.

But Woodward's interest confirmed something important: Chinagate had the potential to be even bigger than Watergate, and Woodward was, in his own surreptitious way, paying me respect. He wanted me as a source in the future, and I would surely oblige if the opportunity struck. It was a good meeting, although neither of us revealed anything of significance to the other.

Around this time, I had to tend to my private law firm business as well. Judicial Watch was still a volunteer organization without any revenue stream, and my family and I needed to eat. A few weeks after Huang was deposed, I traveled to New York City to try a commercial lawsuit on behalf of the same Italian-owned company I had represented on the trip to Reno when I learned of Ron Brown's death.

The case had been going on for some years, and it had been reassigned to a new Clinton appointee, Judge Denny Chin, in federal court. I did not think of it at the time, but Judge Chin was the first Asian-American judge ever to have been appointed to the federal bench. Prior to assuming his post, he was active in antidiscrimination cases involving Asian Americans as the head of the Asian-American Bar Association and Asian-American Defense League.

On the first day of trial, when I entered the courtroom with my client, it was packed with Chinese onlookers. I found this strange; why were they interested in a simple commercial case involving an Italian-owned company? But then it dawned on me: All the press over the Huang deposition and the Chinagate scandal had created a curiosity about me. The DNC and even the president himself were still calling the brewing scandal an attack against Asian Americans. Had the judge invited them to attend to intimidate me?

During the judge-tried case, Judge Chin, who constantly chewed gum while on the bench, was extremely belligerent and disrespectful to my client and me. At the end of the trial, which we unsurprisingly lost, I made an objection for the record and he shot back: "Tell it to the Second Circuit, not my court," a reference to the appellate court. The proof for my client had been strong, and

I was upset not only about the verdict, but by the way we had been treated, so I responded in kind with a remark that the case had not been wellhandled. The judge sneered, much as Keller had done in the Frank Su case, and stormed off the bench.

About a week later, I was in San Francisco to take the deposition of one of John Huang's collaborators at the Commerce Department, a Ms. Melinda Yee. She was not only reported to be involved in the money-laundering side of the scandal, but she had been in charge of the Brown trade missions to China. Yee was also a close friend of the Riadys, and thus a very important witness. Indeed, during her deposition, Yee revealed that she had destroyed, while still a deputy to Ron Brown, all of her documents about the China trade missions.

There was an added bonus. In preparing for her deposition, I reviewed newly produced Commerce documents, which included press reports that Judge Chin had been recommended for the federal bench by John Huang, and that Huang had effectively gotten Chin and other Asian Americans their jobs in the administration. Now, the nasty and belligerent behavior and the ruling of Judge Chin made sense, I thought.

When I returned to Washington, I consulted with the associate in my law firm and we decided to send a letter to Judge Chin, which was permitted under the court's rules of practice, asking if he knew Huang and had had any contact with him prior to ruling in our client's case. We also asked if the judge had seen or been aware of any of the publicity coming out of the Clinton administration and the DNC, branding me and others who were then pursuing the Chinagate scandal as racist against Asian Americans. The letter was nonaccusatory and was sent to learn whether, because of potential bias, there were grounds to file post-trial motions to overturn the verdict. If these issues were not raised in the lower court, arguably they could not be raised later as grounds for appeal.

Within days of sending the letter to Judge Chin, we received an order summoning us to New York City for a hearing. I was concerned, since I had seen how hot-headed the judge could be. The reaction was reminiscent of what I had experienced years earlier before Judge Keller, and more surprising and revealing since we had not even asked Chin to recuse himself. As with Keller, I decided to seek the advice of Ramsey Clark, who practiced in New York City.

My associate and I met with Clark and his partner, Larry Schilling, in their office before heading to Chin's hearing. I showed Clark the letter we had sent to Chin and asked him if he saw anything inappropriate about it. He replied no, but counseled us to keep our cool in front of the judge, as he was known to indulge in knee-jerk reactions. Clark added that he would have done the same thing under the circumstances. We got up and left for our date with Chin.

We entered his courtroom that day with trepidation. Our concerns were confirmed when the first thing out of the judge's mouth was, "I am deeply offended by your letter. You sent it only because I am an Asian American, isn't that right, Mr. Klayman?" I was caught off guard by the bluntness and harshness of the inquiry and responded "no." On the defensive, I continued, something I should not have done under the circumstances. Obviously, given his demeanor, there was no way to reason with Chin.

I explained what I had learned while reviewing Commerce documents for the Yee deposition and stated that we had an obligation to make the inquiry to protect our client. Judge Chin then shouted: "Are you asking me to disqualify myself?" It was telling that, up to this point, the judge had not denied his apparent involvement with Huang. But I held my fire. I replied that we were not asking for recusal at this time, but that if there were some involvement, the judge should "search his soul" to determine whether to recuse himself. I thought this a polite and subtle way to place the issue before the court, but went on to point out that, as a Jewish American, I would have to think twice about sitting on a case involving a Palestinian terrorist.

When my associate was then told to get up and asked the same questions by Chin, he confirmed what I had said: Chin had not been singled out because of his Chinese heritage; it was only that there were press reports that Huang had recommended him for the federal bench. The associate, who is of Greek extraction, pointed out that the same standard would apply if Huang and the judge had been Greek.

Chin, his face reddening, stormed off the bench, shouting that he would soon issue an order about this matter. A few days later, he did issue his order, demanding that we show cause why we should not be held in contempt of court for alleged unethical and racist behavior.

I decided to retain Ramsey Clark to defend us. But Chin had already made up his mind, and sanctioned us nevertheless. Having researched my past run-ins with judges, Chin found the prior Keller sanctions orders and virtually copied them verbatim. He removed my *pro hac vice* status to appear on this case. (The Latin phrase, meaning "for this one particular occasion," connotes special permission granted to an out-of-state lawyer to practice on a specified case.) He also banned me from his courtroom forever, ordered that a copy of his ruling be attached to future applications to appear before the entire federal bench in Manhattan and, for good measure, directed that a copy of his decision be sent to every federal court and bar association of which the associate and I were members. Also in his order was a finding that the associate and I had acted as racists toward Asian Americans by posing the questions about Huang and asking him to "search his soul" about possible disqualification. In reading his order, it was clear that Chin's purpose was to destroy my reputation at the height of the Chinagate scandal and perhaps to help Huang and his benefactor—the president who had appointed him. So we moved the court to place the order under seal, but before Chin ruled, it was leaked by him to the press.

Clark appealed the Chin order to the higher court, but it would not intervene, reflecting the true spirit of the federal judiciary. I had learned long before the Keller and Chin episodes that judges will rally around to protect their brethren—hence the need for Judicial Watch. But some years later, when Huang, who had been ordered by Lamberth to be deposed five times as new evidence continued to come to light, was asked if he recommended Judge Chin for the federal bench, he confirmed that he had. I felt vindicated, although I had done nothing wrong in any event!

During the numerous depositions, I asked Huang various questions about his dealings with Bill and Hillary Clinton, and others in their administration, and whether they had conspired to compromise U.S. national security. He took the Fifth Amendment. To this day, more than 150 contempt citations are in place for Huang's refusal to testify on matters the court ruled that he had to address. As a result, there remains the real possibility that Huang may someday be jailed for contempt of court once these issues run their course in appeals.

My associate and I were also cleared by all of the state bar associations that received Chin's order. They found it to be meritless and dismissed his complaint, his effort to discipline us. But, like the Keller episode, the Chin story not only stands as testament to the intrigues of the Chinagate scandal, it also underscores the corruption on the bench that made Judicial Watch a necessity.

⟶ 7 ⟶

FIASCO: THE THOMPSON COMMITTEE HEARINGS

Bill Clinton, the 42nd president of the United States, was sworn in to a second term on January 20, 1997. True to form, the president, Hillary and the administration had shaken down as many Hollywood, corporate and big-labor donors they could get their hands on to pay for all the inaugural galas. But of greater significance was that the Chinagate scandal marched on. In the early months of Clinton's second term, the continuing press frenzy forced the ethically timid U.S. Senate to announce that, in the style of Watergate, it would conduct full-scale investigative hearings. Chairing the Government Affairs Committee assigned to the task was a Republican presidential hopeful, Senator Fred Thompson of Tennessee. Thompson then chose as his head investigative counsel Michael Madigan, a prominent Republican Washington attorney who, coincidentally, lived only two doors down from my townhouse at Georgetown Park, a gated community near Georgetown University Hospital. The ranking Democratic senator on the committee was Senator Joseph Lieberman of Connecticut; Lieberman and his wife also lived at Georgetown Park. The announced mandate of what came to be called the Thompson Committee was fairly broad. Investigating and suggesting fixes for the broken campaign finance system was essential, of course. But the committee also was to examine fund-raising irregularities and the possible breaches of national security revealed in the press. And, if necessary, it would work with the Justice Department in seeking prosecutions of alleged lawbreakers.

By this time, Ken Starr had been appointed to replace Robert Fiske as independent counsel in the Whitewater investigation, and the administration was plainly worried about yet another investigation into yet another scandal. So the Clinton White House asked its attorney general, Janet Reno, to open an inquiry that seemed an obvious ploy to deflect any damage that might result from the investigations on Capitol Hill. By conducting its own investigation, the Clinton administration could upstage the Senate and steal its thunder. Reno's probe could also be used to keep crucial evidence under wraps since the Justice Department could claim that Congress should not have access to the information lest its criminal investigation be compromised. Taking evidence "off the market" in this way was an age-old Washington legal maneuver to cover up administration wrongdoing. As a result, the appointment of an independent counsel was being called for by myself and others; although from my standpoint, observing Starr's poor performance in Whitewater, this was not much of a solution. I, therefore, was determined to use Judicial Watch's case before Judge Lamberth to pursue as many leads as possible.

Shortly after his appointment as chief counsel of the Thompson committee, Madigan called me. He said that he wanted to meet to go over Judicial Watch's Chinagate evidence. By that time, Lamberth's orders had resulted in the production of hundreds of thousands of documents which proved that seats on Commerce Department trade missions had indeed been sold illegally in exchange for political campaign contributions.

I met with Madigan over lunch and arranged for a future visit to our office for his staff. Although Madigan himself did not participate, he did send a few low-level researchers to Judicial Watch to pore over the documents. They took a few copies with them, and never returned. Nor did I ever hear from Madigan again. Interestingly, during this early period of the Thompson Committee's investigation, Madigan threw a party for his new staff at his Georgetown bachelor townhouse. Despite being his next-door neighbor and the head of Judicial Watch, the group that sparked the Chinagate scandal and had helped his researchers, I was not invited. As the Thompson Committee hearings progressed, I came to understand why.

Shortly after the Madigan soiree, I held a small party of my own one Friday night. Two of my friends, Blanquita Collum, a nationally syndicated conservative radio talk show host, and Jayne Planck, the former Republican mayor of Kensington, Maryland, joined me for dinner at Café Atlantico, a trendy Latin restaurant across from the Justice Department. As we were seated on the second story of the modern edifice for drinks before dinner, Attorney General Janet Reno strolled in with two young girls at her side. All three were dressed in identical denim blue outfits, and they sat down just a few tables away from us.

Despite my years in Miami, I had never met Reno while she was state's attorney there. Blanquita, smiling wryly at the spectacle of the denim triplets, whispered in my ear: "Why don't you send her a complimentary cocktail, Larry?"

Thinking Blanquita's suggestion a devilishly excellent idea, I called the waiter and ordered up a martini for Ms. Reno. Scribbling "Compliments of Larry Klayman" on my Judicial Watch business card, I asked him to deliver it with the drink to my nemesis, the Queen of Justice. Then, as we were about to savor the moment, in walked Senator Fred Thompson.

Taking a table on the third tier of the restaurant and in full view of the other patrons, thanks to the center atrium, Senator Thompson appeared to be waiting for his date. It had been recently reported in *The Washington Post*'s Style section that he was seeing Kelly Ann Fitzpatrick, a young blond Republican pollster with a flair for television. I decided to introduce myself to Senator Thompson before Reno's martini was delivered. When I got to his table, it was clear the senator recognized me, probably from all my television appearances. "How ya doing, Larry? Nice to meet you," he drawled with a heavy Southern accent and friendly demeanor. I responded in kind. Then I asked how his committee was faring. "Good," he said, "except for that damn Ickes"—referring to Harold Ickes, Jr., the former deputy White House chief of staff and close confidant of Hillary Clinton. Ickes had been implicated in the foreign money-laundering aspect of the growing Chinagate scandal. "He won't cooperate," Thompson said.

As I told the senator that Judicial Watch also would seek Ickes' testimony, he spotted Reno out of the corner of his eye seated in the tier below. "How ya doing, good to see you," Thompson shouted out, waving at her and getting a wave back in return. Even by Washington standards, I found the chumminess a bit too much to stomach. Saying my goodbyes to the senator, I offered to help him in his investigation, pointing out that I had already met with his buddy Madigan, and then made my way down the stairs to introduce myself to Reno.

When I got to her table, I held out my hand, leaned over and said in soft and intentionally understated cadence, "Ms. Reno, I just want to introduce myself. Perhaps you've heard of me. My name is Larry Klayman." Not wanting to miss Reno's reaction, Blanquita had strolled over from our table and was now standing right behind me.

Grabbing my left hand with both of hers, Reno replied, "Larry, of course I've heard of you. I can't accept this drink. But I think you are doing a great job."

I was flabbergasted. Thinking that perhaps Reno had not recognized my name, I repeated the introduction, this time adding that I was the Judicial Watch lawyer who had recently deposed John Huang and had her attorney on the case sanctioned for misconduct. In response, Reno looked me straight in the eyes, again grabbed my hand in both of hers and reconfirmed what she'd already said: "Larry, of course I know who you are. You are doing a great job. Keep it up!" Blanquita at that point was close to hysterical laughter, but we both controlled ourselves and walked back to join Jayne at our table.

An hour and a half later, after Reno had finished dinner, the denim-clad triplets got up in unison to leave. On their way out, they stopped at our table, and in a warm and friendly voice, Reno wished us all a great weekend.

I learned that night that Janet Reno was a great actor, perhaps even a better one than Bill Clinton. Her tenure as Clinton's attorney general had been marked by disastrous missteps and crises—the Branch Davidian catastrophe at Waco, Texas, that resulted in the deaths of 83 women and children, the aftermath of the Ruby Ridge incident, and more. Still, the media had largely given her a free ride. Now I understood why: She was extremely warm and likeable in person, something that never came across on television where she had a Joe Friday-like demeanor. In fact, as the years passed at Judicial Watch, most of the Clinton people that I deposed or came in contact with had this quality—a charming and slick exterior that hid the ruthlessness with which they operated. Reno was no exception.

As Judicial Watch continued to take deposition after deposition in the Commerce case before Lamberth, learning more and more about Brown's misuse of department resources for fund raising and other illegal purposes, the Thompson Committee was cranking up its activities. In the spring of 1997, the hearings finally got underway and, by that point, the Chinagate scandal seemed to have all the elements of a movie—foreign money laundering, bribery, extortion and, yes, even treason. It was so big and so riveting that all of the major cable networks decided to cover the hearings live. I was drafted by a new conservative cable network, National Empowerment Television, or NET as it was called at the time, to do the legal analysis of the hearings. A conservative icon and friend, Paul Weyrich, who headed the network, convinced me to come on board for the hearings. My co-commentators were two young conservatives, Tom Fitton and Maryanne Lombardi, both of whom had done political commentary for Weyrich before, particularly on a late night show called "The

Youngbloods." (Yes, this was the same Tom Fitton I would later hire to run Judicial Watch, much to my regret.) Other rising television reporters, such as Norah O'Donnell, later a chief White House correspondent for NBC News, and Major Garrett, later also a chief White House correspondent for Fox News, had cut their teeth on this show as well.

As I sat there with Tom and Maryanne watching the NET monitors in the studio just east of Union Station and 500 yards from the Capitol building itself, waiting for the first day of the much-anticipated hearings to start, I wondered if they ultimately would lead to the impeachment of a president. It was now evident not only from my investigation at Judicial Watch, but also from media reports, that the Clinton White House and the DNC had engaged in massive money laundering for Chinese interests. And while the press reports pointed to illegal campaign contributions and illegal transfers of cash into the Clintons' legal defense funds, the first of which I had challenged at the outset of the administration, I thought that even more damning revelations were sure to follow. By the spring of 1997, I did not yet have the level of cynicism about the Washington political elite that I hold today.

Finally, Senator Thompson entered the hearing room, chitchatted with his colleagues for about five minutes, posed for photos—evoking his career as a movie actor—and called the hearings to order. In his opening statement, he garbled and even slurred his words, at times to the point of incoherence. Maybe he had a hangover, I thought. Somewhere in the middle of his speech, Thompson praised the honesty and forthrightness of the lead witness that day, a Democrat and Clinton hack who obviously lied through his teeth after he was placed under oath. Thompson had been a trial lawyer in Tennessee before launching his acting career, but his approach did not seem in tune with a sharp litigator.

As the hearings wore on, things went from bad to worse. What began as an inquiry into illegal foreign money laundering from China into the DNC and Clinton-Gore reelection campaign, evolved into a counterinvestigation of allegedly illegal Republican money laundering through the chairman of the Republican National Committee, Haley Barbour, who had indulged in some questionable fund-raising maneuvers with Hong Kong businessmen. The Democrats on the Thompson Committee—a band of partisans that included now disgraced ex-Senator Robert Torricelli of New Jersey, and Senators John Glenn of Ohio, Daniel Akaka of Hawaii, Dick Durbin of Illinois and ranking member Joe Lieberman of Connecticut—seized on the Barbour indiscretion to checkmate their Republican counterparts. It wasn't too difficult to do. Some of the Republicans—Senator Don Nickles of Oklahoma, for one—had also taken campaign money from John Huang. Not to be one-upped by Nickles, Senator Arlen Specter of Pennsylvania, as the hearings went on, was caught by no less than the conservative *Washington Times* taking campaign money from the corrupt Teamsters Union in return for favors to its then-president, Ron Carey.

The Thompson hearings proved to be such a fiasco that Democrats and Republicans were happy to shut them down within a few weeks, opting instead to push for so-called campaign finance reform. In effect, they were saying to the American people, pass new laws and stop me before I kill again. The entire proceeding proved to be so farcical and transparent that it ended any hope Thompson had harbored to run for the presidency in 2000, and he later retired from the U.S. Senate, a broken man politically. When he attempted a comeback and ran for president in 2008, he again faltered, showing no real drive or energy. The voters responded accordingly.

During the Thompson Committee hearings, I was never contacted by Madigan or anyone on his staff, although I would leave messages on Madigan's voice mail when I thought that evidence Judicial Watch had gathered before Lamberth could be of use to him. The only call I ever got was from Senator John McCain of Arizona, who had sat on the Thompson Committee and developed a reputation as a Republican maverick. But that call came weeks after the hearings had ended.

I traveled to Capitol Hill to meet with him and was gratified that, even though the hearings had been shut down, someone was willing to listen to what Judicial Watch had uncovered. As I sat in the lobby of McCain's office, I wondered if a high-level politician finally would do something to get to the bottom of the Chinagate scandal. After a few minutes of waiting, McCain emerged from his office. With a big smile and friendly manner, he held out his hand and said, "Larry, I feel as if we're old friends; I've seen you so much on television." When I shook his hand, I could feel how it had been disfigured and crushed by the North Vietnamese when he was a prisoner in the Hanoi Hilton during the Vietnam War.

He invited me to sit down on the sofa in his office and took a plush chair opposite me. Leaning over, he asked me what I could tell him about Chinagate. I reached into my briefcase and pulled out the documents I had uncovered showing that seats on trade missions, judgeships and Clinton administration appointments, and a potpourri of other government perks, had been advertised for sale by the DNC in exchange for $100,000 in soft money campaign contributions. It was like a Chinese menu, I joked; choose one from column A, B, or the combo meal in column C. McCain nervously laughed. I also showed him the DNC donor list, which we had found in the Commerce Department files of a top Brown deputy. This underscored that the Clinton Commerce Department was illegally soliciting campaign contributions from political donors in exchange for seats on trade missions, and perhaps worse. "My God, these are smoking guns," McCain exclaimed. The senator then offered to use the documents in upcoming oversight hearings he was intending to hold concerning the Commerce Department.

I asked him why the Thompson Committee hearings had ended in failure. Was it because both political parties had checkmated each other? McCain agreed, muttering, "Yes, my party is involved as well in the illegal fund raising. It's a disgrace."

In fact, during later depositions of John Huang, I learned that he had illegally laundered foreign Chinese money to Republican Senators Alphonse D'Amato of New York and Mitch McConnell of Kentucky. Incredibly, the person who had assisted Huang in his efforts was Elaine Chao, then the Labor Secretary-designate of the newly elected Bush administration. Chao was the attractive wife of McConnell, a powerful politician who had staked his career on opposing campaign finance reform. Despite my protests, Republicans and Democrats alike voted to confirm Chao.

I really liked McCain that day, and I felt buoyed by his commitment to investigate the illegal fund raising at the Commerce Department. But while the senator later did ask a few questions at oversight hearings, he never called upon me to testify. From time to time, he would mention the illegal Commerce trade missions as one of the fund-raising abuses of the Clinton administration, particularly when he and other senators pushed their so-called campaign finance reform legislation, which became known as the McCain-Feingold bill. But he never went beyond that. And when he later decided to run for president in 2000, he avoided appearing on Judicial Watch's radio show to discuss Chinagate or any other issue. By that time, McCain's seeming independence from his own Republican Party, and his feud with his opponent, Governor George W. Bush of Texas, had made him the darling of the liberal media. He was not going to jeopardize his standing by getting too close to

Judicial Watch or Larry Klayman, who by that time had been labeled by the media as a member of the great right-wing conspiracy.

Like everyone else on Capitol Hill, McCain proved to be a hypocrite. And, while his campaign finance legislation eventually passed, in years to come it proved to be a joke. Rather than pushing for bribery prosecutions, McCain and his gutless, compromised colleagues on both sides of the aisle opted for caution in the extreme. The legislation had more holes than a Swiss cheese, and both political parties would happily use them during the elections of 2004. Later, in upholding the constitutionality of McCain's campaign finance legislation, the U.S. Supreme Court made a none-too-veiled reference to the Chinagate scandals as a reason why the need to curb corruption would have to trump free speech concerns about limiting the amount donors could give. By exposing Chinagate, I had given the Supreme Court license to avoid addressing the real issue—the need to prosecute politicians for bribery as the only effective deterrent to corruption.

With Thompson and his committee neutered, and Janet Reno's Justice Department covering up the Chinagate scandal, Judicial Watch and I pressed on in the case before Lamberth. Through deposition questioning, I learned that John Huang had actually kept a diary of his activities at Commerce. When we asked that it be produced, Hegyi and the Justice Department provided only an illegible copy. As justification for not producing the original, Attorney General Janet Reno provided a sworn statement claiming that the original could not be inspected since it was now part of Justice's criminal investigation. Seeing through the charade, Lamberth granted me leave to serve a subpoena on Reno for the original diary. At this point, the attorney general's political capital was very low; several of her deputies, such as Charles La Bella and FBI Director Louis Freeh, were becoming quite vocal, suggesting that she was stonewalling the department's Chinagate investigation. Their comments implied that Reno was actually obstructing justice, so Lamberth had some cover when he took this rather unusual action.

To serve Reno herself, I sent two Judicial Watch legal interns from George Mason University School of Law, one male, the other female, and both very good-looking. They had no difficulty getting into the Justice Department and entering Reno's suite. But when Reno's secretary discovered that they had come to serve her boss, the interns were quickly told to go to another room, where someone would accept the subpoena for the attorney general. When they did, one of Reno's young assistants came out of his office and, seeing my two interns, whispered, "No one knows it, but I'm the only Republican here. I really like what Judicial Watch is doing." He accepted service of the subpoena for Huang's diary, and the attorney general was forced to hand over the crucial document.

When the Huang diary was eventually produced, it provided a road map of his illegal activities at Commerce and the DNC. It was everything I could have hoped for. But something else would soon happen that would prove to be even more significant in uncovering the true story of Chinagate.

8

NOLANDA HILL'S
REMARKABLE STORY

A former employee of Judicial Watch, Andy Thibault, had gotten to know Nolanda Hill, one of the reputed girlfriends of Ron Brown, over the years since I had sued Commerce. Andy had visited Ron Brown's gravesite with Nolanda after the Commerce Secretary was buried at Arlington National Cemetery. While no longer with Judicial Watch, Andy was fascinated by the Chinagate scandal and Ron Brown; in fact, I had hired him to work for Judicial Watch after he left *The Washington Times*, where he had been writing about the scandal as a national reporter.

Calling me one day, Andy asked whether I would like to meet Nolanda. Needless to say I jumped at the opportunity. She, like Brown, had been the subject of an independent counsel investigation, run by now-deceased Miami attorney Daniel Pierson, over allegations that Brown had misled government investigators during his confirmation process by filing a false financial disclosure statement. The matter concerned a communications company that Nolanda and Brown jointly owned, but which had not been fully divulged.

Andy explained that Nolanda wanted to meet me because she believed that Ron Brown's death was not an accident and that her own life might be in jeopardy, too. She was also concerned that, to shut her up, she would soon be indicted by the Justice Department on a trumped-up income tax evasion charge. She wanted my help, so Andy set up a meeting at the same Latin restaurant, Café Atlantico, where I had bumped into Senator Thompson and Janet Reno and her girlfriends.

By sheer coincidence, we were seated by the maitre d' at the same table that Blanquita, Jayne and I had shared weeks earlier. At Café Atlantico and later at the bar of the Four Seasons in Georgetown, Brown's ex-girlfriend poured out her life story to me.

My first impression of Nolanda was that an attractive and vivacious woman who had suffered a good deal of wear and tear. Now in her mid-50s, she clearly had been quite a beauty in her younger years, but time and stress seemed to have caught up with her. Indeed, she told me right off that things of late had been rough, and that she feared not only for her own life, but also for the well-being of her teenage son.

Nolanda said that Judicial Watch's case against Commerce was a cause of real concern, if not a fixation, in the Clinton White House. Chief of Staff Leon Panetta, she said, had told Brown to "soft-pedal the case"—that is, to obstruct justice before Lamberth's court. (Later, in discovery, we found documents that confirmed what Nolanda had said about Panetta—who incredibly is now CIA director in the Obama administration.)

Over several bottles of wine, Nolanda launched into her relationship with Brown. From her revelations, it was clear that she loved him deeply and was his number one confidante—much more so than his wife Alma—and played a major role in his professional success. Not only was Brown her lover, but also her business partner in the communications venture that had come under investigation by Pierson, the independent counsel.

While Nolanda was proud of being a Democrat, she claimed to have an admiration for my work at Judicial Watch and said that she had followed my career from afar. Not blaming me for looking into what Ron, as she called him, was doing at the Commerce Department, Nolanda insisted that she had many of the same concerns. According to her, Ron was a dreamer, not a realist. And money was never his primary motivation, which explained why he blew through a lot of it and why Nolanda frequently had to bail him out of debt. To my surprise, she insisted that although Ron played a key role in Bill Clinton's election as president, he never really liked him. Clinton's closest African-American friend, she said, was Vernon Jordan, who would later get into trouble for trying to find Monica Lewinsky a job to shut her up. Ron was treated as the "black sheep" by Clinton. (This was later confirmed by another Brown girlfriend I would get to know, Lilliana Madsen, a Haitian-born woman Brown kept in a townhouse owned by him and his son Michael in a northwest Washington neighborhood just off fashionable Foxhall Road.) But Clinton was Ron's ticket to becoming a major Washington star although, according to Nolanda, it was Hillary who pushed Ron into illegally selling seats on trade missions. Ron apparently resented this and used to say, "I'm not Hillary's mother-fucking tour guide!"

But a tour guide he became—his dues for admission to the Clinton mafia—and that wasn't all. In increasingly emotional terms, Nolanda told me that during his days at Commerce, Ron had been forced to get into bed with Chinese intelligence agents such as Wang Jun, also a Chinese arms dealer. The Hillary-induced scam was to work with Jun, John Huang and others to lower the export barriers on sensitive high-technology equipment to China in exchange for the Chinese pumping money into the Democratic Party and the Clinton-Gore 1996 Reelection Campaign, as well as the Clintons' legal defense fund. To grease the skids, ultimate government approval for the granting of export licenses to transfer this technology was moved from the Defense Department to Commerce, where Brown could make the decisions. Nolanda stressed that she had warned Brown not to play with fire, no matter what Hillary and her consigliere, Harold Ickes, then deputy White House chief of staff, wanted him to do. But Brown wouldn't listen, Nolanda said, and for this he paid with his life, even as Hillary and company compromised national security by selling state secrets to the Chinese in exchange for laundered campaign contributions. As Nolanda finished with this remarkable statement, she burst into tears. I was taken aback. What was she saying? That the Clintons had ordered a hit on Ron? I asked her point blank. "Exactly," she replied. To back this up, she then told me what had happened in the few weeks leading up to Brown's fatal trade mission to the Balkans.

One evening, according to Nolanda, about two weeks before going overseas, Brown went to see Bill Clinton at the White House. In fact, it was Nolanda who had driven Ron to meet with the president. While she waited in her car, Ron went in and met up with Clinton in his study. The president sat down in his favorite armchair. As Ron began to speak of the hardship on his family caused by the independent counsel's investigation, Clinton looked stern, his arms folded, his bare feet up on a footstool.

Ron told the president that he was going to have to cut a deal if he wanted to avoid his family being dragged into the investigation, in particular his son Michael, who was close to indictment for helping his father. They were very close, although, according to Nolanda, Michael was "dumb as a rock." Brown's daughter, Tracy, who was smart, was also under investigation for allegedly having furthered Ron's illegal activities. In exchange for the deal, Brown told Clinton that he was being asked by the independent counsel to tell what he knew about Judicial Watch's allegations related to Chinagate, including illegal sales of trade mission seats and John Huang's various involvements. As an aside, Nolanda mentioned that Ron never really wanted Huang placed at the Commerce Department because he was part of the Clinton mafia and his loyalties could not be trusted.

When Ron told Clinton that he had no choice but to cut a deal if the White House could not get Pierson off his back—a legal impossibility—the response was a terse "That's nice." Brown felt a chill in the room and left quickly to join Nolanda in the car, where he related what had just occurred.

With little warning Ron was sent on the trade mission to Bosnia and Croatia. Nolanda was afraid for him and for good luck gave him a water pipe, since she was part Native American and very proud of her heritage.

As was their routine, Ron called Nolanda each day. Before getting on the plane to travel from Paris to Dubrovnik airport, Ron telephoned on his government-issued cell phone. The next call she got was from Joe Rieder, the assistant secretary of the Navy, who broke the news that Ron's plane had gone down. Rieder was an old Texas friend of Nolanda's (and by coincidence, Judge Lamberth's), and he added that the plane had crashed in the Adriatic Sea. The water pipe turned up—among the effects brought back from the crash site.

Later, Nolanda learned that the plane had actually crashed on a mountain. From this contradictory account of the fatal accident, as well as what she thought were Bill and Hillary Clinton's "obvious" motives for killing Brown to shut him up, Nolanda became suspicious, ultimately concluding that they must have been involved in some way. She reiterated that she feared for her own life, or thought the administration might try to silence her in other ways as well. Perhaps, she offered, they would have her indicted by the independent counsel, since she had helped Ron fill out his Commerce disclosure statement, which deliberately understated his income. Nolanda said she wanted my help and, because there was no love lost between her and the Clintons, would tell Judge Lamberth what she knew about Ron's activities at the Department.

What she knew, she said, was that I was right about the trade missions. Ron had showed her a pack of documents—the very ones Judicial Watch had been seeking to obtain from inside the secretary's office. They included letters by Melissa Moss, the Brown deputy who had called me at the outset of the case, soliciting business executives for campaign contributions in exchange for participation on trade missions. Some of the letters thanked the businessmen for their generosity.

Nolanda insisted that she had warned Ron about Melissa and advised him to get rid of her. While she did not say so, it was clear that Nolanda was jealous of Melissa and thought that perhaps she and Brown were intimate. In any event, Nolanda stated that after his death, the documents, which Brown hid inside a desk drawer in his office, had disappeared. Nolanda concluded that they were the smoking guns that Judicial Watch had been seeking all these years.

I asked Nolanda if she would come to Judicial Watch's offices the next day, a Saturday, to tell me what else she knew about the Clintons. She obliged and spilled her heart out to my associate, Don Bustian, and me. And to make good on her offer to provide the information about Ron, Melissa and Commerce to Judge Lamberth, she signed a sworn affidavit, which we promised would be submitted in confidence to the court.

When we filed the affidavit with Lamberth the next Monday, we asked for a confidential *in camera* status conference and an order barring Hegyi and his colleagues in the federal programs branch of the Justice Department from sharing it with the Tax Division, which was investigating Nolanda for tax evasion. We were understandably concerned that Nolanda might be indicted in retaliation for her cooperation with us.

Shortly after the Nolanda pleadings were filed with the clerk's office, Bustian dropped off complimentary copies in Lamberth's chambers and happened to later see the judge in the corridor outside his office. Don said Lamberth looked ecstatic, running down the hallway like a kid with a new ball. Indeed, the games were set to begin.

Judge Lamberth held the requested status conference and ordered an immediate evidentiary hearing. But rather than keeping Nolanda's affidavit confidential, he made it public, on the grounds that it was in the interest of the American people to know what she had revealed.

Within weeks, the court held a full-blown trial, where Nolanda was placed under oath and Hegyi had a chance to cross-examine her. By this time, Reno's Tax Division was threatening to indict her, an obvious warning to keep her mouth shut. Through Reno's deputy attorney general, Eric Holder—incredibly now President Obama's attorney general—word had been passed to Nolanda's lawyer, Stephen Charles, that there would be consequences if she testified. So now she refused to make good on her promise. It was only when Lamberth ordered Nolanda to testify, promising that there would be hell to pay if Justice retaliated, that she took the stand.

But Reno and Holder did not heed Lamberth's warning, and Nolanda was charged with tax evasion. That was the hallmark of Janet Reno, Eric Holder and the Clinton Justice Department: To use every "legal" means to try to silence administration adversaries and critics. The need to take this approach became even more acute because Nolanda had just provided the first eyewitness testimony that Hillary Clinton, Harold Ickes and others had been taking bribes in exchange for illegally selling seats on trade missions, and compromising national security in the process. Much of the press was covering the unfolding story as the Clinton administration, even before the Lewinsky scandal broke, was being brought to its ethical knees. Something had to be done to shut down our case before Judge Lamberth, or so the Clintons and their henchmen obviously concluded. Ongoing discovery was prying open more than a can of worms; it was putting high administration officials at risk of criminal indictment. They must have thought that Lamberth's case, unrestrained, could expose more dirty laundry and even lead ultimately to articles of impeachment against the president himself. So they brought out every trick in their legal arsenal.

9

MOVING TOWARD
BILL CLINTON'S
IMPEACHMENT

The opening for Clinton's Justice Department to make its move to end the case came when Lamberth granted me leave to take the deposition of the CIA agent who, according to columnist William Safire, had been briefing John Huang on national security matters. I asked for this opportunity on the grounds that trade missions may have been involved in the briefings. Lamberth agreed, and ordered that the deposition be taken underground in a secure area of the courthouse. While the agent's "cover" had already been lifted by the CIA, Lamberth was taking an extra precautionary step to avoid appearing too willing to expose a former case officer to public scrutiny. (Lamberth wanted the appearance of being especially careful because he was then the head of the Foreign Intelligence Surveillance Court, the secret tribunal that can grant national security wiretaps. The court, which came into being under the Federal Intelligence Surveillance Act of 1978, is the one that President George W. Bush illegally bypassed in authorizing wiretaps on American citizens by the National Security Agency in an effort to track terrorist suspects at home and abroad.)

In taking the agent's deposition, I was confronted with another CIA operative, whom Lamberth allowed to sit in. His role was that of a "judge." Before questions were answered, he would make nonbinding rulings, subject to Lamberth's review if I disagreed, on whether the response would reveal classified national security information. This sounded reasonable, so I did not object to the procedure. But during the deposition, the CIA judge was extremely belligerent, acting as if I did not have the right to be questioning the agent at all. His demeanor grew threatening as each hour of the deposition passed, despite my constant reminders that I was on his side, particularly since we were concerned that John Huang had compromised national security.

The conduct of the CIA judge was not entirely unexpected, I thought at the time. In my years of practice both inside and outside of the government, I had come to understand how those in power do not like to admit to screw-ups, and the national security briefings the CIA had dished out to Huang were significant blunders—not in the league with the intelligence catastrophes that preceded the 9/11 attacks, but very serious nonetheless. The CIA judge was just covering the agency's proverbial ass.

However, when the deposition ended and I returned to my office that evening, I got a call from Hegyi. "You're in big trouble," he gleefully purred. I sternly asked why. Hegyi then offered that when the CIA agent left the courthouse that evening, a television news crew came up and filmed both him and the CIA judge. Revealing the identity of the agent was a crime, according to Hegyi. (This was akin to the "outing" of CIA agent Valerie Plame in 2003, an episode that actually wound up sending a journalist, Judith Miller of *The New York Times*, to jail for not revealing her sources—even though she wasn't the reporter who mentioned Plame's name in print.)

Accusing me of orchestrating the filming, Hegyi said that he would call Lamberth and ask for an immediate hearing, then call back. He did a few minutes later, boasting happily that Lamberth would hear the matter immediately. I left for the courthouse with Don Bustian, who had assisted me at the deposition; when we arrived, we were escorted by Lamberth's law clerk inside the secure room where we had deposed the CIA agent earlier that day.

Hegyi opened the hearing by telling Lamberth that national security had been breached. He added that revealing the identity of the CIA agent effectively exposed him to possible death, since he was a secret case officer whose identity was protected. My sins were not quite at the level of the "Pentagon Papers," Hegyi said. In that case, criminal charges were brought against Daniel Ellsberg, a Pentagon employee during the Vietnam War, after he leaked classified information. Still, he said, the Justice Department would have to pursue "independent action." What Hegyi was saying to Lamberth was that Justice was going to open a criminal investigation over my alleged conduct, regardless of how Lamberth might rule in the ongoing Commerce civil case. This threat made it clear that Hegyi and the Clinton Justice Department would use the incident to later argue before Lamberth that the case should be shut down. At a minimum, Hegyi must have thought that this would put Lamberth on the defensive about allowing my wide-ranging discovery to continue.

As Hegyi made his presentation, Don and I sat there quietly, my colleague whispering in my ear from time to time, joking nervously that they were going to take us away. For his part, Lamberth sat there silently, seeing through the ruse and turning red as the integrity of his court and his national security expertise were being called into question.

At the end of Hegyi's speech, I asked Lamberth if I could defend myself. He tersely said okay, but only briefly. I simply denied the accusations. Then, Lamberth looked sternly at Hegyi and the CIA judge who had accompanied him to the hearing, and in a serious voice told them to file a motion if they had something else to say—in effect, to put up or shut up.

As the judge left through a side exit and Don and I filed out of the main door, Hegyi and the CIA judge walked over to us. "Larry, do you now want to settle this case?" Hegyi asked, smiling with a Cheshire cat's grin. I was startled. Reno's hack lawyer and his CIA minion had just used the threat of criminal prosecution as leverage to shut down the case. Under the Code of Professional Responsibility for lawyers, this was unethical. But it showed me once again how ruthless Reno's Justice Department was. Losing my cool, I shot back, "Go fuck yourself!" and Don and I stormed out.

Hegyi made good on his threat and filed the motion before Lamberth. As the court pondered what to do, the CIA and likely others in the administration engaged in what I took to be an orchestrated campaign of intimidation to get me to end the matter.

First, there was the constant clicking on Judicial Watch's telephones. After that, white men wearing black leather pilot jackets and aviator sunglasses were seen on the street outside of Judicial Watch's headquarters, which was located in a predominantly black neighborhood of southwest Washington. Some of our employees, including Don Bustian, were followed home by these white men in sunshades. And it was reported by the security guard at my Georgetown gated community that "D.C. tax appraisers" had gained entry to photograph my townhouse. When I asked if anyone else's house was being photographed, the guard couldn't think of any. Finally, one day, I even got a call from the CIA judge himself, snidely asking me for a video copy of one of my recent television appearances, where I had discussed the CIA agent. He sarcastically said his mother would like it as a memento.

When Lamberth ultimately threw out Hegyi's motion to have me sanctioned, and it was apparent that the threats and intimidation would not get me to back off, Reno's Justice Department and its client, the Clinton Commerce Department, pulled one more card from their sleeves to try to shut the case down. In a bizarre maneuver, Hegyi filed an unprecedented motion for summary judgment by the court against his own client, the Commerce Department. Reno's Justice Department even asked the court to order Commerce to pay all of Judicial Watch's attorney's fees and costs, which by that time exceeded two million dollars. (Judicial Watch collected about $1 million in fees and costs years later, after I left to run for the U.S. Senate in Florida.) In effect, the Clinton administration thought that it was making an offer that neither Lamberth nor Judicial Watch could refuse—a Hail Mary pass to end the agony of further discovery and scandalous revelations about Chinagate.

In fact, the offer was tempting. Judicial Watch had not yet become a fund-raising behemoth, and we needed the money. Many of my colleagues and friends urged me to take the money and run. But I could not bring myself to do it. I had started Judicial Watch because I believed that the nation was in jeopardy of falling into an ethical abyss; I would not sell out. The Clintons must have thought that, like them, I could be bought. They didn't know me very well.

Lamberth set down Commerce's request to enter summary judgment against itself for a hearing. I was worried that, given the brouhaha over the CIA agent, the judge was now on the defensive. So in my closing argument, I challenged Lamberth. I argued passionately that while Judicial Watch could use the award of attorneys' fees and costs, we would not sell out. And if I would not sell out, neither should the court. The judge was the American people's last hope, I stressed. To a packed courtroom of reporters, I then got up and returned to counsel's table, knowing that Lamberth would hold fast. I was certain that the Clintons and their crooked Justice Department had lost again, and the Chinagate scandal would continue to unfold. Sure enough, months later, Lamberth denied the motion. By then the administration was desperate. The media had uncovered other potentially treasonous indiscretions, and Chinagate looked like it truly would undo the presidency of Bill Clinton.

Among other revelations, it emerged that Bernard Schwartz, who had bragged about paying $100,000 to the DNC and then being invited on a trade mission to China, had been allowed by the Clinton Commerce Department to export crucial satellite technology to the Chinese through his company, Loral Corp. This high-tech gear, made in America, had allowed the Chinese to learn how to more accurately target their nuclear- tipped missiles on major U.S. metropolitan areas. Not unexpectedly, the revelation caused a furor. But since Janet "Stonewall" Reno obviously would not investigate it, I needed to find a creative legal way to address this new element in the Chinagate scandal. I decided to find a shareholder of Loral to bring a lawsuit against the company for trashing its name and reputation and embroiling it in the widening Chinagate probe. This, I thought, would allow me to investigate the matter through discovery. Again, through the grace of God, the case was assigned to Judge Lamberth.

During this time, I also had the opportunity to meet Johnny Chung, the Taiwanese businessman who had testified before the Thompson Committee that the Clinton White House was akin to a turnstile: Put your money in, gain entry and receive favors. Lamberth had granted me leave to depose Chung, and he appeared with his lawyer, Brian Sun, an Asian American who had gained a reputation as being a Clinton advocate who liked to play the race card. In fact, he was viewed in some circles as the Asian-American equivalent of Johnny Cochran. I would later encounter Sun again in another case I filed, this one against Wen Ho Lee, a Chinese scientist at Los Alamos Nuclear Laboratory in New Mexico. Lee illegally downloaded nuclear codes from the lab's computers; then, when his caper was exposed, he accused Notra Trulock, the Energy Department official who opened the investigation that led to Lee's indictment, of having racist motives. I filed suit for Trulock against Lee for defamation and, true to form, the Reno Justice Department used every trick in the book to shut the case down.

Chung apparently liked my style of direct and respectful questioning. During a break in my deposing of him, I told him how I had defended Chinese people before and stood up for their civil rights as an international trade lawyer. After the deposition, he approached me and asked if I would represent him in the future; the truth was, he said, he didn't really trust Sun. His concern, I thought, probably had to do with Sun's ties to the Clinton administration. After all, Chung had testified that he believed President Clinton and Chinese leaders were trying to silence him through prosecutions and threats. Reno's Justice Department had indicted him after he revealed that he had given a $50,000 bribe to Hillary Clinton in the White House, and that the money had been laundered through Chinese intelligence. This obviously did not win him friends in Washington or in Beijing. He believed that hit squads were out to get him; indeed, press reports said that he had been in hiding.

Later, I filed suit against the Justice Department on Chung's behalf. Justice had leaked protected material about his whereabouts to the newspapers, thus violating provisions of the Privacy Act of 1974. The reason for the leaks, he thought, might have been to tip off Chinese agents that wanted to do him in. Chung's belief about the hit squads came from a message sent to him through a Chinese intermediary in Los Angeles that "our two presidents are working together."

During his deposition I had asked Chung if he thought Ron Brown's death was an accident. Chung replied, looking somewhat frightened, that he believed it was not—that it had been arranged by Clinton and the Chinese president, implying that Brown also knew too much. Chung's belief that Brown had been killed came on the heels of Nolanda Hill's similar assessment. And even that wasn't the last word.

A short time later, a photographer from the Armed Forces Institute of Pathology contacted me at Judicial Watch. Kathleen Janoski was an attractive, middle-aged lieutenant commander in the Navy. She told me, as she had explained to reporter Christopher Ruddy of the *Pittsburgh Tribune-Review* a week or so earlier, that she had been present when Brown's body was returned from Croatia. She said she found it odd when she overheard laboratory doctors being warned not to conduct an autopsy, especially since Brown was a high-level presidential appointee and cabinet secretary. What made this doubly suspicious, she said, was that the pathologists who combed over Brown's body found a hole in his head the size of a 45-caliber bullet. Why then, would an autopsy not be ordered?

Fearing that something untoward was occurring, Janoski had photographed the X-rays of Brown's skull that were hanging on light boxes, thinking that they might later disappear. Sure enough, they did vanish. And when she and at least two other pathologists complained that there appeared to be a cover-up, they all were threatened by military brass to keep their mouths shut. Fearful of retaliation and being drummed out of the Navy, Janoski contacted me for help.

My decision to represent Kathleen and her colleague, Dr. Steven Cogswell, resulted in more than just publicity; in the book "Ron Brown's Body," by Jack Cashill, Janoski credits me with saving her life. Indeed, her superiors at one point threatened her with court martial, which at its extreme carries a death penalty, if she spoke publicly about what she had observed. It took the utmost pressure I could mount to keep the military brass off her and Cogswell's backs. But despite my keeping them from being punished with the severest of sanctions for their revelations, they both ultimately retired from the military in disgust.

Jack Cashill's account of the episode is so complete that I will not belabor it here. What struck me most about this aspect of the Chinagate scandal was the attention it was getting in the black community. It was often featured by Tavis Smiley on his show on Black Entertainment Television, earning me more appearances in a two-week period than any white man in the history of the network. And the Congressional Black Caucus was plainly concerned. Congressman John Conyers of Michigan and Congresswoman Maxine Waters of California, two staunch liberal Democrats, were even calling for a full-blown investigation. The outcry in the black community came from the belief that there must have been foul play. Brown was a cabinet secretary, but he had been denied an autopsy. Conyers, Waters and other members of the Caucus reasoned that surely a white cabinet secretary would have been treated differently. Whatever their perception, support from liberal black Democrats would be crucial, I thought. So I asked Congressman Conyers if he would have dinner to discuss the situation.

We weren't strangers. I had come to know Conyers just before deposing John Huang because he had leased excess space from me in Judicial Watch's offices. (In fact, he still owes me unpaid rent.) During the Huang deposition, he had been in his section of the suite with his newly born child, unaware of what was going on in my conference room nearby. On one occasion, he had even invited me to one of his fund-raisers in the Virginia suburbs. Being exposed to donors who undoubtedly were Ron Brown supporters, I found the whole scene so intriguing and entertaining that I decided to donate $200 to Conyers in appreciation—the last time I ever made a political contribution.

Conyers and I dined at—you guessed it—Café Atlantico, the restaurant that had come to symbolize my life as a crime fighter. I explained to Conyers how it would be good if he met with my clients, Janoski and Cogswell. I also told him about my investigations of Brown at Commerce—the illegal sale of seats on trade missions and high technology to the Chinese. With his characteristic grin and "Detroit drawl," Conyers replied, "It doesn't surprise me. Ron was a scallywag." He added that, frankly, nothing that Clinton and

Brown did would surprise him, and he agreed to meet with my clients in his House offices.

I really liked John Conyers at that time. He was refreshing and not what he sometimes appeared to be on television. In private, he realized that not all issues were clear-cut. Brown and Clinton were corrupt birds of a feather. But as important, Conyers had conceded during our dinner discussion that neither of them had done much to advance the cause of black people during the administration's tenure. It was therefore clear to me that Conyers and his Congressional colleagues could become great allies in my campaign against Clinton corruption.

A few days later, Janoski, Cogswell and I met with Conyers in his office. Taking us to an underground House recording studio, he asked if he could tape the interview. We agreed. At the end of the session, the congressman promised to take action to pursue a vigorous investigation. We were pleased. What made us ever more optimistic was Conyers' praise. He complimented me for my work and stressed that not all was kosher in the Clinton administration. Here was a valuable ally, we thought.

Later, I was approached by the Washington chapter of the NAACP and comedian Dick Gregory. Like Conyers, they too wanted a complete investigation of Brown's death. I agreed to prepare a petition to be presented to the three-judge panel that oversaw the appointment and administration of independent counsels, asking for an inquest. In an unprecedented filing, the NAACP joined Judicial Watch. For his part, Dick Gregory attended press conferences and spoke out strongly about the need for a full airing of the facts. It was clear that the black community did not trust the Clintons. If this traditional Democratic stalwart could be turned, I thought, we could make real progress in bringing Bill and Hillary to justice for their apparent crimes.

Through our actions and by default, Judicial Watch and I were becoming a virtual Justice Department because no one else seemed willing to seriously investigate, much less prosecute, the players in the ever-growing Chinagate scandal. But Judicial Watch's voice was echoed elsewhere as the list of Clinton-era scandals lengthened. Beyond Chinagate, there was the misuse of the Internal Revenue Service to audit critics. There was Travelgate and Filegate and a host of other sleazy intrigues. The outcry among conservatives, people of faith, political moderates, and even a few liberals, like columnist Nat Hentoff and pundit Christopher Hitchens, was reaching a fever pitch.

In the spring of 1997, I was contacted by Howard Phillips, one of the founders of the modern conservative movement and the head of the Conservative Caucus and the Constitution Party. I had come to know Howard as a friend and fellow member of the Council for National Policy (CNP), a group of predominantly religious conservatives that I had joined. Howard was a great admirer of Judicial Watch, and we often spoke about issues of the day. Interestingly, we also had similar backgrounds. Like me, he was born a Jew and his grandparents had also fled Ukraine. But Howard had become a devout Christian, while I had not as yet made the leap to fully accepting Christ. Still, our common roots probably had something to do with our personal and intellectual connection.

When Howard told me that he wanted to get together a group of prominent conservatives to push for the impeachment of Bill Clinton, my first reaction was skepticism. I had seen the hypocrisy and cowardice of Congress during the Thompson hearings. Why, I asked him, would Congress now act? Still, despite my doubts, I pledged to support Howard in his quest and offered to help him. Obviously, my involvement would be crucial, given my status as Clinton's chief antagonist. Judicial Watch also had the evidence, Howard correctly argued, to get the president impeached and convicted. We decided to go see a mutual CNP member and friend, then Republican Congressman Bob Barr from Georgia, since Bob always seemed to have the guts to stand for principle.

A few days later, we visited Bob's office on Capitol Hill. With a few staff members at his side, Bob listened intently as we laid out the case for impeachment, stressing how Clinton had violated the public's trust in ways that dwarfed what Nixon had been accused of in Watergate. After we finished, in a quiet but determined way, Bob agreed to spearhead the effort. He instructed his staff to work with Howard and me to draft articles of impeachment. We would decide later when they should be introduced before the House of Representatives.

But Howard, Bob and I knew that we could not mount even a credible impeachment effort without the support of our other prominent conservative friends, most of whom headed powerful public interest groups. So we decided to gather together a meeting at the next CNP conference, to be held in Charleston, South Carolina. We met several weeks later, in a room offsite from the CNP conference. Present were Paul Weyrich of the Free Congress Foundation, Phyllis Schafly of the Eagle Forum, Wayne LaPierre of the National Rifle Association and many other powerful leaders of the conservative community. Howard, Weyrich and I each made a presentation. Then it was time to take a vote. On that evening in Charleston, the "vast right-wing conspiracy," in the words Hillary Clinton would later use on the "Today" show, was born. We voted to remove the 42nd president of the United States by whatever legal and ethical means were necessary. All agreed that the future of the Republic hung in the balance and that treasonous acts uncovered by the press and, frankly, Judicial Watch and me, could not go unpunished.

In the winter of 1997, as my infant daughter Isabelle was being born, Bob Barr was on television announcing that he had introduced articles of impeachment to the House of Representatives. They did not as yet contain any charges concerning Monica Lewinsky, because that particular Clinton scandal had yet to break. As the right-wing conspiracy hatched in Charleston had agreed, the primary basis of the effort rested then on Chinagate and other indiscretions by the Clintons. I made Bob Isabelle's honorary godfather.

Indeed, there was a vast right-wing conspiracy during those Clinton years, not out of design but out of necessity. Few Democrats and liberals gave a damn about Clinton corruption; instead, most of them paid slavish allegiance to the ethically challenged president and first lady. But many conservative leaders demonstrated a double standard when it came to wrongdoing in the administration that succeeded the Clintons—the presidency of George W. Bush. Take the Valerie Plame episode. The leaking of her name—probably caused by Karl Rove, either directly or indirectly—to get back at her husband, Joseph Wilson, a Democrat who accused the administration of fabricating evidence of Saddam Hussein's so-called nuclear program, was simply indefensible. Democrats and liberals who defended Clinton now attacked the Republican White House. But where were the Republican voices? Their hypocritical silence was deafening. For both Democrats and Republicans, politics too often trumps national security and the best interests of the American people.

10

FAMILY VALUES AND A TALE OF TWO CITIES

In March of 1997, as I was deeply embroiled in the growing Chinagate investigation, a scandal of sorts touched my own family. My grandmother, Yetta, then 89 years old, had fallen out of bed at her nursing home and broken her hip. It was bad enough for my grandmother that she had been placed in a nursing home. Her dream, for when she got old, was to be cared for by her daughter, my mother Shirley.

I got a frantic call from Yetta's younger sister and my great aunt, Gussie, to go to my grandmother's bedside in a remote part of northeast Philadelphia, since she was near death in a hospital there. My mother and her husband, Irv Feinberg, were then in Los Angeles visiting my brother, Steven, and his family.

I dropped what I was doing at Judicial Watch and rushed to see my grandmother. When I entered the room, my heart sank. She looked like a cadaver, her skeleton starkly delineated against her ash-gray skin, her hair completely white and uncombed. I nearly collapsed. Stephanie, my second wife, whom I had married in July 1996, had to prop me up. I summoned enough strength to go over to her bed, lean down, and whisper in her ear, "It's Larry, Nanny. I love you."

After a few minutes, my grandmother opened her eyes and whispered in a faint and gravelly voice: "Larry, my darling grandson, I'm so glad you're here. I love you, you know. You were always my favorite. Is mom here?"

Yetta and I had a special relationship. When I was young, she was the one who essentially raised me, living with us until I was about 10. Since I was her first grandchild and named after her husband Louis, the bond between us was very strong. My grandmother took me everywhere with her. On Saturdays, we would hop on the bus and elevated train—the El—to downtown Philadelphia to see a movie and then have an early dinner at Horn & Hardarts, a favorite restaurant of my other grandparents as well. After my mom had taken me to see "The Wizard of Oz," I had recurrent nightmares of the Wicked Witch of the West slipping into my bedroom and tickling me. When I was scared, I would sleep in her bed. Nanny was always there, and when my parents sometimes fought, she would comfort me.

At the hospital, tears were running down my face when my grandmother called out for my mother. I knew that without Shirley at her side, she might not last. So I immediately called my mother in Los Angeles and told her that she needed to come home right away, that Nanny desperately needed her.

But my mother inexplicably balked. "I've done so much for your grandmother. Enough is enough. I need a vacation," she replied. I was stunned. How could my mother abandon my grandmother in her hour of need? I did not know at the time that my mother was suffering from the onset of dementia, which years later would develop into acute Alzheimer's disease and ultimately lead to her death.

I also did not realize as yet that her husband, Irv Feinberg, had persuaded my grandmother to turn over her life's savings to my mother—about $80,000. That was a fortune for Yetta, who had led a frugal life. Even her meals at restaurants rarely cost more than three or four dollars. On the telephone, I asked my mother how much Nanny had saved, because it was clear that I would need to fill out a financial statement to secure her rehabilitative services at a nursing home once she was released from the hospital. But my mother replied tersely that she didn't know what Nanny was worth: "I think she lost all of her money in the Mexican stock market."

I never really liked Irv, not because he followed my real father Herman as my mother's husband, but because he always seemed to be a leech. Even before they were married, Irv had moved into my mother's house in Penn Valley, appropriated one of its rooms as his office, and then obtained an insurance adjuster's license. Day and night, Irv would listen to a police radio he had purchased; hearing of a new fire, he would race to the scene of the tragedy to offer his services, signing up victims, then inflating insurance claims on their behalf. Irv was very proud of his new profession, although he could not have survived financially without my mother's support; she ran a successful art gallery. The word "nebbish"—Yiddish for "zero"— described him perfectly. My brother Steven and sister Janine felt much the same as I did about Irv: He was a loser and we knew it. But he claimed to deeply love my mother, and she believed him; so we kept our mouths mostly shut for many years.

Ironically, my grandmother liked Irv in the period before she broke her hip. He had tended to her years earlier after she had tripped and fallen in front of her modest row house in Oxford Circle, breaking both of her arms. He and my mother also helped Yetta pay her bills and perform other tasks. Perhaps it was Irv's calculated "kindness" that gave rise to my grandmother's entrusting him with her money.

This trust was misplaced. In my conversation with my mother, I learned that not only had Yetta's money disappeared, but that her health insurance had been allowed to lapse. Apparently, Irv had not paid the premiums. This made it all the more important that I locate my grandmother's life savings, since she needed immediate care. Because of a technicality, she did not qualify for rehabilitative Medicaid. So when my mother did not return from Los Angeles, I had no choice but to get my grandmother into a rehabilitative nursing home and personally guarantee the health care, even though Stephanie and I had little spare cash and could not finance Yetta's needs by ourselves. The facility was close to my mother's home. But this was only a temporary solution. My personal guarantee would have to be backed up with cash payments, because the cost of care would run to more than $5,000 a month. So I asked Steven and Janine for help in having Shirley identify where Nanny's life savings could be found.

But instead of help, my brother and sister declined to get involved. Either they did not believe that Irv had stolen the money, or were too busy in their own lives. Nor did they seem to appreciate the gravity of the situation and our grandmother's will to live. Janine believed that Yetta's 89 years on this earth had been enough. I was deeply offended by their attitude. I knew that Steven and Janine were not pro-life, but I never thought that their philosophy would extend to their living grandmother. Not only could I not get them to intervene, but they harshly criticized me for crying foul and putting pressure on Irv and my mother to disclose where they had stashed Yetta's money.

Steven and Janine visited Nanny only once each in her new rehabilitative nursing home. And after their return from California, my mother and Irv rarely showed up, despite living only three miles from the facility. From my mother's perspective, perhaps she saw in my grandmother her own eventual fate and was scared to confront her mortality. Or maybe it was the incipient dementia that clouded her thinking. For his part, Irv obviously didn't give a damn, having already pried the money loose.

So at the height of the Chinagate scandal, with all hell breaking loose, Stephanie and I would drive nearly every evening from Washington to Philadelphia, and on weekends as well, to be with my grandmother and comfort her. In the early days of her convalescence, we slept in her room to make sure that she felt loved and was getting adequate care. Later, when we could not be there all the time, we hired nurses to be with her round the clock. We personally had to guarantee payment, since my mother and Irv steadfastly refused to tell us where Yetta's assets could be found. It would be an understatement to say that I was a nervous wreck.

After several weeks, when it became apparent that my mother would not tend to Yetta, I proposed to her and Irv that my grandmother be moved to Washington, where Stephanie and I could care for her daily. After a few disagreements, my mother finally relented and Yetta was placed in a similar rehabilitative home in northwest Washington, not far from our Georgetown townhouse.

Over the next five months, my mother visited Yetta exactly once. And despite having relatives in the area, few other family members came to see her. For our part, Stephanie and I continued to visit her, often twice a day. We ate meals with Nanny and joked with her. But during this time, without my mother present, my grandmother's condition worsened. Her heart was broken that her daughter was not by her side.

Also worsening was the financial situation. Finally, I had no choice but to bring suit on my grandmother's behalf to recoup the money Irv had obviously stolen from her. I had become a public figure as head of Judicial Watch and did not want to attract attention or give the Clintons a chance to drag my family's name through the mud, so I came up with a clever way to file the case. Assigning the mounting debt to Accounts, Inc., a company I founded to collect unpaid legal fees at my law firm, I filed suit in its name—in Pennsylvania, rather than in the public glare of Washington, D.C.

Irv had cunningly placed the assets in my mother's name, thinking he could then not be accused of embezzlement. The result: I had no choice but to sue my own mother.

Once the complaint was filed, my mother's lawyer—a friend of Irv's, of course—moved to dismiss, arguing that the Feinbergs had not taken Yetta's assets. During the hearing, however, I successfully got the court to question my mother and she admitted that, in fact, about $80,000 was in her name—money Irv had taken from my grandmother.

The judge used the opportunity of our being all together to hold a conference in his chambers and tried to settle the matter. When he asked me sarcastically, "What's the problem?" I told him the story: How Irv, through my mother, had taken all of my grandmother's money and allowed her private health insurance to lapse, and how she now could not pay for crucial health care. The judge responded tersely, "I don't see any issue. Everyone takes their parents' money so they can qualify for government Medicaid." I was incredulous; the judge had just advocated committing a fraud on the government because "everyone" does it.

"I don't condone fraud and, as a judge, neither should you," I shot back. Needless to say, we did not settle the case that day.

The incident reminded me once again why I had founded Judicial Watch. This was yet one more example of the ethical bankruptcy on the bench. But more important for my grandmother, at least, I had uncovered the truth about the money taken from her. I returned to Washington prepared to file a motion for summary judgment to get Yetta's money back so we could pay the creditors. Fortunately, the court had granted my request ordering that these assets not be moved or disbursed, freezing the status quo until it could dispose of the case in its entirety.

Around this time, I was attracting even more attention in the national press. There was Chinagate, of course. But several other lawsuits against the Clintons also were gathering steam, including Filegate, a class action that involved the Clinton administration illegally obtaining and misusing confidential government files to smear political adversaries. In this case, I was deposing many Clinton administration officials, from former White House communications czar George Stephanopoulos to Chief of Staff Mack McLarty and even political consultant James Carville. In Stephanopoulos' case, Lamberth had sanctioned him with monetary penalties for lying under oath. As a result, the newspapers and weekly news magazines were writing major stories about me. Most of these publications had a liberal pro-Clinton bent, and the pieces were hardly flattering, although I did take pride that Judicial Watch's anticorruption efforts now had the full attention of the mainstream media. If nothing else, the attention showed respect, if not fear, that my efforts endangered the continued political existence of Bill and Hillary Clinton and their enablers.

But given my family situation, this notoriety was not a cause of great pleasure. I became exceedingly agitated one evening when I received a call from reporter Daniel Klaidman, who had written a recent *Newsweek* profile about me.

"Larry, I got a tip that you sued your own mother. Is this true?" he asked with delight. Not knowing what to say, and wondering how he had found out, I asked him where he had heard this. He responded that he could not say, that it came from a confidential source.

I explained to Klaidman the basic facts behind the story, and left it at that, naively thinking that perhaps he had understood the unfortunate circumstances and would respect my family's privacy and not print it. But a few days later I got another call, this time from a supporter. He told me that Chris Matthews had just named me "Loser of the Week" in his MSNBC "Hardball" program.

I immediately called Matthews' producer and asked him what this was all about, and he explained that, based on a *Newsweek* story by Daniel Klaidman, the show had learned that I had sued my own mother. Thus, the "award." Shortly after Hardball had aired the story, it was also broadcast on Charles Grodin's MSNBC show. Grodin couldn't resist the opportunity to take a further shot at me, mocking conservatives for their emphasis on "family values."

Incensed, I immediately wrote a stiff letter to MSNBC asking for equal time. But before long, the story was all over television and radio. I became known as "Larry Klayman, the guy who sued his own mother." Later, when I redeposed Carville, who had also been sanctioned by Lamberth for lying, he boasted how he was the one who coined this phase, calling it the "comma" technique. The intent was to portray me as an overly litigious, crazed maniac who was out of control.

To their credit, Matthews and Grodin both put me on their shows and gave me equal time. When I explained the whole story, they praised me for coming to the defense of my grandmother. But the Carville comma lived on nonetheless. In a strange twist, political scientist Larry Sabato of the University of Virginia once gave an interview to *Legal Times* magazine, where he argued that the "mother tag" had benefited me. "If someone can sue his own mother," Sabato was quoted, "then anything is possible." The professor and frequent television commentator was making the point that I had developed a fear factor that served me well, much like insect repellent, in keeping the political cockroaches in Washington, D.C., at bay.

Interestingly, while Matthews and Grodin were quick to run with the "mother story," Geraldo Rivera of the same NBC-affiliated network never used it. Geraldo was the strongest of the pro-Clinton advocates during those years, and the two of us sparred often. But the tabloid reporter had a deep respect for me, which he often voiced off camera. And despite his air and reputation for being "in your face," I found him to be the most straightforward of all the cable hosts I encountered. We both had a lot of fun during the Clinton years jousting with one another, but it never got personal.

Throughout the smear campaign begun by Daniel Klaidman, I believed that Clinton private investigators had found the court file of my case against my mother. But after a little digging, I learned the sad truth. It was my own brother, Steven, who had given the story to *Newsweek*. Indeed, in Klaidman's piece, Steven was "cutely" quoted as saying that he would not comment on the case for fear that I would sue him, too. So when I learned from my father that Steven had admitted to being the source, I was not completely surprised. My younger brother—I am nine years his senior—has always had an older brother complex, particularly since his own career as a would-be screenwriter had not yet materialized as hoped. I once made the mistake of comparing him, in jest, to Roger Clinton, Bill Clinton's tortured younger brother. While he did not find the comparison particularly funny, Steven, who prides himself as a comedian, smiled nevertheless.

Years later, after we had reconciled, I asked Steven why he had exposed the family's sad story in the media. He denied being the source and claimed that "some gay guy he had been working with gave the tip to Klaidman." "Larry, you don't know how hard it is to be your brother working in Hollywood," he pleaded. I responded by asking Steven how that guy had learned of the matter in the first place. Notwithstanding the lack of credibility in my brother's defense, it was curious that he would blame a gay man. Never during my tenure at Judicial Watch was I involved in gay rights issues, and I am not homophobic. The fact that Steven used this defense spoke only to the continuing misconception that if you are a conservative, then you must be a threat to traditionally liberal groups. This polarization was never more intense than it was during the Clinton years, with the fallout continuing to this very day.

In the meantime, my grandmother's troubles grew worse. Her will to carry on eroded in the absence of my mother's attention; she refused rehabilitation in the nursing home and developed circulation problems in her legs. When the circulation issues became acute, and gangrene set in, Yetta had to be transferred to nearby Georgetown Hospital for emergency care. Without medical insurance and a reliable flow of income—the court had yet to rule on my case to get Yetta's money returned to her—the Catholic, pro-life Georgetown Hospital had little interest in providing her with quality care or, for that matter, even keeping her alive. In a series of missteps, the hospital allowed my grandmother's condition to worsen and she eventually slipped into a coma.

I called my mother to tell her of Nanny's declining condition; it might be her last chance to visit with her own mother. Dutifully, Shirley took the train to Washington and stayed with Stephanie and me at our Georgetown townhouse.

I thought that perhaps the strain and sadness of the situation might cause us to reconcile, but I was wrong. While visiting my grandmother in the hospital that day, my mother had requested, at Irv's suggestion, that a "do not resuscitate" order be placed on Yetta's medical charts. As next of kin, she had the legal right to do this, but at least she could have discussed it with me first. I found out about the order through one of the nurses whom I had hired to look out for my grandmother, not trusting the cash-hungry hospital. When I confronted my mother with the revelation, she said that she did not know what I was talking about—again, perhaps the result of her advancing dementia. After a heated discussion, she left our townhouse and returned to Philadelphia.

But I could not let this stand. Nanny was not gone yet, and I intended to find out myself whether she could be brought back to consciousness. I asked the hospital to give me access to her medical records, but was told that my mother had ordered them not to provide the information. By this time, my grandmother's blood pressure was falling rapidly, and it was apparent that she might not live more than a few days. So, on a Friday morning, the day I became aware of the problem, I was forced to file yet another suit to try to lift the "do not resuscitate" order and gain access to my grandmother's medical records. After filing a complaint, I moved that the court provide emergency relief because I worried that Nanny might not make it through the weekend. Despite waiting at the courthouse during the day, and constantly asking the judge's clerk to make sure I could be heard, the judge walked off the bench at the 5:00 p.m. closing time, in the full knowledge that my grandmother could die in the next 48 hours.

I was frantic. The hospital also had been ordered to stop providing food to my grandmother. This was illegal, I thought. So, I called the Washington, D.C. police department's homicide division and reported the matter to a police officer. He reacted immediately and visited the hospital. His inquiry generated a newfound desire by the "pro-life" Catholic institution to provide the medical records to me. I enlisted an internist to read them and he learned that, lo and behold, my grandmother's condition was reversible since she was suffering from kidney failure that could be treated with dialysis.

When I heard the good news, I quickly called my mother to get her permission to allow my grandmother to get medical treatment. By this time, it was a Sunday. Shirley and Irv were most likely on the golf course enjoying themselves, I thought. So I called directory assistance and asked for the home phone number of the judge who had walked off the bench on Friday afternoon. It was unlisted. I then asked the operator to contact the judge herself to explain the need for an emergency court order. After speaking with the operator, the judge refused to talk with me.

The time was growing late for my grandmother. It was the evening of August 24, 1997. Her blood pressure was very low and she lay still, her eyes closed in a hospital room that overlooked my townhouse across the street. I kept calling my mother on my cell phone, but to no avail. Finally, I got through. I begged my mother to allow for Nanny to be treated. In exasperation she finally relented, saying, "OK, do what you want!" I told the head nurse that my mother had given the go-ahead and put the nurse on the phone with her. The nurse, after listening to my mother, replied that this was not what my mother was now telling her.

I ran back into my grandmother's hospital room to check on her. There were two orderlies standing over her. They were pulling the sheets over her head. My grandmother had just died.

I called my mother once again. "Mom, please order them to try to revive Nanny. She just died," I begged her through my tears. I got no response, only silence. I kissed my grandmother goodbye and told her that I loved her. I went home dazed and emotionally spent,

About a week later, Stephanie and I went to Philadelphia for my grandmother's funeral. Georgetown Hospital at least had had the courtesy to arrange for the body to be shipped back to Yetta's hometown. As she was lowered into the ground, next to her beloved Louis in a remote section of the cemetery near the house where she'd lived, I stared at my mother, Irv and my brother and sister. I could not believe what had occurred and, frankly, I had no desire to speak with them. After the rabbi read his final prayer, Stephanie and I walked off and did not have any contact with any of them for several years.

In late 2002, I got a call from Steven. He pleaded with me to listen to him. Mom had moved to San Diego and purchased a condo with Nanny's money. Now, Steven told me, she too had been robbed by Irv, who had forged her signature on divorce documents. To make matters worse, Irv had abandoned Mom, admitting her to a nursing home for Alzheimer's patients. Her condition was bad. Steven also told me that he had tried to have Irv arrested, since he had become an alcoholic and abusive to our mother. He apologized for the past and admitted that I was right about Irv. I got a similar call from my sister Janine a few days later. She apologized as well.

I took no solace in the apologies or in what had happened to my mother in the intervening years. I love her and never wished her any harm. But when Steven later sent me the medical records from my mother's caregivers, indicating that she had fallen victim to the onset of dementia as early as January of 1997, a few months before Yetta's tragic fall and death, it helped to explain in part her conduct toward my grandmother. The information helped me come to grips with what had occurred.

When her condition worsened, my mother spent the next few years in a nursing home close to my brother in Los Angeles. He visited her frequently and cared for her as I had for Nanny. I visited her, too. My sister, who owns and runs a horse farm outside of Chicago, was deeply involved with the legal effort to straighten out my mother's affairs and recoup the money Irv had stolen yet again. The money was needed to pay for my mother's Alzheimer's care, as it had been in 1997 for my grandmother. Irv had allowed my mother's private health care policy to lapse as well.

A few years later, Irv died of a heart attack and my mother soon followed suit in 2006, her nervous system totally destroyed by this deadly disease. Janine, without asking Steven or me, had her body cremated, and the ashes spread over areas of her hometown of Philadephia that she loved so much.

Scars still remain among Steven, Janine and me over Nanny, but at least some small good has come out of all of this; my sister and brother apologized and family relations at least were restored somewhat during my mother's final years.

In 2003, in honor of Yetta and my mother, I founded another non-profit organization, The Respect Foundation, to care for the elderly who have been abandoned by their own families. I asked Rodney "I can't get no respect" Dangerfield, one of my favorite comedians, to be the spokesperson, and he agreed. Unfortunately, he was already critically ill at the time and died soon after undergoing surgery for heart valve replacement.

In this world we live in, few people get the respect they deserve. My grandmother and mother certainly never did. In fighting two battles at the height of the Clinton scandals, one with a bunch of crooks in the White House and one with a crook in my own family, I learned not only that life is more complicated and difficult than I ever expected as a young boy, but also that steadfast principles do matter. My family experience prepared me for the road ahead, and it was one reason why, several years later, I would assist the Schindler family in trying to save the life of their daughter Terri Schiavo, a brain-damaged woman who was put to death by our flawed system of so-called justice.

About nine years after my grandmother's death, I had a long heart to heart talk with my brother Steven about this sad episode in our family's history. This conversation occurred just after one of my periodic visits to my mother at her Glendale, California nursing home. As always, it was painful to see her lying in a semicomatose state. Saddened, I reflected with my brother that perhaps, despite the urgency of the situation at the time, I could have tried to use other means to try to save my grandmother before filing suit, but I have always held true to the principle that only God can decide life or death decisions.

11

THE LEWINSKY
LIGHTNING ROD

As the Chinagate scandal was reaching critical mass, underscored by the introduction of articles of impeachment through Bob Barr, a miracle for Bill Clinton occurred: The Lewinsky scandal. Yes, it was a miracle. With its sex, lies and the semen-stained dress revealed for all to see, the media, seeing a chance to exploit the prurient angle of the scandal and boost ratings, quickly left Chinagate behind for the story of an intern giving oral sex to the president of the United States in a room just off the Oval Office. Much as with the death of Ron Brown, I felt sick. No pun intended, but my brother Steven's "Moby Dick" analogy came to my mind. Had the scandal of the century just washed ashore? The answer proved to be yes.

While appropriately accused of many things, Clinton Attorney General Janet Reno was not stupid. She assigned the Lewinsky investigation to independent counsel Ken Starr. After a lackluster and suspect investigation of the death of White House counsel Vince Foster, Starr had just rubber-stamped the episode as a suicide. And his thrashing about in the Whitewater matter hardly inspired hope and confidence. He also had no prior experience as a prosecutor and there were doubts he would go the distance and indict Clinton for the lies he told in the Lewinsky affair. Starr had become the whipping boy of the media, including some conservative voices and outlets.

Coupled with this was the hard fact that the Lewinsky scandal, billed as being primarily about sex, was never going to be the vehicle to impeach and convict Bill Clinton. It just did not rise to the level of seriousness of other Clinton scandals such as Chinagate, Filegate, the misuse of the IRS and the misappropriation of taxpayer money through illegal "legal" defense funds. Indeed, the difficulty with the Lewinsky scandal was that it just could not be taken seriously as an impeachable offense, no matter how hard anyone tried. So, for Bill Clinton, it was the lightning rod—no pun intended—that drew attention away from his more egregious abuses of power.

In any event, I decided to take a stab at justice. I instructed my staff at Judicial Watch to prepare an "Interim Impeachment Report" of our own, focusing on the "other" scandals. With great fanfare, I publicly filed the report with the House Judiciary Committee, the congressional committee assigned to consider impeachment. Congressman Bob Barr then formally introduced it into the House impeachment record. In fact, I remember vividly when he did so. I was walking into the Fox News studios in Washington and encountered Tony Snow and Carl Cameron, two of the network's top anchors, leaving after a day of commentary about the impeachment hearings. The two congratulated me on Barr's introduction of Judicial Watch's Interim Impeachment Report into the Congressional Record. They told me that Barr had been successful in his effort thanks to his having made a motion just before dinner. The Democrats, anxious to eat, apparently did not pay much attention and allowed the motion to pass.

But even Barr's clever introduction of Judicial Watch's Interim Impeachment Report into the Congressional Record did not mean that the House Judiciary Committee would widen the scope of its inquiry beyond Lewinsky. So I had Barr set up a meeting with the legal counsel heading the probe. David Schippers was a Democrat, but he had been picked by the Republican head of the Judiciary Committee, Henry Hyde, based not only on his hard hitting-reputation as a crime fighter while with the Justice Department in Chicago, but also on his independence.

Barr, Schippers and I met in the same Judicial Watch conference room where I had been deposing various Clinton and Democratic officials. Backed up by Barr, I laid out the seriousness of the other Clinton scandals —in particular, Chinagate—and made a formal pitch to widen the impeachment scope. I also told Barr and Schippers the story about one of my newest clients, Dolly Kyle Browning.

Not long before the meeting, Dolly, who claimed in the media to have been Bill Clinton's high school girlfriend and then his lover for more than 20 years, had contacted me. According to her story, she had written a book, "Passions of the Heart," which in truth was a fictionalized account of her years with Bill. After it became known that she was writing the book, Dolly said, she was threatened by Clinton henchman Deputy White House Counsel Bruce Lindsey, who told her she would be "destroyed" if her novel were ever published. As a result, Dolly believed that the Clintons and their agents had intervened to prevent a major publisher from buying and distributing the book. In addition, they had publicly branded her a liar about her alleged affair with the president. The story was important in the context of the Lewinsky impeachment investigation because it was yet another example of Bill Clinton lying about an affair. And since Dolly had become an issue in the Paula Jones sexual-harassment case, it could be argued that Clinton and his lawyer, Bob Bennett, had also obstructed justice. This pattern of similar conduct would raise an evidentiary inference that they had lied about Lewinsky as well.

The day that Dolly walked into Judicial Watch's office, I was taken aback. Not only was Dolly beautiful, she looked like Bill Clinton. I even mentioned the resemblance to my secretary; Dolly's chin, cheekbones, nose and hand structure were virtually identical to Billy's, as Dolly called the president. Never shy about disclosing personal details of her life, Dolly told me that Clinton's father had had an affair with her mother. They were, she said, half brother and sister. Dolly supported this claim with a picture of her son, Anthony, who looked identical to Bill Clinton at a young age. Indeed, the famous picture of Bill Clinton shaking the hand of President John F. Kennedy, when juxtaposed with a picture of Tony at the same age, showed startling similarities. I never doubted Dolly's claim. In the wonderful world of Arkansas, just about anything had proved possible.

I laid out Dolly's story to Barr and Schippers and they both immediately seized on it. Schippers, in particular, wanted to meet with her. I told him that we would quickly set up a meeting with him and his investigators. But even more important, I thought at the time, was their commitment to push for a wider impeachment probe, one involving Chinagate and the other scandals set forth in Judicial Watch's Interim Impeachment Report.

The meeting with Dolly soon took place. It was clear that Schippers really liked her and that there was a tremendous personal rapport between them. This affinity grew even stronger when Schippers' investigators checked out her sources and came back with a resounding confirmation that she had been truthful with them.

But Barr and Schippers were having difficulty convincing Congressman Henry Hyde to widen the impeachment hearings to include Chinagate and the other scandals. They told me that House Republicans, and in particular Speaker Newt Gingrich, were blocking the bigger investigation. Barr and Schippers both felt frustration and anger; it was apparent to them, as it was to anyone with common sense, much less a sense of the political climate, that Bill Clinton would never be impeached and convicted on oral sex alone, despite his false testimony under oath. Nevertheless, the two continued to hold out some hope and asked if Dolly could be made available to testify before the House Judiciary Committee to support the "pattern of similar conduct" strategy. I immediately contacted Dolly and she responded with an enthusiastic yes.

Barr, Schippers and I all agreed that the Republicans did not want to widen the impeachment inquiry because they were fearful that it would actually result in Bill Clinton's conviction. If that happened, Vice President Al Gore would be installed as president and then the party would be facing an incumbent in the upcoming 2000 presidential elections. And, while it was not known at the time, Gingrich himself was having an affair with a female staff member of former Republican Congressman Steve Gunderson of Wisconsin. Gingrich, I would later learn from former California Congressman Bob Dornan, was being blackmailed in effect by Congressman Barney Frank of Massachusetts. Gunderson had told Frank about the Speaker's affair, and Frank was putting pressure on Gingrich not to push too hard on Clinton. Frank and Gunderson were close, owing in part to their public disclosure of their gay lifestyle—a rare admission on Capitol Hill. Consequently, Gingrich did all he could to thwart meaningful and effective impeachment proceedings.

Meanwhile, the Democrats, through collaborative efforts with porno-grapher Larry Flynt, were busy "outing" a number of prominent Republi-cans, including Henry Hyde himself, for extramarital dalliances. Working with Flynt was James Carville and a host of other Clinton smearmeisters. The result was that the Republicans lost any nerve they might otherwise have had to legally cut off the head of the king. While congressmen like Tom DeLay of Texas, then the majority whip, would huff and puff that FBI and other government files were being used to dig up dirt on lawmakers to deflect Congress from doing its duty, they never had the guts to probe further. In fact, I offered Judicial Watch's assistance to DeLay after he called for a formal FBI inquiry into the outings, but he never took me up on it. I had pointed out to him, nicely, how futile, if not ridiculous, it was for him to ask the FBI to investigate itself for the misuse of FBI files. Instead, I urged him to send staff members over to Judicial Watch's offices to pore over the documentation we had obtained about the illegal use of FBI and other government files by the Clinton administration.

I never heard back from him—another indication of how the Republican leadership was only using the Lewinsky scandal to politically weaken the president, not knock him out. I concluded that DeLay, a favorite of the Christian conservative community, was simply using the Clinton scandals for his own political purposes.

Years later, it would become clear how damaging to the country this strategy was. By leaving Bill Clinton in office, preoccupying him with a sex scandal and diverting attention away from the growing threat of bin Laden, Al Qaeda and terrorism in general, the Republican leadership laid the foundation for a serious cancer to grow—one that ultimately metastasized into September 11, 2001.

So when Dolly was finally called upon by Schippers to testify before the House Judiciary Committee, the handwriting was already on the wall. She dutifully traveled to Washington at Judicial Watch's expense, but we were not hopeful that her testimony would make a real difference. In fact, it didn't even get that far. At the last minute, Henry Hyde, probably on instructions from the Republican House leadership, prevented her from testifying and then tried to stiff Judicial Watch with the bill for her travel. Schippers, a man of his word and, in my opinion, a true American hero, at least made sure that Congress paid up.

In subsequent years, the House managers who tried the impeachment case against Bill Clinton would brag about their role in a "historic event." With the exception of Bob Barr and David Schippers, the only two officials who truly wanted to widen the impeachment into Chinagate and the other scandals that would have required conviction, these House managers participated in what was, in effect, a conspiracy to sell out the country. While the House managers were patting themselves on the back for what they had done, or rather, for what their gutless Senate colleagues had not done, Osama bin Laden was hard at work, and the nation was too preoccupied with a sex scandal to know who was really being screwed.

12

WRECKAGE: ALL THE PRESIDENT'S WOMEN

I had become a regular on the prime-time CNBC show "Geraldo Live," the strongest of the pro-Clinton cable programs during the Lewinsky sex scandal. The House had voted to impeach the president and the matter was being referred to the U.S. Senate for trial. Host Geraldo Rivera was doing a retrospective on how the issue had grown, and how it was threatening the continued term of his friend, Bill Clinton. As I sat in the studio chair, "miked up" and waiting for Geraldo to introduce me and the other guests to discuss the day's events, I couldn't help but think that he would pull something out of his hat and try to put me on the spot, as was his practice. Geraldo did not disappoint.

At the beginning of the show he announced the theme, which was an explanation of why the Paula Jones case had not been settled sooner, sparing Bill Clinton from deposition and the perjury charges leading to his impeachment. To set the debate, Geraldo flashed onto the screen the statement of an unnamed source in the White House, whose thesis was: If they had settled the Jones matter, that lunatic Larry Klayman would have wound up representing all of the other Clinton women to make trouble anyway.

Flattered by Geraldo's obsessive fixation on my perceived role in what I truly believed was a second-rate scandal, I smiled at the claim. If nothing else, it showed how much the Clinton administration had come to fear me, no matter what issue was involved. In addition to providing commentary on the Lewinsky scandal, Geraldo showcased video footage of many of the depositions I had been taking in the far more serious Chinagate and Filegate scandals. The footage was amusing and entertaining, if nothing else. Characters such as James

91

Carville, Harold Ickes, George Stephanopoulos and John Huang seemed to play villainous roles right out of a Batman episode. While Geraldo supported the Clinton administration, he could not resist being the showman and went along for the ride.

But there was some truth in the anonymous statement from that White House source. I had already filed suit on behalf of Dolly Kyle Browning over the threats made to prevent her from publishing her fact-based fiction. And at the time, I was in preliminary discussions with another of Bill Clinton's paramours, the better known Gennifer Flowers, the woman who had first confirmed publicly during the 1992 presidential campaign that the future leader of the free world cheated on his wife. Gennifer, a nightclub lounge singer by trade, also had been harmed by Clinton's henchmen for telling the story about her relationship with then-Arkansas Governor Clinton. Instead of having a book deal squelched, Clinton and his "friends" had intervened with Gennifer's potential employers to prevent her from obtaining singing engagements.

Through press accounts, I had learned that many of the other so-called Clinton women also had been threatened, accosted and harassed, frequently by Clinton's private detectives, to try to keep them from telling all they knew about the president's proclivities. Frankly, the thought had dawned on me to bring a class action for all of the president's women. A class action suit could unleash a torrent of complaints by Clinton's victims, making the Jones case look like child's play.

What enraged me was not so much that many of these women had either consensual or nonconsensual sexual encounters with Bill Clinton, but that their privacy and other rights had been violated. While most of the so-called women's groups had been supporting Bill Clinton, doubtless because he was pro-choice and a liberal Democrat, this violation of his victims was truly a travesty. Paula Jones had not only been harassed, she had been audited and trashed in the media with information dug up by private detectives. Juanita Broaddrick, the woman who claimed she had been raped by Clinton, had her home broken into and her reputation smeared. She was later audited by the IRS as well. Kathleen Willey, who had allegedly been accosted in a pantry just off the Oval Office, saw her children threatened and her former marriage tarnished. As I sat there listening to Geraldo effectively blame me for the growing Lewinsky scandal, I thought that the list of Clinton's women victims must be far greater than known. I would be the protector of true "women's rights," I thought. The Clinton White House source might have his supposition come true after all.

After the show, determined to round up all of the Clinton women, I got the word out in the community of people who could help make it happen.

A few weeks after my appearance on Geraldo's show, I was in Dallas with two of my Judicial Watch colleagues, Tom Fitton and Heather Thurmon. We were there in part to meet with Dolly, who called Dallas home. The Sunday evening that we arrived, Tom, Heather and I decided to visit the spot where President John F. Kennedy had been shot in 1963, followed by dinner downtown. I had been to the scene of the assassination many years earlier when I was a Justice Department lawyer, but Tom had never seen it and wanted to experience this important site of American history first-hand.

As we drove down the expressway from our hotel toward downtown Dallas and the scene of the crime, a car suddenly swerved into our lane, swiping our left side. Heather, who was driving, panicked and hit the brake hard, sending our car into a 360-degree spin. As we finally came to a dead stop, the vehicle that had hit us raced off into the night. It was a close call. If this accident had happened at another time, particularly during a period of heavy traffic, we would have been hit by oncoming cars and perhaps killed.

Shaken and thanking God that we had survived, Heather, Tom and I continued downtown to have dinner, our car damaged but drivable. My two colleagues and I had trouble eating that evening, and it was not because the Texas barbecue lacked flavor. We all had an uneasy feeling that maybe the incident was not accidental.

Our fears were heightened later that evening, while listening to the radio. Matt Drudge, the Internet reporter who first broke the Lewinsky scandal by publishing news of the president's dalliance on his website, inexplicably announced on his Sunday night show that I was in Dallas to meet with all of the Clinton women to plan a class action suit. If the resourceful Drudge had gotten wind of my long range plans as well as my trip to Dallas, might Clinton investigators have done the same? The thought wasn't inconceivable—given the mysterious deaths of Ron Brown, Vince Foster and dozens of witnesses in the Clinton years. I had been repeatedly threatened in an attempt to intimidate me. To this day, I do not know if the frightening near miss of that Sunday night was just a simple automobile accident or a failed hit.

While the Clintonistas had always denied that they were responsible for any of the alleged murders of witnesses in their scandals, they certainly wanted their adversaries to believe that they were. In the case of Linda Tripp, a list of 80-plus dead was left on her Defense Department chair as she was revealing Monica Lewinsky's affair with Bill Clinton to the independent counsel. The same scare tactic was used later on with other Clinton White House whistle-blowers, for example the computer room operators who discovered that hundreds of thousands of e-mails were suppressed by the executive office of the president rather than produced and delivered to Judicial Watch, Ken Starr and Congress. But whatever the case, I was determined not to be intimidated in my crusade for justice. I felt, as my grandfather used to say, that God had his hand on my shoulder.

Unrelated to the Dallas incident, I decided not to pursue a class action strategy; however, I planned to file separate lawsuits for each of the Clinton women who asked for help. The first to do so after Dolly was Gennifer Flowers. I immediately flew to Las Vegas, Nevada, where she had recently moved to try to find work in the casino lounges, and checked into the Venetian Hotel, a relatively new complex on the main drag.

While we had spoken over the phone, I had never met Gennifer. I called her after I got to my hotel suite, and she and her husband, Finis Shelnutt, decided to come over to the Venetian for dinner.

I will always remember my first impression of Gennifer. Her reputation had taken a beating by the likes of Clinton henchmen James Carville and George Stephanopoulos who, during their 1992 campaign War Room days, took pains to paint her as nothing less than a whore. So what struck me when I opened the door was her classy appearance and soft and polite greeting. Only five foot two and about 50 years old, she was not only beautiful but extremely poised. "Hello, Larry, I'm Gennifer Flowers. I'm extremely pleased and honored to meet you," she cooed. While Dolly had a home-spun quality, Gennifer was more like a little lady. Despite their differences, both women were impressive. What they had in common back then was their unfortunate involvement with a future president; Clinton was having affairs with both of them at the same time, with neither woman knowing about the existence of the other.

After Gennifer introduced me to her husband, we went downstairs to have dinner at a steak restaurant just off of the casino floor. Over red wine and red meat, Gennifer told me her life story with Bill. I found it interesting that while

Dolly called Clinton by the diminutive "Billy," Gennifer stuck to "Bill," the more formal nickname for William. As I had with Dolly, I asked Gennifer out of curiosity if Clinton had offered any justification for cheating on his wife. I was hardly surprised by the response. Gennifer echoed Dolly, saying that Bill had told her Hillary was really gay. This defense, if it can be called that, had been used by Dick Morris, then Clinton's top political adviser, at the height of the Lewinsky scandal, but it never was given any real credence in the media. Still, the stories were out there. For example, White House whistle-blowers who sought my assistance said that Secret Service agents claimed to have facilitated Hillary's frequent encounters with other women. I never used the information publicly during all of my years fighting the Clintons. But I found it very interesting nevertheless, particularly when the well-known liberal investigative journalist Seymour Hersh told me the same thing during a meeting in Judicial Watch's offices. Clearly, Hersh had no ax to grind and no reason to make up the story, which he claimed was common knowledge on the left.

Indeed, the joke in Washington has always been, "What do Bill and Hillary have in common? They both date the same women."

If Hillary is indeed gay, and frankly I couldn't care less on a personal level, it may help to explain why she has never really advocated nor spoken out for gay rights issues. Given her leftist views, the gay community is a natural constituency for her. Speaking out might do little more than engender a political backlash among those skeptical of the gay rights agenda.

Also interesting was the revelation by Gennifer's husband that he was the former brother-in-law of Webster Hubbell, once the Clinton Justice Department deputy attorney general and a onetime partner of Hillary's at the Rose Law Firm in Little Rock. Hubbell had recently been indicted and convicted of tax fraud and other illegalities and was in prison. Finis revealed that during his earlier days in Little Rock, he had been present when his former brother-in-law and Bill Clinton snorted cocaine, another widely held belief on the right. (Later, I would also learn from White House whistle-blowers in the e-mail scandal that Secret Service agents had observed Bill Clinton and Marsha Scott, chief of staff in the White House personnel office, using cocaine in the White House movie theater. Scott was described by the Secret Service as being one of Bill's "in house" tryst partners.) Both Gennifer's and Finis's insights, while not relevant to the potential case at hand, were fascinating because they seemed to confirm rumors that had been rampant for years about the Clintons. It was like landing on Mars and finding that extraterrestrial life did exist after all, following years of speculation and rumor.

Then, Gennifer, Finis and I got to the matter at hand. With Finis looking on intently, Gennifer told me that she had had enough and wanted to fight back. Her career had been ruined, she said; she believed that Clinton and his people had intervened with nightclub owners to keep her from singing. And she was tired of being threatened and smeared by the president's henchmen, in particular James Carville and George Stephanopoulos, who had accused her of doctoring audiotapes to prove that she had had a relationship with Bill Clinton. The charge was untrue, she said, but it had destroyed her credibility and reputation. Gennifer then asked if Judicial Watch would represent her and file a case against the two Clintonistas. I agreed enthusiastically, and the suit was soon prepared and filed in the U.S. District Court for the District of Nevada—the federal court in Las Vegas. I believed then, as I still do now, that this was the best venue, since showgirls would likely be among the jurors and obviously identify more with Gennifer than with the likes of Carville and Stephanopoulos. If these two Clinton aides wanted to continue to paint her as a Las Vegas showgirl, then let the Strip's showgirls decide their fate.

The case was assigned to Judge Philip Pro, who was appointed by the first President Bush. While Pro had a good reputation in commercial cases, it was clear from the initial status conference that he found the lawsuit too hot to handle. Without any legal basis, he dismissed it on phony statute-of-limitations grounds. By then we had added Hillary Clinton as a defendant, as evidence emerged that she was behind the smear campaign executed by Carville and Stephanopoulos. When we challenged the dismissal, the famously liberal U.S. Court of Appeals for the Ninth Circuit in San Francisco reversed the lower court's decision; it was so flawed that even a Clinton-appointed appellate judge was compelled to rule in our favor. This judicial misconduct, as I learned all too well during the Clinton years, was part and parcel of our politicized and often incompetent federal judiciary.

The next suit I filed was on behalf of Juanita Broaddrick, a sweet, down-to-earth nursing home operator from Fort Smith, Arkansas, whom Clinton had allegedly raped earlier in his political career. To learn more about her story, I flew to her home, a sprawling farm located just outside of Fort Smith, a beautiful mountain-lined town in the western part of the state. It was apparent from our initial meeting that she was truly an honest and gentle lady, and that her then-husband David was a gentleman. But they clearly resented what had happened to them. Someone had broken into their home, a tape on their telephone answering machine had been stolen and their privacy had been violated by what they believed to be Clinton's private investigators. Indeed, when Lisa Myers of NBC first broke the story about the rape on national television, the Clinton agents followed a familiar pattern, ramping up a smear campaign against Juanita and her family. For good measure, they most likely were also behind having her audited by the Internal Revenue Service—a rite of passage of many Clinton adversaries and critics, and an ordeal that I played a hand in successfully combating. So, as with Dolly and Gennifer, I agreed to file suit on her behalf for violation of privacy.

Then there was Kathleen Willey, an attractive and elegant brunette who, shortly after her first husband committed suicide, asked President Bill Clinton for employment. In turn, when she worked in the White House, the grieving and vulnerable widow was assaulted sexually in the Oval Office pantry. When I first met Kathleen, with her new husband, Bill Swicker, I was struck by her credibility, just as I had been with Juanita. She, too, had no ax to grind, despite having been the victim of the Clinton smear machine. And she, too, asked for my assistance. Kathleen's case was not only easy to prove, but potentially devastating for Bill Clinton.

Her name had already come up in the Filegate class action suit, which turned on the administration's illegally obtaining and misusing confidential government files in violation of the Privacy Act. This law requires that documents kept and maintained in government files cannot be released publicly unless the subject of the papers gives his or her consent. In Willey's case, to try to blunt her charge that he had accosted her, the president himself had unilaterally ordered the release of Kathleen's letters, which allegedly showed that she wanted to be employed by him even after the assault. I had learned of this in a deposition of James Carville during the Filegate suit, when Judge Lamberth had allowed me to get into this area, since it was related to the similar misuse of FBI files by the Clinton White House to smear adversaries. Subsequently, Lambreth had made a ruling that the release by Bill Clinton of the letters written to him by Kathleen—kept and maintained in official White House files—was a criminal violation of the Privacy Act.

The ruling that Bill Clinton had committed a crime came in the context of a discovery issue. But it would be binding on the president, through the legal doctrine of collateral estoppel, should Willey file a civil suit for damages under the Privacy Act, which carried both civil and criminal penalties. As a result, Kathleen and her husband both authorized me to file suit against the president. It was a chip shot, I thought, given Lamberth's already binding ruling. The Swickers were very happy that finally, justice would be served.

But just weeks after this potent case was filed as a related suit before no-nonsense Judge Lamberth, I was unexpectedly ordered by Kathleen to withdraw it. A month or so later, appearing on Fox News' "Hannity & Colmes," she told Sean Hannity, the conservative half of the television duo, that she had recently been threatened by Clinton. I then understood why she had bailed out. Kathleen, unlike Gennifer and Dolly, was not a fighter. The poor lady had gone through so much after the death of her first husband that she was vulnerable to continued intimidation. While I do not know with absolute certainty that this was the reason for her dismissal order, I will always believe it to be. Kathleen and Bill Swicker, after my initial representation, never really wanted to discuss the case further. I wish them both well.

Around the same time that I filed suit for Dolly, Gennifer, Juanita and Kathleen, I was also asked by none other than Paula Jones to file a privacy case on her behalf. Her situation was similar to the others in that she had been smeared and audited, and had her privacy violated, as part of the retaliatory effort by the administration's agents to silence all the president's women before, during and even after the Lewinsky impeachment hearings. To try to cheer her up, I even invited Paula on Judicial Watch's annual "Cruise to Clean Up Corruption," where supporters and donors joined us aboard ship to hear Clinton victims and others speak about the need to restore ethics in government. When I first asked Paula to join us, she exclaimed, "My God, how can I go? I don't even have short shorts," I couldn't help laughing out loud at her response and put her in touch with our office manager to see if this "problem" could be addressed, but in the end Paula never joined us on the cruise. During the week of the cruise, she had to tend to family business. Her young son, it seems, had difficulties in school with one of his teachers, who was apparently a big fan of the president. However, she did call into the ship and spoke to Judicial Watch supporters by speaker phone. I will always remember Paula as the innocent young victim of Bill Clinton's voracious Jabba the Hutt-like appetite for young women.

Finally, I was approached by yet another female victim of the Clinton smear machine, Katherine Prudhomme, who confronted Al Gore—at the height of his 2000 presidential campaign—over Bill Clinton's treatment of women, asking him at a town hall meeting whether he condoned the president's behavior. The confrontation caused a great stir on national television, especially when Gore dodged the question for fear of angering his mentor. Shortly after the incident Katherine got a letter from the Internal Revenue Service—a notice of an audit. She retained me as her counsel and fortunately the IRS backed off.

These acts of terrorism—what else to call them?—aimed at the so-called Clinton women by the president and his smear machine were unprecedented in American history. This was the real story as far as they and the nation were concerned, more important than the consensual oral sex in the Oval Office. As a source at the Clinton White House had mused to Geraldo Rivera, the women victims eventually found their way to me, in part because by then I had developed a reputation for taking on difficult cases and challenging the powerful government elite. In all likelihood, few others would be willing to do the same for fear that they, too, would be destroyed.

⸺ 13 ⸺

MEDIA WHORES

B ill Clinton was very good to the "scandal industry." His 40-plus ethical
lapses not only generated enormous work for Judicial Watch, Ken Starr
and Congress, but also provoked banner headlines and endless material for cable
talk shows. For better or worse, the nation was obsessed with the Clintons, and
the media capitalized on it.

Indeed, the Clintons' presidency—Hillary was a full partner in crime—
ushered in the age of tabloid television journalism, turned mainstream print
media into a gossip mill and made conservative talk radio the giant it remains
today. Nothing sells better than scandal. Just ask the owners of the *National
Enquirer* and *Globe*, whose tabloid circulation dwarfs all other magazines. With
the flood of Clinton's transgressions, the media moguls had a field day.

In the early days of the Clinton scandals, during the immediate aftermath of
Bill's election in 1992, there were two conservative cable networks. One, National
Empowerment Television (NET), was operated by my friend Paul Weyrich, the
founder of the Heritage Foundation and then head of the Free Congress Foundation,
both conservative think tanks. The other was the emerging Fox News, started
under the direction of Roger Ailes, the Republican ad man who was instrumental
in electing President Ronald Reagan, and financed by the media tycoon Rupert
Murdoch. During the Thompson hearings, I was a legal analyst for NET, and
the ratings of the fledgling and underfinanced network did quite well due to the
sensational allegations of treason in the Chinagate scandal. But then NET ran into
trouble, collapsing under a host of financial and personnel problems. NET was a
true conservative media outlet, but it could never quite get off the ground.

Fox News, on the other hand, was well-financed, thanks to Murdoch, a man
with no real ideology other than the love of money; and Ailes' swashbuckling
leadership was tailor-made for the Clinton scandal era. While more
Republican in style than truly conservative, Fox News was close enough for

most conservative viewers who had been starved for what the network would label "fair and balanced" reporting. (Although by now it should really change its motto, "We report, your decide," to "We brainwash, you decide.")

Fox's competitor, CNN, owned by the eccentric liberal Ted Turner, had a decidedly leftist slant, even if it tried to appear evenhanded by hiring a few token conservative journalists, such as Robert Novak and Pat Buchanan, for its premier political talk show "Crossfire." Indeed, during the 1990s, CNN was derisively dismissed in conservative circles as the "Clinton News Network," an image enhanced when Rick Kaplan, a pal of the president, became its chief operating officer. In yet another scandal, it was reported that Kaplan had made large campaign contributions to the Clinton-Gore and Democratic reelection campaigns in return for the privilege of sleeping in the White House's famous Lincoln Bedroom. It was no wonder that during Kaplan's reign, I was rarely invited onto the network.

But even with CNN's pro-Clinton tilt, the real success story of the cable news networks was Fox. Today, thanks to the Republican and conservative following built up during the Clinton years, it has eclipsed all of its cable competitors in viewership and revenue. In my opinion, it has become the official TV press organ of the now decimated Republican Party. In another take on its obvious bias, the popular political comedian Jon Stewart has named Fox the "Al Jazeera" of American cable news. While such characterizations provoke strong reactions, the dirty little truth is that Ailes and his minions know where their bread is buttered and, like their hated competitors CNN and MSNBC on the left, they have learned to exploit public opinion at every turn.

During the early years of the Clinton administration, the exposure I got on Fox was not only welcome, it also helped Judicial Watch gain stature. Since the media is, in my opinion, the strongest branch of "government"—hence the name "The Fourth Estate"—and since the other branches react to its power in influencing the public, it was important for Judicial Watch and me to publicize our cases in order to create a favorable climate for decision makers.

While Geraldo Rivera, who now works for Fox and who apparently underwent a miraculous epiphany that converted him to a more conservative perspective on things, was mocking the Judicial Watch depositions he aired on CNBC in the various Clinton scandals, Fox was showing them with ideological glee. Without Fox, and its print media equivalent *The Washington Times*, neither Judicial Watch nor Larry Klayman would be where we are today. But there is another story to be told about Fox—a petty and ethically challenged aspect of its personality that the conservative world never knew about or fully appreciated. While I am more ideologically in tune with Fox, I never liked its underhanded and even dishonest style.

I first noticed this split personality at Fox during the Lewinsky scandal, when many of my female clients were being solicited to come on the air. Because they had active lawsuits, it was important that I appear with them to prevent something being said that could haunt them at trial. While I made this known to the producers who booked guests on the shows, and asked them to always run the appearances through me or my press office at Judicial Watch, Fox continuously contacted my clients directly in efforts to lure them in front of the camera without me. On at least one occasion, Fox producers succeeded: They got Dolly Kyle Browning to appear alone in prime time on "Hannity & Colmes" to answer questions about her lawsuit against Bill Clinton. When I asked Dolly why she had accepted the invitation without advising me, she replied that Sean Hannity had asked her to do it as a "personal favor."

This was not the first time that Fox and Hannity had not been straight with me. During the time I was rumored to be planning the class action suit for the women victims, Hannity called to tell me that he had lined them all up for a joint television appearance and that I might as well cooperate in insuring that they all show up for his special. When I checked with Dolly, Gennifer and the other women, I learned that this was not true and concluded that Fox and Hannity were simply trying to trick me into getting them all to come on the air together.

I came to perceive Hannity as a shallow and insincere Rush Limbaugh wannabe. In contrast, his television co-host, Alan Colmes, a Jewish liberal, was actually a mensch, even though I rarely agreed with him politically. But my problems with Fox did not stop with Sean Hannity.

At the height of the Lewinsky scandal, Dolly had been invited to appear on "The O'Reilly Factor." I liked Bill O'Reilly and even then, before his ratings really took off, considered him to be the most talented of the Fox news anchors. Indeed, during these early days, Bill would borrow many of the issues that Judicial Watch posted on its website to use as themes for his nightly show. I was flattered and frankly thought this was good for our clients. And Bill was not afraid to call a spade a spade. Unlike Hannity, O'Reilly had no desire to become the darling of the Republican Party.

But when Dolly made her first appearance on his show, which was being broadcast from Miami Beach during the run-up to the Super Bowl, O'Reilly started the interview by asking if she had abused her children. When Dolly, who was connected by satellite hookup from Dallas, looked stupefied and shocked by the outrageous and irrelevant question, O'Reilly pressed on, declaring that he had just spoken with her ex-husband—in fact, Dolly had three ex-husbands—and been informed of her abusive behavior. I was hooked up to the broadcast in Fox's Washington studio, and I remember seeing Dolly turn red and refuse to answer any more questions or, for that matter, to speak at all. The interview abruptly ended, but the incident did not.

Dolly called me crying and screaming as soon as the interview ended. She told me that this former husband was a drug addict and had lied. She threatened to sue Fox if the clip was not removed from the interview. In those days, the O'Reilly show was taped; it was possible to edit what had transpired. So I immediately called Roger Ailes and told him what had happened. I speculated that this was unlike the Bill O'Reilly I had admired. Ailes appeared sympathetic, particularly after I advised him, at Dolly's direction, of the consequences of not editing the interview. I further demanded that Dolly be put back on the air that week, this time during a personal O'Reilly interview in Fox's New York City studio, to clear up the mess, since it looked bad that her Miami Beach interview had abruptly ended. To his credit, Ailes did edit the segment for that evening and agreed to have her go back on "The O'Reilly Factor" from New York later that week.

Following up on my conversation with Ailes, I contacted O'Reilly's producer, David Brown, and he agreed to have Fox pay Dolly's New York travel and lodging expenses. Brown said that he would take care of the flight reservations and have Fox buy an e-ticket. But when Dolly arrived at the Dallas airport, no such ticket had been purchased by Fox. She called me frantically and I had to foot the bill on Judicial Watch's credit card.

Dolly did reappear that week on "The O'Reilly Factor," but Fox reneged on its commitment to pay for her airfare, even when I brought the matter to Ailes's attention. In response, and without my knowledge, Dolly, who was still mad about what had occurred in Miami Beach, sent Ailes a letter threatening to write about the incident in her second book about Bill Clinton. I got a letter back from Fox's in-house lawyer, Dianne Brandi, raising the specter of retaliation against Dolly and me if my client took any further action. To this day, Judicial Watch has not been reimbursed for Dolly's travel. The entire affair was unnecessary and avoidable, but it was, regrettably, what I was beginning to learn was textbook Fox News pettiness.

Another Fox double-cross came at the hands of Paula Zahn, one of the network's prime-time hosts before she moved on to CNN. Zahn's producers had wanted her to interview another of my clients, Donato Dalrymple, the so-called fisherman—he actually was a house cleaner—who saved Elian Gonzalez from near-certain death. Elian and his mother had fled the hell of Fidel Castro's Cuba on a boat that eventually capsized. The mother drowned, but Elian survived. Donato found the brave little Cuban boy miraculously floating in an inner tube off the coast of South Florida.

I told Fox that I would have to appear with my client, since he had brought suit against Clinton Attorney General Janet Reno over the infamous raid on the home of Elian's Miami relatives. Donato had been assaulted at gunpoint by Reno's storm-trooper immigration agents and, along with others, was suing over the use of excessive force in violation of his constitutional rights.

As I was being miked up for the interview to discuss the case, I had a funny feeling because my chair was being positioned about three feet away from Donato's seat. The funny feeling turned to surprise when Zahn introduced the topic and guests for the segment, but didn't mention me. As Zahn began to question Donato about the case, and my client gave his typically rambling responses, some of which were not helpful to his case, I felt obliged to try to step in and set the record straight. Anything Donato said could be used by Reno as evidence in court—perhaps, in lawyer language, as "an admission against interest." But when I tried to intervene, Zahn just continued to interview Donato as if I were not even there. The audio feed to my mike had been cut and I was utterly helpless!

I was livid. So I wrote a letter to Ailes in an effort to reach an understanding of how we would proceed should Fox want to interview my clients and me in the future. In light of the Dolly incident, I was sensitive to not appearing overly aggressive or demanding. Despite my diplomacy, Ailes never got back to me. Later, when I sent him a modest Christmas gift, he returned it with a terse note saying that it was the policy of the network not to accept Christmas gifts.

Over my 10 years at Judicial Watch, others also would learn of the strange and petty tactics of Roger Ailes and Fox. Matt Drudge, whom he hired to host a television show at the height of the Clinton-Lewinsky scandal, left in a huff when Ailes would not let him air a photo of an aborted infant and then tried to embarrass him in the media over it. Catherine Crier, the classy former Texas judge who had preceded Paula Zahn, also left the network abruptly, after she reportedly had been mistreated. There were more examples, and the brusque, arrogant style of Fox News, the tone having been set by its CEO Ailes, became widely known in the industry. To Ailes's commercial credit, however, ratings have continued to soar, and one has to give him his due for being a marketing genius, if not a media whore like his megalomaniacal owner Rupert Murdoch.

His savvy for promotion will always stick in my mind over two off-the-cuff comments he made when we were still on friendly terms. On one occasion, I noticed on the television monitor just outside Ailes's office that former Governor Mario Cuomo's youngest and most handsome son, Chris Cuomo, was doing commentary for the network. It appeared to me that Cuomo the younger, still in his 20s, was out of his depth and knew little about the issues he was being asked to address, so I asked Ailes why he had hired him to do commentary. He replied, "If I'm going to put on some goddamned liberal, I might as well get the dumbest fuck I can find!" On another occasion, I jokingly asked Roger if the wide shots of Catherine Crier's lower body were intended to exploit her looks, since she had great legs. His response was, "If I need to put two dogs having sex on the air to boost ratings, I'll do it!" This, in a nutshell, is what "fair and balanced" is all about at Roger Ailes's Fox News Network.

Years later, when I decided to run for the Senate in Florida, I called Ailes and told him the news. He wished me well, said that we were friends and professed no hard feelings. It was good to hear, since my appearances on Fox had evaporated in the wake of our previous conflicts. But toward the end of my Senate campaign, when Geraldo Rivera wanted to put me on his show along with Gennifer Flowers, who was supporting me, his producer called to cancel only a day after he had booked us. "The higher-ups killed it," he said apologetically, and he couldn't figure out why. He added that "Geraldo was very disappointed and still considers himself your admirer and friend." I wrote again to Ailes and pretended that there must have been some misunderstanding that he would want to straighten out. Typically, I got no response.

To this day, I have been boycotted by Ailes and Fox, and no matter what news I make in my public interest efforts, the network will not carry it. As discussed later, I also have reason to believe that Fox's owner Rupert

Murdoch tried to kill the publication of this book, given its criticism of him, Roger Ailes and their network.

Fox News and CNN were not the only television networks with peccadilloes. During the Clinton years in particular, Chris Matthews, whose "Hardball" show started on CNBC before it migrated to MSNBC, not only went after me over the "suing my mother" story, but he rarely had me on. This was no accident. One day, Matthews, who is a liberal Democrat but had been taking an anti-Clinton line, perhaps as the network's marketing counterweight to Geraldo Rivera's then pro-Clinton tilt, called me to ask about my Filegate case. At the time, I was representing Republicans and others who had their FBI files illegally taken and misused by the administration. Matthews wanted to know if there was a file on him, since he was concerned that he might be viewed as an adversary over his stinging criticism of the Lewinsky affair. I told him that I would keep my eye out, but did not know of any such file. During later depositions of Clinton officials in the case, I would ask if Matthews was ever a subject of White House scrutiny, but his name never popped up in questioning or in any of the documents the administration was forced to cough up. Nevertheless, Matthews's concern underscored two important points about many in the media. First, they were intimidated by the Clintons and were obviously scared to push too hard for the president's removal from office. Second, Matthews's paranoia helped to explain why I was not being invited onto his show; he, too, apparently feared that my appearance might trigger retaliation by the Clinton White House.

But there was another phenomenon at play. Despite all of my television appearances on cable, none of the traditional commercial networks—ABC, NBC or CBS—ever had me on their Sunday morning news shows. I can only speculate that they were scared either of government retaliation, or that the Clinton White House would refuse to send top-notch guests. Moreover, I sensed the old elitist system at work. The major networks, like much of Washington, simply would not give credit to a self-styled independent counsel who, in effect, had created his own Justice Department. The concept was so foreign to the Washington establishment that it could not bring itself to give me full due.

Instead, the Sunday shows rounded up the usual suspects—congressmen and senators like Arlen Specter, Fred Thompson and others—all establishment Republicans who talked a good game about getting justice during the Clinton years, but didn't do much about it. This was just plain frustrating, and even though my complaints may sound ego-driven, that wasn't the case then, nor is it today. To make meaningful change and have a significant impact, the use of the media is critical: How else can you reach the American people? My being snubbed only strengthened my resolve to take on the establishments—in politics, law and the media—and beat them at their own game. My satisfaction as the outsider, the upstart, the gadfly became more pronounced as I was continually boycotted by the elite mainstream media.

In time, however, a curious reverse phenomenon began to occur. While the establishment media kept me at a distance during the Clinton years, their counterparts in Hollywood found my exploits interesting fodder for prime-time television drama.

One night, near the end of the Clinton presidency in the early spring of 2000, after I put my daughter Isabelle to bed, I got a call from one of my clients, Jack Daly, a naval counterintelligence officer. Jack had been hit by a laser from a Russian vessel in Puget Sound while he was surveying and photographing the ship from a helicopter as it tried to spy on U.S. Navy nuclear submarines. I had brought a lawsuit for Jack against the Russian front company that owned the vessel, the *Kapitan Man*. Jack was excited: "Turn on NBC. The show 'The West Wing' has you on," he exclaimed. I didn't know what he was talking about. Rather than explain, he yelled over the phone, "Just turn it on!"

When I did, I saw a dark-haired lawyer questioning a White House official over the alleged use of drugs by the White House chief of staff. The scene was reminiscent of one of my Judicial Watch depositions of Clinton officials. Placed behind the lawyer, played by John Diehl, was a videographer with his camera trained on the witness, and to the left of the lawyer sat a legal assistant. The setup was exactly how I conducted my proceedings.

As I watched more, I realized what Jack was talking about. The hit NBC series "The West Wing," a liberal drama about a presidency similar to Bill Clinton's, with the commander in chief played by Martin Sheen, had created a character based on my work as chairman of Judicial Watch. Indeed, I heard my fictitious counterpart referred to as "Harry Claypool of Freedom Watch."

As the deposition session concluded in rancor over how Freedom Watch had obtained administration documents proving the drug use, the White House deputy chief of staff approached Claypool, grabbed him by the throat, slammed him against the wall next to the exit door, and threatened to bust him "like a piñata" if he continued with the case. The scene reminded me of the time I had

108

been threatened with criminal prosecution in Judge Lamberth's court by Bruce Hegyi over allegedly exposing the identity of the CIA agent who briefed John Huang with classified national security information. I was pleased to see that, as I had done with Hegyi, Claypool told the White House deputy to take a hike and turned away with a smirk and swagger to gather up his things.

"The West Wing," a show with its ultra-liberal executive writer-producer, Aaron Sorkin, was obviously mocking my role as a gadfly. But it was also elevating my importance in the eyes of popular culture. That, I realized, could further Judicial Watch's mission and help to spark popular support for our efforts to restore ethics in government and the legal profession. The creation of television character Harry Claypool of Freedom Watch marked a rite of passage for Judicial Watch and me. My years of work at the public interest foundation had been noticed and now I was becoming part of the pop culture. If I could reach the mainstream American, then perhaps we could really make a difference by influencing public opinion.

In later episodes, Harry Claypool returned to "The West Wing. "Among his exploits were taking on a White House official who was having an affair with a congressman. The portrayal continued to be somewhat mocking in style; not surprising, considering that several retired Clinton White House officials such as former Press Secretary Dee Dee Myers were writers or consultants for the show. But the simple fact that "Freedom Watch" and Harry Claypool had become a sometime presence on the show underscored two crucial factors— that Judicial Watch and I were seen as thorns in the side of the establishment left and that we were making an impact.

Around this time in early 2000, Judicial Watch's influence and my public persona, thanks to several recent developments in our cases, were reaching their highest levels. Judge Lamberth had just returned the finding that Bill Clinton had committed a crime in releasing the Privacy Act-protected White House employment letters of Kathleen Willey. White House computer room whistle-blowers had revealed to me and the court the suppression of hundreds of thousands of missing and incriminating administration e-mails. And I had blocked the preferential mortgage on the Clintons' first attempt to buy a mansion in Chappaqua, New York, as a prelude to Hillary taking up residency in New York and running for the U.S. Senate. The pressure on the Clintons in the media was intense, so much so that during a White House news conference, a reporter asked the president what he thought about my having blocked his house financing deal.

The legal basis for my suit was similar to the case I had brought against the Clinton legal defense fund; neither a president nor any other federal official can accept a gratuity, in this case a below-market mortgage loan from Deutsche Bank, while in office. My case caused such a stir that Deutsche Bank withdrew its cut-rate loan offer. I imagine Hillary was livid. From what I came to learn about her personality through the White House e-mail whistle-blowers, she probably cursed profusely at Bill. I smiled at the thought.

So it was no wonder that when the reporter asked the President about me, on national television, Bill Clinton exploded, accusing the media of being just like "the political press world of Larry Klayman, where truth is fiction and fiction is truth." When the White House press corps snickered, perhaps thinking that he had in a Nixonian fashion finally gone off his rocker, the president added, with a smirk and Freudian slip, "You know, your president has just committed the truth!"

Never before had Bill Clinton attacked me in public. Indeed, it was obvious that he had been told by his advisers never to utter my name, for fear that it would elevate my status, provide oxygen to my crusade against him and Hillary, and embolden contributors to support Judicial Watch with further financial contributions to pay for cases against the Clintons. So when he lost his cool, the president made a major public relations gaffe.

Clinton's advisers were correct. It would be an extreme understatement to say that the attack helped fund raising. At Judicial Watch, we began to amass a substantial war chest. At $28 million or so in 2000, we managed to raise even more than the prestigious conservative Heritage Foundation. I inwardly thanked Bill Clinton for the gift that kept on giving. The money was badly needed to fight the bipartisan scourge of government corruption.

To show my appreciation, I decided to attend, for the first time, the annual black-tie dinner of the White House Correspondents' Association, the most prominent insider press gathering of the political season. The gala was always attended by the president and first lady. Annually held at the Washington Hilton in late April or early May, for official Washington, the dinner is the equivalent of the Academy Awards—the place to see and be seen. Tickets to the event are in high demand. Since I never thought of myself as part of the Washington elite, I had previously had little interest in attending. But given Judicial Watch's expanding role and my emergence as a pop-culture character, I thought it would be amusing to see how the beautiful people of Washington might react to me. Paul Rodriguez, then the managing editor of *Insight Magazine* and my best friend, invited me to sit at the conservative publication's table next to Matt Drudge, whom he had also invited.

I'd met Matt before, as I had appeared frequently on his Fox News television show before the network began its boycott of me. An eccentric and fearless individualist, Matt had asked to be seated next to me, not only to try to pry some gossip from me, but because he thought I was the hottest conservative figure in town, or so Paul told me. Matt also wanted to report on the reactions of the Clinton people to my presence at the dinner. Accordingly, he proposed that we circulate throughout the reception area and later in the banquet hall and introduce ourselves to the leftist friends of the president and first lady. We were an unusual pair: I was wearing a tuxedo, but Matt, true to form, dispensed with the dress code and wore his trademark pork pie hat and a tee shirt depicting Donato Dalrymple being held at gunpoint by an INS agent during the Elian Gonzalez raid on his family's Miami home.

Matt first confronted Janet Reno by flashing his tee shirt at her while she was seated at a table in the middle of the banquet hall. Then he suggested that we go over and say hello to Gregory Craig, a former Clinton State Department official who, like so many other Clintonistas, now has a high position in the Obama administration as White House counsel. Craig was the lawyer representing the leftist National Council of Churches, which I believed to be a front for Fidel Castro and which had worked to get Elian Gonzalez returned to Cuba. When I said hello to him, with Matt standing behind me, I was surprised by his broad smile and friendliness. Then it dawned on me that my coming to the dinner could be perceived as seeking to join the so-called Washington club. And if that were the case, then my role as a private attorney general would be compromised. So while I was taken aback by Craig's friendliness, and wanted to respond in kind, I held back. Instead, I smiled, held out my hand and said with some sarcasm that "I always wanted to meet the man the press says charges over $2,000 per hour." Craig laughed, and Matt and I went on our way.

That encounter, similar to what I experienced with other Clintonistas throughout the evening, highlighted an interesting phenomenon. The president's people, many of whom I had either sued or deposed, or both, were generally quite personable. But then, so too was the devil. This was how they had wooed much of the media elite, notwithstanding the bias in their favor to begin with. It reminded me of my earlier run-in with Janet Reno at the Café Atlantico restaurant, where her warmth and friendliness had also taken me by surprise.

Another example was Terry McAuliffe, the premier Democrat fund-raiser and "Friend of Bill." I ran into him later that evening at a post-dinner party, hosted by Michael Bloomberg, now mayor of New York City, at the Russian Embassy across the street. McAuliffe, whom I had deposed in the Chinagate case, and whose demeanor had struck me as similar to the Joker in the Batman comics, came up to me and put his arm around my shoulders. "Lar, howya doing? Good to see ya here," he said with his southern Florida drawl and warmly mocking style. "Ter," I responded, again not wanting to be taken as a member of the club, "good to see ya out of a deposition room." He laughed, and laughed again when I told him to make sure not to put his hands, then on my shoulders, into my pockets. Later, I would sue McAuliffe on behalf of the shareholders of Global Crossing, a company that bilked its investors with fraudulent accounting. The head of Global Crossing, Gary Winnick, a close friend of Clinton's and McAuliffe's, had given a few thousand shares of stock to Terry that had netted him millions of dollars.

At the gala, I also ran into Clinton White House Press Secretary Joe Lockhart. A rotund and tough little guy who frequently attacked me in the media, Lockhart noticeably jumped when I put my arm on his shoulder and said, "Hope you're doing well, Joe!" He grimaced and abruptly walked away.

But the most interesting encounter of the evening occurred when Matt and I went over to the table of the cast of "The West Wing," which had been invited, along with Jay Leno, then host of "The Tonight Show," as the featured Hollywood guests at the event. It was Matt's idea for me to meet the executive producer, Aaron Sorkin, who had created the Harry Claypool character on the hit series. The cast was at a table right next to the dais of the president and first lady.

As Matt and I drew near the "West Wing" table, we noticed that Sorkin was not there. Seeing Martin Sheen, who played President Bartlett on the show, I bent down, put my arm around him and said, with my face close to his, "Martin, I thought you might like to meet the real Harry Claypool." I then added, "I just wanted to know if y'all are going to bust me like a piñata this season," a reference to the threat against Claypool by the White House lawyer in the first episode. Calm and debonair, Sheen looked up, grinned and said, "Nice to meet you, Larry, but we're more worried about ourselves getting busted," an amusing reference to Sorkin's recent drug arrest on a cocaine charge. I must concede that I was impressed by his quick sense of humor!

As we finished our exchange, I looked up at the dais to see if I could get Bill Clinton's attention, curious how he would react to my presence after his having railed against me in public. So with Matt in tow, I walked over to within 15 feet of the president and stood just behind the barrier that prevented anyone from approaching the dais. As Hillary was having a merry old time flirting with the woman seated to her right, I just stared at the president. Sensing that he was being watched, Clinton cocked his head toward me with a leftward tilt and, with a pronounced grimace, stared right back. I was transfixed.

It was the first face-to-face encounter I had ever had with Bill Clinton and I will always remember his reaction. He stared at me like a gorilla in a cage. Just as memorable is what happened shortly afterward. A few minutes after Matt and I returned to the *Insight Magazine* table and sat down to resume dinner, we were surrounded by Secret Service agents whispering into their miked lapels. At a time when Judicial Watch's impact had reached new heights, and I had caused the president and Hillary major problems, Bill Clinton wanted to send a signal that he was still boss. The message was clear: Don't mess with me any more!

When I later met host and comedian Jay Leno at the Bloomberg post-dinner party, he looked at me and laughed. With all of my television appearances and my newfound pop-culture status, he had recognized me. In jest, I asked him, "Do I know you from somewhere? Are you Johnny Carson?"

The White House Correspondents' Association dinner of 2000 reminded me that all of the glitter of Washington, or for that matter Hollywood, was just that. I enjoyed the experience, but it also highlighted for me why I would never want to join this club of superficiality, hypocrisy and glitz, lest my role as an independent ethical watchdog be compromised.

As I left Bloomberg's party that night, I stopped at a Porta-John just outside to relieve myself. When I opened the door, there was a woman inside, buck-naked from the waist down. Seeing me looking directly at her, she screamed. I quickly closed the door in shock, thinking I had just stumbled into "The Vagina Monologues." What kind of wacky roller-coaster ride was I on anyway? I got into a cab to return home wondering if I ever wrote a book about all of this, would anyone believe me?

My experience with the elite media was an important education. I admit that it is easy to get caught up in the notoriety and fame. But as the Clinton-era scandals wore on, I became less and less impressed by the press culture—and frankly, less impressed with myself, too. It was a surreal world, and Judicial Watch and I had unfinished and difficult business to conduct. While the media could be instrumental in lubricating the wheels of justice, and while there are a number of honest and talented journalists in the trade, it would never lead to change on its own. And the hypocrisy I witnessed among many members of the Fourth Estate continued to underscore why simply feeding the media beast could never be my real or ultimate objective.

——14——

AN OMINOUS BEGINNING TO THE BUSH YEARS

After the White House Correspondents' Association dinner, the administration's last formal farewell to the Washington press corps, one would have thought that the Clintons' penchant for shameless behavior might have died down. They had, after all, only about eight months left in office. But Bill and Hillary didn't disappoint the scandal mongers. They slogged on, racking up one new outrage after another. Capping off their eight years, and perhaps bent on establishing a new world record, they proceeded to illegally sell presidential pardons and steal the people's furniture, loading it onto a moving van and later having to give it back after a public outcry. For added good measure on the way out the door, their staff trashed the White House office equipment. I always marveled at the Clintons' chutzpah; ethically rotten to the core, there truly was no crime that was beneath them!

But despite the howls and screeches that came in protest even from the liberal element of the media, the Clintons pressed on. Their corrupt ways infected many others. Al Gore, for example, became a victim of their disreputable doings. Previously conservative leaning and thought of as ethical before he signed on as vice president, he prostituted himself and became a Clinton wannabe with presidential aspirations. For example, in his famous "ice tea" press conference after the Chinagate scandal broke, Gore claimed that he wasn't present at times during a crucial meeting where the illegal campaign contributions were discussed because he had gone to the bathroom after drinking too much ice tea. Following his television outing, I received a call from David Kendall, the principal lawyer of the Clintons, asking for an extension of time in one of our cases. Trying to be charming to get my consent, he quipped referring to the press conference, "Have you ever seen a worse performance in your whole life?" Then

115

he added, "Maybe we should get together for lunch one of these days and trade stories." I didn't respond and let the conversation trail off. His remarks were uncharacteristic for him. He normally was a very cautious operator, however engaging, and rarely let his hair down. Perhaps he was upset because Gore excusing himself implicated Clinton in the wrongdoing.

As the nation was then approaching the run-up to the presidential election of 2000, one would have thought that the Republican Party would try to capitalize on the continuing stench emanating from the Oval Office. But apparently still shell-shocked by what had occurred during the Chinagate and Lewinsky scandals, when Democrats quickly called the Republicans' bluff by digging up dirt on them as well, the Grand Old Party remained impotent. The fat elephant had been neutered by a ruthless organized crime operation known as the Clinton White House and its co-conspirator, the Democratic National Committee.

But there were other reasons why the Republicans did not aggressively seek to capitalize on the Clinton-Gore scandals: in just three words—the Bush family. George W. Bush, the popular governor of Texas, was likely to be the party's nominee for the presidency, and there were plenty of skeletons in the closet of this venerable political dynasty. There was, for example, the senior President Bush's closeness to the Saudi Arabian royal family, a fact that would later emerge after September 11, 2001, and become a major theme in Michael Moore's movie "Fahrenheit 9/ll." And then there was the cronyism and influence-peddling the Bush sons had engaged in for years during their dad's years as vice president and president. Without real experience or expertise, Neil, Jeb, Marvin and W. himself all miraculously found themselves heading major corporations, put in place by sleazy entrepreneurs who were ready, willing and able to make them stars. And they all, at one point or another, had gotten themselves into hot water over their questionable dealings with their father's administration on behalf of those corporate interests. As a result, the Republicans understood full well that it could be disastrous if they were seen to be exploiting the ethical lapses of the Clinton-Gore years. So they relied on others instead to do their dirty work for them.

But if they thought that I would play ball and be one of their lackeys, they were mistaken. I wanted the Republican and other candidates for president to explain to the American people what they intended to do, in concrete terms, and to restore ethics to the White House and the government as a whole. Only Republicans Alan Keyes and Gary Bauer, and Howard Phillips of the

Constitution Party, were specifically addressing the ethics issue; the others were just spewing the usual platitudes about the need for honest government. So I made it a point to invite all of the presidential candidates on Judicial Watch's weekly national radio show. Keyes, Bauer, Phillips, Republican Steve Forbes and the Libertarian and Reform Party candidates accepted. But noticeably absent from our list of guests were John McCain, the self-styled Republican reformer, Al Gore, the presumptive Democratic nominee, Ralph Nader of the Green Party, and, yes, George W. Bush. In Bush's case, his staff offered to send a surrogate. I declined, responding with a message that the American people were not prepared to elect a surrogate as president, so I had no interest in having one, whoever it might be, appear on our radio show! At the time, I thought that Governor Bush's offer might have been due to his inarticulate style and inexperience with the issues, but I later learned otherwise.

As the presidential campaign wore on, W. and his surrogates refused to seriously address the pardon scandal and the stealing of furniture. In fact, they did not really discuss any of the Clinton-Gore scandals. Frustrated, I decided that Judicial Watch would organize a nationally televised presidential debate. Again, I invited all the candidates for an event scheduled to take place just weeks before the November elections at the newly constructed Reagan Building in the heart of downtown Washington.

To my surprise, the first to accept the invitation was Vice President Al Gore. While this was obviously a tactic to make Gore appear unafraid of the ethics issue, it had the added advantage of calling Bush's bluff. At the time, Gore was proposing many presidential debates, believing, incorrectly as it later turned out, that he was a far superior orator compared to his clumsy and ill-informed counterpart. Following Gore's acceptance came the acceptances of Howard Phillips of the Constitution Party, Pat Buchanan of the Reform Party, Harry Brown of the Libertarian Party and John Haeglin of a rival faction of the Reform Party. The role I played in setting up this debate, which was to be dedicated solely to the ethics issue, received major play in the media, and I hoped that it would influence the nation's consciousness about the need for honesty in government. Since the debate was to take place the night before Judicial Watch's Sixth Annual Conference, also in Washington, it drew many of our fans and backers to the nation's capital. One supporter, who appeared at the conference and is now a good friend, was Morgan Brittany, the vixen on the TV show "Dallas" who shot and killed Bobby Ewing near the end of the series. Morgan, a

Christian conservative, would later tell me how she had experienced retaliation in Hollywood for her religious and political views. This underscored why the public needed to understand, unfiltered by the elitist media and Hollywood, why an ethical government was crucial for our nation's survival.

By the time the debate rolled around, Gore and Bush had cut a deal to do only three Presidential Commission debates, and Gore reneged on his offer to show up. Also absent from the forum was Pat Buchanan, who begged off when John Haeglin, his Reform Party rival, accepted. At the time, Buchanan was busy debating the Green Party's presidential candidate, Ralph Nader, on television. He apparently did not want to dilute his outsider status by appearing with what he must have viewed as a bunch of also-rans.

I decided to move forward nonetheless and opened the debate by reminding the viewers that our founding fathers, and in particular John Adams, our second president, had preached that without ethics, morality and religion, there will be no lasting liberty. Despite being characterized by the snobbish Washington press corps as losers, Phillips, Brown and Haeglin acquitted themselves extremely well and the debate was widely televised on C-SPAN and MSNBC throughout the United States. At least in terms of educating the American people on the need for ethics in government, I was pleased.

I was disappointed, however, that Bush had not shown up, and I lost a great deal of respect for the future president. It would take September 11, its aftermath and Bush's leadership for me to regain that respect in some small measure. As for Gore reneging on his promise to appear, I expected as much from him, and his later performances in the Presidential Commission debates proved my point. He came off as not only shallow and disingenuous, but robotic and buffoonish. In retrospect, Bush and Gore deserved each other; sadly the American people did not.

Three days before the election the reason for Bush's reluctance to address the ethics issues became clear. Leaked from a sealed court file in Maine, documents revealed a drunken driving criminal conviction of the future president. Given my years of experience in fighting the Clintons, and our Filegate case, it was not hard to figure out how and why this breach had occurred. As a result, W.'s modest lead evaporated and the incident almost cost him the election. The outing also was a strong warning to him not to pursue justice against the Clintons, should he take over the reins of government. The message was that there was more where those drunken-driving documents had come from!

And sure enough, after the election battle was won, the new president made nice with the Clintons. First, he suggested that Bill and Hillary should not be prosecuted for their many crimes and that the independent counsels should end their investigations. Next, he ignored the continuing controversy over the illegal pardons that the Clintons had sold. Then there was the sickening scene of the Bushes going to the White House to have tea with Bill and Hillary, followed by effusive praise from the Republican victors. And if this were not enough, *The Washington Post* uncovered and reported a year or so later that Republicans and Democrats, just after the 2000 elections, had cut an under-the-table deal that neither party would again pursue serious ethics investigations against the other. The whole scene was so rife with insider deceit, hypocrisy and corruption that I felt like throwing up. This self-inflicted neutering of the Republican Party and George W. Bush may have been good for Judicial Watch business, since I literally remained the only game in town after the independent counsels dutifully followed Bush's advice and shut down their probes. But I was truly afraid for the future of the nation.

The ultimate irony was that while Bush and his party had taken a dive regarding the Clinton scandals, they owed their election to them. According to exit polls, 44% of the American people based their votes on a disgust over the Clinton scandals. What they got in their new president was hardly what they wanted, but W. was their only alternative to the corrupt Al Gore and his entourage of Clinton criminals who would have continued to infest the White House like so many cockroaches. The Orkin Man may have been better suited for the job.

After the inauguration, I thought Judicial Watch would give it one last college try to communicate with Bush's people to see if we could work together to bring the Clintons to justice and preserve a sense of honest and ethical government for the nation. Indeed, the publication *Legal Times*, the gossip rag read by most Washington lawyers and other practitioners around the country, ran an article after former Republican Senator John Ashcroft was nominated as attorney general, stating that the Justice Department would probably now try to settle many of my clients' cases.

I had been thinking the same thing, so I contacted some of my conservative evangelical friends, religious leaders such as James Dobson of Focus on the Family, Jerry Falwell, Chancellor of Liberty University, and Paul Weyrich of the Free Congress Foundation. They had been instrumental in getting Ashcroft his nomination. I asked my fellow religious conservatives to urge Ashcroft to meet with me to plan for early settlements. But the call from Ashcroft or his people never came. Ashcroft was a religious conservative himself, and he had obviously foreseen serious problems in his confirmation process before the left-leaning Senate Judiciary Committee. In light of those problems, it was likely that he decided it would be unwise to link up publicly with religious conservatives before he was confirmed.

─── 15 ───

ENTER, PETER PAUL
PART 1

It was late February of 2001, and someone by the name of Peter Paul was calling Judicial Watch's headquarters incessantly from Brazil. I was wrapped up in a lot of matters, and since I did not ordinarily answer the initial inquiry of someone apparently seeking legal assistance, I asked Judicial Watch's investigation department to call him back.

What they heard was an astounding tale. The man who identified himself as Peter Paul claimed to have given in-kind, hard-money campaign contributions totalling $2 million to Hillary Clinton's successful New York Senate campaign for the Hollywood Tribute to Bill Clinton, a widely publicized extravaganza in Beverly Hills. This gala was, in reality, a fund-raiser that, according to Paul, generated over $1.5 million for Hillary's campaign. Paul had paid for the entertainment, which included performers such as Dionne Warwick; for the catering, which included chefs such as Wolfgang Puck; and for a number of other things necessary to stage the event. Hillary never reported Paul's $2 million contribution to the Federal Election Commission.

Paul had thank you notes from both Clintons, which they sent after Hillary's Senate victory, crediting him with helping her win. Such in-kind donations constituted "hard-money" campaign contributions since they went directly to pay for the candidate's election, and they far exceeded the normal limit, which was then $1,000 per donor. Paul added that the money was generated through a company that he had founded as a silent partner with the creator of Spiderman, Stan Lee. The company was appropriately named Stan Lee Media.

Paul also told my investigators that he had the cancelled checks of the money used to finance Hillary's fund-raiser, as well as copies of the thank you notes, among other smoking-gun documents. He wanted to meet with me quickly, since he was fearful that he was about to be indicted for alleged stock fraud at Stan Lee Media. In exchange for our legal defense, he would blow the whistle on the Clintons.

I was intrigued but somewhat skeptical about the credibility of Paul's story. The Clintons had eluded the grasp of several independent counsels and Congress. Was it possible that we could now finally catch them red-handed with irrefutable evidence?

I called Paul back myself, with my assistants at Judicial Watch listening in on speaker phone. He sounded credible and so we agreed to meet in Miami within days. Not only was Miami my home at this point, but Judicial Watch had an office there. Before meeting with us, however, Paul suggested that we meet with one of his "friends," who he claimed could be instrumental in his legal defense on possible stock fraud charges. His friend's name was Stanley Myatt and, after taking his telephone number from Paul, we arranged to meet with him at the Sheraton Biscayne Bay Hotel off Brickell Avenue in downtown Miami.

As two Judicial Watch investigators and I waited for Myatt in the bar area of the Sheraton, we couldn't help but wonder what he had to do with Paul's story. Soon, a man in his 60s wearing a black leather coat bobbed into the lounge area. He held out his hand and, with a wiseguy demeanor and New Jersey accent, said, "You must be Klayman. I know all about you." We sat down at a table near the bar, with Myatt on my left. I asked him how he knew all about me and he replied, "Don't worry, I have my sources. I hear you're fucking OK."

Myatt went on to explain his relationship with Paul. He began by telling us that Paul owed him more than $800,000, and that the last person who owed him money was no longer around. He added that because he liked Peter Paul, whom he nonetheless described as a pathological liar, he was somewhat flexible on the timetable for debt repayment—but he still wanted to get paid quickly. Myatt then launched into the reason he had come to meet with us, his head continuing to bob like a character in a Martin Scorcese movie. It was apparent to me that he was some kind of Mafia figure. He told us that Paul was in trouble, since he was under investigation for stock fraud by the feds. I asked Myatt how he knew this, but he dodged the question. Instead, he asked me how I intended to defend Paul, obviously having been briefed by Paul in advance that we were considering taking his case.

I explained to Myatt that the logical way to proceed would be to try to cut a deal with the Justice Department to grant Paul immunity in exchange for his cooperation in exposing the illegal, unreported $2 million in campaign contributions to Hillary Clinton. I added that it would be best to try to negotiate this deal with Attorney General-designate John Ashcroft himself, since he was a conservative and we knew the leaders in the community who had pushed for his nomination. Ashcroft, I added, would be the best chance to get favorable action.

Myatt looked perturbed. "Don't go to Ashcroft," he said. "Take it from me, go to the U.S. Attorney for the district of New Jersey. There you can get something done."

I challenged him, "Why would I want to go to a lower-level official when I can go to the top?"

"Just take it from me!" Myatt snapped back.

While it was clear to me that Myatt was some underworld figure, I did not fully appreciate at the time why he was pointing me in the direction of a U.S. attorney in New Jersey. The meeting, which was cordial but always had an edge, ended a short time later. I told Myatt that we'd stay in touch. But I wanted to hear from Paul himself about this Myatt character before deciding whether or not to deal with him. I was looking forward to the meeting we had scheduled with Paul in Judicial Watch's Miami offices for the next morning.

Paul arrived early the next day, having flown in the night before from Brazil, where he had a home and another company, called Mondo English, an online concern that taught English over the Internet. When Paul walked into Judicial Watch's offices, my first impression of him was not favorable. He was short and somewhat unkempt, with a dark, scraggly beard. But, as my staff and I talked with him, we could see that he possessed considerable charm and personality. Paul was very likeable and energetic, a real promoter. But being a promoter was not a virtue for the issue at hand; I wanted to see hard proof of his claims.

Paul had brought along a slew of photographs of his encounters with the president and the first lady before, during and after the Hollywood Tribute to Bill Clinton, and the originals of the thank you letters from them. Paul told us his life story. He had grown up in Miami, become a lawyer, gotten into bed with the CIA, pulled off a few capers against Fidel Castro, and been previously convicted and disbarred for cocaine possession and use of a false identity. Despite his checkered past, including two stints in federal prisons, he had always emerged as a friend of the rich and powerful, which spoke volumes not only about Paul's charm, but also about our culture. He produced evidence of awards or accolades he'd been given by U.S. Supreme Court Justice Warren Berger, whom he had assisted on the commission that planned America's 200th birthday party for the Constitution. And he helped Gerald Ford and Ronald Reagan with political fund raising. But Paul was a nonpartisan and equal-opportunity ex-con, and he had decided to get his hooks into Bill and Hillary Clinton around the same time that he was helping Stan Lee get back on his feet after he had hit the financial skids.

Following his two prison sentences, Paul had moved to Los Angeles and become a Hollywood promoter. He claimed to be responsible for launching the career of Fabio and a host of others. It was there that he met Stan Lee and had gotten the bright idea to resurrect the comic book king. But with his prior convictions, he could not be in the spotlight, and thus became the brains and silent partner of Stan Lee Media.

To boost the fortunes of that company, Paul explained that he had gotten the idea of bringing Bill Clinton in as a member of the board. But to make the offer, Paul had to get to know Clinton first, and it was then that he conceived of the Hollywood Tribute. He made contact through mutual Hollywood friends, who put him in touch with Democratic National Committee chairman and former Philadelphia Mayor Ed Rendell, whom he used as a conduit for the funds. Paul offered Clinton not only the money to put on the gala, but also more than $17 million in stock options in Stan Lee Media after Clinton left office. The president, through his surrogates, expressed great interest and ultimately a deal was struck. That was acknowledged by no less than Chelsea Clinton on the night of the Hollywood Tribute, when she told Paul that her dad looked forward to working with him and Stan Lee after he left office. (After the deal was struck, Ed Rendell hit up Paul for another $150,000 to get him a pardon from the president for his two convictions, Paul insisted.)

After the gala, Lloyd Grove, then the political gossip columnist of *The Washington Post*, got wind that Paul, the twice-convicted felon, was behind the financing of the Hollywood Tribute and published an article in the paper's style section. That piece caused the Clintons to distance themselves from him and to renege on their support of Stan Lee Media. Worse, Paul said that he had reason to believe that he was now under investigation by the Justice Department and possibly the Securities and Exchange Commission for stock fraud at Stan Lee Media, which he had used to generate the funds to pay for the Hollywood Tribute. He needed our help.

Paul then detailed his relationship with Myatt, whom he described as someone who lives in that netherworld between the government and the Mafia. Myatt, it seemed, had been Paul's handler from his early, pre-disbarment years as a Miami international lawyer pulling CIA stunts against Fidel Castro and others. In fact, the CIA, Myatt and Paul had tried to cheat Castro out of $8 million, a "crime" according to the Carter administration, for which Paul was convicted. Later, when he tried to cross the border from Canada, after he had been convicted for another Myatt-inspired scheme—the sale of cocaine to finance CIA operations—Paul was arrested and convicted again for use of a false identity (that of Myatt's brother). According to Paul, Myatt was not only a CIA operative, who had participated in the assassination of the leftist Chilean President Salvador Allende in 1973, he was a Mafia hit man—part of the Meyer Lansky organization. In fact, he had once been on trial for murder in secret proceedings in Fort Lauderdale federal court, but got off because of his work for the government.

With his pull, Myatt had also been instrumental in having Paul released early from his two prison terms. In recent years, Myatt's trade was to investigate companies for the Justice Department through its Northeastern Crime Task Force, and then by himself, without official agency approval, extort money from these companies by selling what in effect was Mafia insurance. Myatt had also been a silent partner in Stan Lee Media and it was in this context that Paul, who needed cash for its early operations, borrowed money through him. It was clear that the $800,000 Paul allegedly owed Myatt was Mafia money.

But despite Myatt's sordid underworld connections, he continued to have clout at the Justice Department. It was for that reason, Paul explained, that Myatt had suggested approaching the U.S. attorney for the district of New Jersey, since this was where Myatt's "juice" was. Myatt worked directly under this branch of the Justice Department and had been dealing with an FBI agent there who promised to smooth things over for Paul. Myatt's primary interest in getting him out of the fix he was in, Paul figured, was to allow him to repay the Mafia loan.

During the meeting, Paul also discussed the stock transactions that led to the Justice Department investigation and perhaps the SEC's as well. He made a convincing case that, from a legal standpoint, he had committed no crime. But he needed me to make a proffer to the U.S. Attorney in New Jersey, as Myatt had suggested, to give him the Clintons' heads on a platter in exchange for immunity.

Paul stressed that Myatt and his FBI agent friend could be instrumental in getting this immunity deal.

I voiced reservations to Paul about making an offer to the U.S. Attorney, since it could backfire. But Paul said that he even had a tape recording of a telephone conversation with Myatt, in which the mobster had assured him that New Jersey would offer him "protection" from prosecution. He was adamant about the plan, despite the risk of providing the information that could ultimately lead to his indictment if the evidence that Paul offered about the Clintons was not "saleable" to a highly politicized Justice Department.

After the meeting, which ended with our agreement to represent him, I got a call from an assistant U.S. attorney (AUSA) in the New Jersey district. It was obvious that the call had been somehow arranged by Myatt and his FBI agent friend. The AUSA wanted to meet; this only strengthened Paul's belief that we should make the proffer.

The AUSA arranged for the meeting in his offices and invited assistant U.S. attorneys from other interested districts. They included the southern district of New York, which had been investigating the illegal sale of pardons by the Clinton administration, and the eastern district of New York, which had jurisdiction over some of Paul's stock transactions. The central district of California also made the list: It likely would get involved if the Hollywood Tribute to Bill Clinton and related matters ever became an issue in any possible prosecution, notwithstanding the securities allegations.

The meeting took place within a week or so after our conversation with Paul. As we laid out the legality of our client's stock transactions for Stan Lee Media, and as I offered to turn in those who had broken the law, Myatt's FBI agent friend, who also was present, glanced in our direction and nodded with approval. He looked pleased when we launched into what we could offer concerning the Clintons' illegalities.

At the time, I decided, on behalf of Paul, to play along with Myatt and the FBI agent. Clearly, once Attorney General John Ashcroft was confirmed and installed as the head of the Justice Department, we would have to bring the Myatt situation to his attention, as this was a huge internal scandal for Justice. A similar scandal had erupted previously in Boston, where Mafia hit men were also found to have been FBI operatives. But for the time being, following the instructions of our client, Paul, we wanted to see what we could get by doing it Myatt's way.

Unfortunately, Paul grossly miscalculated. Rather than offering him immunity and beginning a criminal investigation of the Clintons, the U.S. attorney for the eastern district of New York, Alan Vinegrad, who had assumed primary jurisdiction, indicted Paul instead. In the process, he grandstanded his prosecution with a press release mocking our client's Hollywood past. It was clear that Vinegrad was doing the bidding of Hillary Clinton; he was an interim Bush appointee following the resignation of the prior U.S. attorney, who had left at the end of the Clinton administration, and he wanted to be installed permanently. To succeed, he would need Senator Clinton's approval. Senators nominate and have veto power over the appointment of U.S. attorneys in their states.

As a result, the initial proffer, which I had viewed with some skepticism, turned into a nightmare for Paul. I had seen the pattern before. Rather than prosecute the Washington elite, the Justice Department burns the little guy. And the strategy was brilliant: Indict and then smear Peter Paul in the media before he could say or do anything that could harm Hillary and Bill, thereby undercutting his credibility with the public. In exchange, Vinegrad would get Hillary's approval to be made permanent U.S. attorney. It reminded me of why I had quit the Department in the early 1980s and had gone into private practice. Our own Justice Department remained rife with political corruption.

At the time that Paul was indicted, he was still living in Brazil. Predictably, the AUSA called and demanded that he be brought back to the United States. Fearing that he might be killed by Myatt's Mafia friends or others in an American prison as he awaited trial, Paul was hesitant to return voluntarily. And extradition wasn't a foregone conclusion; it would require the Brazilian authorities to determine if Paul should be sent back to the United States. At a minimum, Brazil, under its treaty with the United States, could not extradite Paul for crimes that did not exist in Brazil. Paul had been indicted on some counts which appeared not to "translate" into a Brazilian equivalent under its legal system of justice. So, after careful consideration, Paul decided to fight extradition.

In the interim, he was free "on his own recognizance" to live in his plush compound on the outskirts of São Paulo. But it was not long before he was arrested by Brazilian authorities; the U.S. Justice Department had invoked its powers under the extradition treaty to have Paul picked up and incarcerated. Rather than disappearing in some remote part of the Amazon, Paul played it straight and was taken into custody while vacationing with his wife, Andrea, and their young child, at a resort hotel in São Paulo. While I would have never counseled Paul to bury himself in the Amazon, the man obviously did not think like a criminal, or he would not have exposed himself to be arrested in public. I joked with my Judicial Watch colleagues that our client was one of the dumbest "criminals" on the face of the earth. In fact, Paul was highly intelligent; to his credit, he just didn't think like a criminal.

Even before Paul was arrested in Brazil, I had tried to get the Justice Department's new man at the top to order an investigation of the case. By this time, after a bruising confirmation process before the Senate Judiciary Committee that included vicious and unfair accusations by Senator Ted Kennedy and other ultra-leftists that he was a racist, John Ashcroft had finally limped into the job as attorney general.

I again contacted my evangelical friends to urge an early meeting with the new attorney general, explaining that Paul represented the last hope to ensnare the Clintons in a major criminal prosecution that could finally mete out justice. James Dobson, Jerry Falwell and Paul Weyrich made the overture and a meeting was arranged—not with the attorney general, who was apparently still nervous about being seen with religious conservatives, but with the head of the Criminal Division of the Justice Department, Michael Chertoff.

Before going into private practice, Chertoff had been the U.S. attorney for the district of New Jersey many years earlier. It was this U.S. attorney office that, technically speaking, oversaw the capers of Myatt as part of the Northeastern Crime Task Force, although it was an open question whether Chertoff had direct knowledge of them. Later, he had become the chief counsel of Republican Senator Alphonse D'Amato's Whitewater hearings, which was the first investigation of the Clintons and concerned allegations of illegal land and banking deals in Arkansas. Chertoff had a reputation as a straight shooter; I was hopeful, although not overly so, that he would take over the criminal prosecution from U.S. Attorney Alan Vinegrad, grant Paul immunity in exchange for his evidence on Clinton wrongdoing, and begin a serious internal investigation of the role Myatt had played with others in corrupting the Justice Department.

Two investigators of Judicial Watch and I met with Chertoff and his staff in his large conference room adjoining his office at Justice. I was struck by his skeletonlike appearance. We laid out what had transpired with the U.S. attorneys in the northeastern corridor, as well as with the central district of California, and how, rather than starting up a serious criminal investigation of the Clintons, the political hack Vinegrad had indicted Paul instead. We also told Chertoff all about Myatt, even playing audiotapes of his many conversations with Paul, in which he urged Paul to go to the district of New Jersey because it would deep-six any securities investigation.

I emphasized to Chertoff and his staff that the meeting needed to be kept confidential, that the evidence we were providing about Myatt could not get out and that, under the circumstances, control of the prosecution needed to be moved from Vinegrad to his office. I stressed further that if any of this came out in public, Paul's life, the well-being of his family and even my life could be in jeopardy since Myatt was a Mafia hit man and could seek to retaliate. Chertoff and his entourage, which included not only his deputies but a senior lawyer in the inspector general's office, the body that conducts internal Justice Department investigations, all agreed to be discreet. Chertoff even suggested that, if the facts checked out, he would take over the case. I promised to allow Chertoff's people to interview Paul to independently gather and confirm the facts and left the meeting pleased with the initial progress.

But less than 24 hours after my meeting with Chertoff and his minions, Myatt called Paul in Brazil and left a message on his answering machine: "You motherfucker son of a bitch, I'm coming to Brazil to deal with you!" I was outraged. It was clear that Chertoff's staff had leaked our meeting to Vinegrad and his people, who then informed Myatt.

Judicial Watch's investigation department has computer software that can find almost anyone in the United States. So I asked our chief investigator to get Ashcroft's home phone. If he did not have the courage to meet with me, I would instead track him down myself. Sure enough, we located Ashcroft's home telephone number on Capitol Hill and I called him to ask for his immediate intervention. What Chertoff had allowed to happen was itself "criminal," as he had placed our lives in danger and violated the Privacy Act, which should have protected our communications with his office.

When I phoned the attorney general, he would not take the call, even though he was clearly at home. Instead, his son asked me the reason for my call, and so I instructed him to relay this message to his father: "Tell your dad that the head of the Criminal Division, Mike Chertoff, has just placed the life of Larry Klayman and his client, Peter Paul, in danger by leaking evidence about Mafia involvement in the Department's affairs. A Mafia hit man just threatened our lives. Fellow conservatives are not going to take this well. Have your dad contact me immediately, before I have to file suit against his officials and take this public." The edge in my voice was pronounced; I was that close to exploding.

Within minutes I got a call from one of Ashcroft's top deputies, who promised to get hold of Chertoff and find out what happened. He did so, and I was then contacted by Ashcroft's deputy chief of staff, who asked that I come in the next day. They wanted to learn more about the leak and take whatever action was required, he said. Fortunately, Paul had a recording of the threat.

The next day, we played the phone threat to Chertoff's people. While swearing that they were not behind the apparent leak, they decided only to try to gather further evidence about Myatt's actions because, they claimed, the message was not strong enough to merit action: Myatt had "only threatened" to come to Brazil to deal with him, not kill Paul—although it was obvious what he had meant. Through the inspector general's office, a sting was set up in which Peter Paul would call Myatt back and try to get him to threaten him even more directly; the Department would tape the conversation from an office in close proximity to Chertoff's. This taped conversation would be staged in such a way that it could be used as evidence before a grand jury or in court proceedings, or both.

The call was set up and Paul was able to get Myatt on the phone. Again, the experienced Mafioso hit man was cleverly vague, although his meaning would be clear to any experienced law enforcement official. But even without the direct threat, the Justice people were able to get a better feel for Myatt; notwithstanding his professional-grade use of the "F" word, a trademark prerequisite with the underworld, it was clear that he was connected to criminal elements—not only in the Mafia, but also in the U.S. attorney's offices in the northeastern corridor. During the conversation, Myatt also made several references to the money that his sources had loaned Paul, and this buttressed our proffer about what had transpired between the two men.

Even though we did not get conclusive evidence of a threat, Chertoff and company did step up the urgency of their inquiry, if for no other reason than that they were on the legal hot seat. They had been caught leaking our proffer to Myatt, either directly or indirectly. As a result, Chertoff assigned the head of the National Crime Task Force, Bruce Orr, to lead the probe. After several telephone conversations and meetings with Orr, I decided that he seemed to be a person of integrity and that I could deal with him in a serious way.

By this time, Paul had been placed by Brazilian extradition authorities in a small prison in the center of São Paulo. During its less democratic days, the prison was used as a place to torture political prisoners. Orr and his staff decided that it would be helpful if they could fly to Brazil and interview Paul, in our presence, in the jail itself. This was highly unusual under the Department's procedures.

Orr and personnel from his office and the inspector general's met with Peter Paul in the Brazilian prison over the course of two days. During four sessions totaling more than 20 hours, in an underground room as dark as a dungeon, Paul laid out the fine points of the stock transactions at issue, in which we maintained he had not committed a crime. He also described the Clintons' involvement in the illegal money laundering scheme that generated more than $1.5 million in unreported campaign contributions. He further spelled out the criminal past and role of Myatt in excruciating detail. Orr and his people were impressed and promised to independently confirm the proffer through their own investigation.

After several weeks following the sessions in the Brazilian hell hole, I called Orr to check on the Department's progress. While claiming not to be able to discuss details of a criminal investigation, as was Justice's policy, he added that Paul's story was checking out. This was good news and I awaited Orr's promise to contact me with a follow-up plan. Throughout our various conversations, I always prodded Orr with the inevitable question: Given the politics involved with the Clintons and the Bush administration's reported deal to lay off of them and other Democrats, would the Justice Department be able to pursue an immunity deal with Paul and prosecute the former president and first lady if the evidence proved genuine? Orr always assured me that it would. I remained highly skeptical. Nevertheless, we had an obligation to our client to pursue this course. We had to follow his instructions—and in any event, we had no other alternative available to us.

But despite Orr's confidence that justice would be done, over a year passed and Paul remained imprisoned in Brazil. During this period, we had hired a local extradition attorney for Paul, and his case was winding its way through the Brazilian justice system. But despite my many calls and letters, we never really heard anything more from Orr, Chertoff or anyone at Justice, prompting Paul, who had a wry sense of humor, to nickname Chertoff "Michael Jerkoff."

The Department had served a warrant to raid a storage facility in Los Angeles where Paul had kept documents about the Clintons, Myatt and others.

In this paperwork at least one agent swore to possible illegal campaign finance activities by Hillary Clinton. But it was abundantly clear that the investigation had hit the same political wall of internal corruption inside the Department that I had experienced all too often as a government prosecutor and in private practice. Indeed, it was likely, again based on my experience, that the raid on Paul's document warehouse was meant not to pursue justice, but to get hold of and bury documents that would incriminate the Clintons and Myatt.

In the meantime, Paul, who as a former lawyer was always thinking about legal strategy, ordered me to file a civil suit against the Clintons to "get his money back." If nothing else, we could use the case to take discovery, which we could then hand over to the Department to try to kick start its stalled investigation. It was also a way to gather evidence that we could release publicly to try to force Justice's hand. We crafted a case, and filed it in Los Angeles Superior Court asserting, among other counts, that the Clintons had unfairly enriched themselves and Hillary's Senate campaign with unreported and thus illegal campaign contributions. Claiming that Paul had no standing while he was still a "fugitive" in Brazil, an argument we strenuously contested, the Clintons' lawyers convinced the court to throw it out for the time being. It was later reinstated when, after a couple of years of inaction, Paul was extradited back to the United States in 2003 to await trial. At that point, Paul, who was in American custody, was no longer a fugitive, even under the court's strained reasoning.

—16—

EXIT, PETER PAUL
PART 2

Some months before I left Judicial Watch in the fall of 2003 to run for the U.S. Senate in Florida, I learned that Michael Chertoff had been nominated to sit on the U.S. Court of Appeals of the Third Circuit, the judicial circuit that covers the states of New Jersey, Pennsylvania, Maryland and others. For some reason, I had not picked up on this in the press until the day before the Senate Judiciary Committee was scheduled to "vote him out of committee" onto the Senate floor for a vote by all of the senators. Despite the short time frame, it immediately dawned on me that this might present an excellent opportunity to put Chertoff on the spot. If the committee would ask him why he had not acted on the Paul scandals—the Myatt situation and the $2 million in unreported campaign contributions to Hillary—then perhaps we might provoke some action.

After all, Chertoff had been the U.S. attorney for the district of New Jersey during the time that Myatt operated under the aegis of the Northeastern Crime Task Force. This task force in turn worked with Chertoff's staff in the U.S. attorney's office. Questions should therefore be asked of Chertoff about when and where he learned, if ever, of Myatt and his organized crime ties.

Sitting on the Senate Judiciary Committee was none other than my old "friend" Arlen Specter, the senior senator of Pennsylvania. While completely unreliable in the past, Specter had a healthy sense of my ability to make his life miserable through the press if he failed to act, I thought. And then there was the chairman of the Judiciary Committee, Orrin Hatch of Utah, whom I had also given a hard time over the years for his failure to stand up for the confirmation of conservative judges against the liberal Democrats. While he talked a good game, he failed to support Judicial Watch's legal efforts to break the Democratic filibusters that spiked many conservative appointees. I believed Specter and Hatch feared me since they became upset every time I criticized them in the media. But they also respected me. Both appeared on Judicial Watch's radio and television shows, with Hatch even crowing, obviously in jest, that when he finally retired, he would like to join Judicial Watch. Specter offered similar compliments, calling me the "second best lawyer in town." When I asked him who was the best, he replied, "me, of course." Though cynical after my years in the sewers of Washington, I was also the perpetual optimist. Perhaps we could back Specter and Hatch into a corner and force them to confront Chertoff on the Paul scandal issues.

I called Specter and found him in his office one day before the Chertoff hearing. Explaining what was at stake for him—Chertoff was nominated for a judicial seat on the appellate court in Philadelphia, Specter's home town—I asked him to question the Criminal Division chief on the Paul matters before the vote. The conversation was friendly and we also talked about other Judicial Watch cases that Specter had followed. In the end, he promised to have someone from his staff contact me immediately. The call never came, so I decided to write a letter to every member of the committee advising the senators of the situation and asking them to hold up the vote on Chertoff's nomination until the questions about why the Paul-related issues had not been thoroughly investigated were satisfactorily answered. Because the letter was faxed to Democrats as well, I limited the discussion to the Myatt matter involving internal Justice Department corruption; mentioning Hillary Clinton's role in the scandal would have just turned them off.

When I did not get any responses to my letters, I decided to take matters into my own hands and show up in person at the Senate Judiciary Committee hearing. Before the formalities began, the senators were shooting the breeze with the media people and each other, who had stationed television cameras just outside the door to the hearing room. The Chertoff confirmation was not a big media draw, but there were other matters on the committee's agenda that were. It was a perfect opportunity to put all of the senators on the spot.

I walked up to Specter and asked him what he planned to do about my requested inquiry. He looked sick and tried to dodge answering the question. So I approached Hatch and asked him the same thing. When I mentioned Peter Paul's name, he responded: "Isn't that the guy who gave me a hard time with the BCCI matter?" It was a reference to a major international banking scandal in which the senator had been implicated years earlier. Hatch was right. Paul had been involved in the BCCI case as part of his work for the CIA with Myatt.

Hatch's committee had oversight responsibilities for the Justice Department, but he had never been very tough on Clinton Attorney General Janet Reno. One reason, many speculated, was that he feared her ongoing investigation of BCCI and the potential for his own indictment. Despite his reaction to Paul, Hatch assured me that he would personally look into the matter before the full Senate voted on Chertoff's confirmation. Even so, he added, he wanted the nomination to be voted out of committee today.

After Specter and Hatch, I approached Senator Chuck Grassley, a Republican from Iowa, who was also the chairman of the Senate Finance Committee, one of the most powerful posts on Capitol Hill. Grassley, one of the few senators I had found during my years at Judicial Watch with palpable integrity, seemed concerned about what I had outlined in my letter, and he promised to look into the matter. As the hearing was about to begin, I took my place at the front of the gallery overlooking the U-shaped table where the committee members sat.

Hatch gaveled the hearing to order. To my surprise, he immediately launched into the Chertoff confirmation. He obviously realized that if he did not address the Paul matter at the outset, I would walk out of the hearing room and conduct an impromptu press conference with the national television and radio reporters stationed just outside. Revealing to the public that he had just received a letter from me claiming that Chertoff had information about a Justice Department scandal involving an organized crime figure, Hatch promised to have the issue thoroughly investigated. But he added a caveat: He still wanted Chertoff to be voted out of committee today. As he had said to me before the hearing, the investigation would take place between the time of the vote sending Chertoff's confirmation to the Senate floor and the ultimate vote by all members of the Senate.

Specter and Grassley then put in their two cents, supporting Hatch's approach—in effect, ramming the Chertoff nomination through before any investigation could take place. Chertoff, given his days as chief counsel on the Whitewater hearings, had obviously garnered a lot of goodwill with his Republican friends on the Judiciary Committee.

But then an explosion occurred. Much like an estranged wife or husband, the Democrats on the committee took the other tack. Seizing the opportunity to poke a finger into the eye of the Republican elephant, ranking Democrat Senator

Patrick Leahy of Vermont held up a copy of my letter and tried to stall Hatch's plans. He argued forcefully, in a manner intended to embarrass Hatch and the other Republicans, that there was no rush to force a vote on Chertoff before the investigation of the Myatt matter was complete. Chiming in to support Leahy were other leftist Democrats such as Chuck Schumer of New York, Dick Durbin of Illinois, Diane Feinstein of California and even the venerable senior senator from Massachusetts, Ted Kennedy himself. I had to laugh inwardly. I had started a cat fight over Chertoff, and the Democrats were not even aware that the underlying scandal involved their great matron and colleague, Senator Hillary Clinton! This was delicious not only for its irony, but also because the hearing was being widely covered by the national media.

The heated partisan bickering over the vote on Chertoff's nomination continued for about 40 minutes and, in the end, despite vehement objections from the Democrats, Hatch called for a vote on the judicial nominee. With the Democrats refusing to vote, the Republican majority approved his nomination and sent it to the Senate floor. As he had said to me at the outset, and then to the public, Hatch ended the session by promising a thorough investigation of the issues I had raised. I was not holding my breath.

A few days after Chertoff was voted out of the Judiciary Committee, I got a call from a senior person on Hatch's staff. He wanted to meet to discuss the issues I had raised with his boss. A few days later I sat down with several members of Hatch's Judiciary Committee staff and a representative of Leahy's office as well in a conference room of the Hart Senate Office Building.

At the outset, Hatch's senior staff person read the senator's so-called ground rules for the investigation. I would have about 20 minutes to make my case, and the issues could not go beyond the matters raised in my letter. Of course, since I had not discussed the Hillary Clinton aspect of the Paul scandal, this was a real limitation. But even worse was the derisive and condescending tenor of the admonition from Hatch's senior staffer. I exploded. Raising my voice, I told him and his colleagues that this investigation was an obvious sham and that the national press might like to have a full briefing about Chertoff's nomination being steamrolled through and how the issues of Justice Department corruption were being whitewashed. My two investigators and I were prepared to get up and leave, since it was obvious that we were wasting our time. I got up to walk out the door. The Judiciary staffers, visibly upset by the prospect of my departure, asked me to reconsider, promising to seriously listen to our case. Relenting, I went through the evidence, even playing taped conversations between Paul and Myatt, as well as raising for the first time the Clintons' involvement in the scandal. At the conclusion, the staff admitted that the matter was much more substantial than they had been led to believe, and that they would take our evidence back to their senators for further instructions.

But, within a week or so, I learned inadvertently by reading *Roll Call*, the major daily newspaper that covers Capitol Hill, that Hatch had concluded his investigation and found my request to thoroughly question Chertoff about the Paul scandals to be frivolous. As a result, his investigation was concluded and Chertoff's nomination would now be voted upon by the full Senate. The whitewash was complete.

In the fall of 2004, David Rosen, the chief Hillary Clinton fund-raiser who worked with Paul to organize the Hollywood gala, was indicted on charges of underreporting Paul's campaign contributions to the Federal Election Commission. The evidence was so overwhelming that even a timid Bush Justice Department had to act. However, in typical fashion, Hillary herself, the queen of crime, was not charged—another shining example of the pact the Bushes and Clintons had either explicitly or tacitly engineered to protect their respective families and political parties.

The case went to trial in Los Angeles federal court. Predictably, the Bush Justice Department trial attorney argued in his opening statement to the jury that while David Rosen had committed crimes in not fully reporting the extent of Paul's in-kind campaign contributions to Hillary Clinton's Senate campaign, there was not a scintilla of evidence linking her to the offenses. This effort to protect Hillary made no sense to the jury: Why would her chief fund-raiser be held accountable when the beneficiary was not involved? In effect, what would Rosen himself get out of committing a crime for Hillary if she were not part of it? Needless to say, during the trial, Paul was not called as a witness, lest real evidence emerge of Hillary's direct role in the crimes.

Sure enough, in near record time, eclipsing even the botched O.J. Simpson prosecution a decade earlier, Rosen was acquitted. It was yet another confirmation of the inherent corruption in our judicial and political systems.

As for Peter Paul, he ultimately tried to cut a deal with the Justice Department, offering to plead guilty to one count of securities fraud; but incredibly, after many years under house arrest, he was not given credit for time served in an American prison and instead was sentenced to eight years. It would appear that the federal judge, Judge Leonard Wexler, an Al D'Amato-compromised Republican from New York, obligingly put Peter on ice so he could no longer be a threat to Hillary Clinton in particular. I am trying to help Peter to overturn this political sentence.

Because of the information he holds, Paul still holds the keys to bringing the Clintons to justice. He is the Rosetta Stone for their transgressions.

17

DON'T DELAY, LET'S COVER UP!

Less than two weeks after George W. Bush was inaugurated on January 20, 2001, Republicans were carrying on in the Clinton tradition. Not missing a beat, Republican House Majority Whip Tom DeLay, who would become majority leader in two subsequent Congresses, fashioned a plan to raise money for the GOP by selling access to administration representatives on tax policy issues. To implement his scheme, which required a maximum hard-money contribution of $1,000 in exchange for being invited to a meeting with White House leaders during which tax policy would be discussed, the former pest exterminator—nicknamed "the Hammer" for his ability to keep Republicans in line during House votes—went to the airwaves, sending out hundreds of thousands of prerecorded telephone messages to the party faithful.

Having spent the better part of eight years fighting the Clintons for doing the same thing—selling access to the White House and government as a whole for campaign contributions—I did not feel that I could look the other way simply because a professed Christian conservative was now taking up the Clinton mantle. DeLay was very popular in my ideological community; indeed, he was a fellow member of the Council for National Policy (CNP), the group of religious conservatives that I had joined in 1997. But I had to be true to my own beliefs.

By this time, I had finally made the leap of faith from Judaism to a total acceptance of Christ. The catalyst for this was an experience in church on Christmas 1999. Standing in the pew with my wife and two children on the day that celebrates my savior's birth, and my grandfather Isadore's as well, I believed that Christ was communicating with me. As the cross passed by, I felt a tremendous love and warmth. It was as if Christ were conveying to me that I could finally accept Him without feeling that I was betraying my Jewish heritage. From that day forward, I was no longer only a Messianic Jew, but also a Christian. In my view there is nothing inconsistent between Judaism and Christianity. It's the same religion.

My total acceptance of Christianity, however, had not been easy psychologically. I had not wanted to reject my Jewish roots, of which I was and remain very proud. But for some reason, I had gravitated to Christians over the years—I had married two of them and my children were being raised Catholic. My own people, by and large, had not only abandoned me, but continuously attacked me, their leftist love of the Clintons proving more important to them than the ethical principles of the Ten Commandments. Shortly before my communication with Christ, a friend, the Reverend Bob Rieth of Media Fellowship, which counsels public figures under serious work pressures, read me several passages of the Old Testament, in which the coming of Christ was clearly predicted. I had confided in Bob that while I felt Christian, I could not renounce my Jewish heritage. In his warm and friendly way, the pastor assured me that I could remain Jewish and believe in Christ. Now I felt that Jesus was telling me that it was OK to join with Him, a Jewish rabbi who had changed the universe and, like me, had worn a Star of David.

Later, Alice Alyse, who had become a good friend, had a Star of David necklace with a cross on it made for me as a 54th birthday present. This symbolized my coming to grips with my Judeo-Christian roots. I wear it to this day, proudly a Jew who loves Jesus, the greatest Jew that ever was.

With my newfound beliefs, I wasn't trying to pick a fight with DeLay and thought we might be able to discuss the fund-raising issue like Christian gentlemen. I called his office and asked for a meeting. When this did not work, I wrote a letter asking him to not emulate the Clintons and to stop selling access to administration officials. When I again got no response, I contacted some of my evangelical friends—in particular, Paul Weyrich—to see if a meeting could be arranged before I was forced to pull the trigger on the Hammer and go public. But the silence con-tinued. So I had no choice but to threaten to file an ethics complaint. That finally got a response. I received a note from DeLay's lawyer: "Tom DeLay obeys all laws." The terseness of the reply sent a clear message: Fuck off, Klayman.

I promptly made good on my threat and filed a complaint with the House Ethics Committee. Knowing it was probable that the leadership in neither party would take action, the complaint was more useful for its ability to generate media than anything else. In front-page headlines, the *Houston Chronicle*, a left-leaning, Delay-hating newspaper in the Hammer's home district, reported that the conservative group Judicial Watch accused the congressman of bribery. Other articles also appeared in the national media. As a result, the Republican House leadership, which was more than a little embarrassed, put pressure on DeLay to stop. Even Speaker Denny Hastert was forced to intervene, obviously not because he thought that DeLay was doing anything terribly wrong, but to save the skin of his own Republican Party.

Around this time, I encountered my friend Bob Barr at a hearing on Capitol Hill, and he asked me about the DeLay controversy. Bob was not only my friend, but a fellow member of CNP and an arch conservative. "I see you've gone after DeLay," he said with a wry smile. Sensing that he approved, I asked, "Yeah, what do you think, Bob?" Bob's ethical standards were of the highest order, but on this one, he responded with sarcasm: "He's a crook, but he's our crook!"

I paid a price for taking a principled stand against DeLay, who would come under a huge ethical cloud in 2005 and 2006 and would be forced to resign his seat in Congress. The Hammer had many friends and he had done some good on behalf of Christian causes. He also employed a lot of fellow conservatives on his payroll, among them David Keene, the head of the American Conservative Union (ACU), as a political consultant. The ACU is a self-styled conservative think tank that puts on an annual conference in Washington and sends out mailings on various conservative issues the rest of the year. Yet, although it had become quite prominent over the years, it did little more than push the Republican line and raise money, perhaps underscoring the kinship between its leader, David Keene, and Tom DeLay.

Thus, it came as no surprise following the House ethics complaint to see Keene viciously attacking me in an article he wrote for *The Hill* newspaper that, like its competitor *Roll Call*, covers Congress *for* Congress and other media. In the article, Keene conveniently used the Clinton-inspired attack on me for suing my own mother and seemed to suggest that I was crazy and out of control. DeLay had fallen victim to Larry Klayman, just as Klayman's own mother had. Keene's tack was certainly an about-face from his earlier views about me. Indeed, I had previously been invited on several occasions to speak to his national ACU conference, and he had complimented me profusely on my work against the

Clintons. I couldn't allow Keene's attack piece to go unanswered, so I wrote an emotional response for *The Hill* accusing Keene of hypocrisy and a kinship with the cynical political tactics of the Clintons—the unkindest cut of all to a so-called conservative.

But the criticism did not stop. Fellow members of the Council of National Policy, a group of prominent conservatives founded by people like Ronald Reagan, Richard Diguerie, Ed Meese, and others in the conservative community intervened to try to dissuade me from being nonpartisan. In one instance, I remember a well-respected retired judge saying to me, "Larry, can't you just go after Democrats? Why don't you just say that Judicial Watch has limited resources and it can't pursue everything?" In shock, since I had admired this person a great deal, I responded, "That wouldn't be very Christian or principled. If I acted differently, I'd be a hypocrite."

Later, when the National Republican Senatorial Committee (NRSC) emulated DeLay's crass tactics and began selling national security briefings right after the September 11, 2001 attacks, I again intervened and was forced to file Senate ethics complaints against every Republican senator on the NRSC. To his credit, Senator Pete Fitzgerald of Illinois, one of the committee's leaders, quit in disgust.

But wait: How could the NRSC have sold national security briefings in the first place? The answer is that it couldn't; the entire fund-raising campaign was a complete fraud. My intervention put an end to this illegal behavior. With its plan in the glare of the media spotlight, the NRSC caved in and killed its fund-raising scheme.

While I did take flak for standing up to the Hammer, the NRSC and my own Republican Party, I knew in my heart that I was not attacking them so much as attempting to preserve their true ideals. Convinced that I had done the right thing, I vowed to press on, with or without the Clintons in office. And to my satisfaction, the overwhelming majority of Judicial Watch supporters, who had gotten to know me quite well over the years with my appearances in the media and direct-mail newsletters, backed my principled stand against my fellow conservatives. I reflected that I would need this support over the next four years. Bush and his party were too entrenched in the institutionally corrupt ways of the nation's capital to be choir boys, even if, at that time, I thought that their brand of corruption was not likely to rise to the level of the Clintons.

The Bush brand of government ethics indeed proved to be different as the new administration developed. It entailed a paranoia about government secrecy and an arrogance that the people are less worthy than the political elite—in effect, that the rabble do not have a right to know, much less to govern themselves. This Hamiltonian view—that "the people are a great beast"—was manifest in a particularly ugly way with what came to be called the Cheney Energy Task Force.

The task force was established by a Bush executive order to determine the nation's energy policy. Vice President Dick Cheney, the former head of Halliburton—a huge international energy and construction company, and a prominent government contractor—was named to run it. And run it he did, in secret, consulting with other energy-company tycoons such as Enron's Kenneth Lay, who had donated handsomely to both the Bush and Clinton campaigns, and who would later be indicted and convicted after his company collapsed amid accounting scandals. (Lay died of a massive heart attack in early July 2006, a few months before his sentencing.)

It's true that these consultations were informal and that the meetings or conversations did not take place in a government office. But the Federal Advisory Committee Act (FACA), a post-Watergate law, that required all contacts with nongovernment persons in such committees or task forces be disclosed, demanded transparency, at least in my view. The reason for the act was to prevent paid lobbyists and others from getting their financial hooks into presidential task forces and secretly formulating policy.

When the left-leaning press got wind of what was going on with Dick Cheney's Energy Task Force behind closed doors, reporters and columnists went berserk. The most notable article that I read at the time was written by *The Wall Street Journal*'s Washington editor Al Hunt, a liberal and friend of Clinton consigliere Harold Ickes. Hunt published a stinging piece that asked the rhetorical question: Where are Larry Klayman and Judge Royce Lamberth now that Hillary Clinton is not first lady?

Hunt was referring to a widely held perception that I was behind the lawsuit that challenged the secrecy of the presidential advisory committee set up to help Hillary formulate health care policy during the early years of her husband's administration. But he was wrong. When the American Association of Physicians and Surgeons and other interest groups filed suit to pry open the door of secrecy, the case was assigned to Judge Lamberth.

Responding to interrogatories, or written questions about the makeup of the advisory committee, Hillary and company were caught lying, swearing under oath that only government officials sat on the task force and that it was therefore immune from public scrutiny under the law. Lamberth was forced to take action. In fact, lobbyists and other nongovernment influence-peddlers were part of the process. Under the spotlight of Lamberth's court and intense media scrutiny, "Hillary Health Care," as it derisively came to be called, fell apart. So Hunt's article challenged me not to be a hypocrite and to apply the same open government standards to the Cheney task force on energy, which also had representatives from outside the government.

In fact, at the time that the Hillary case was filed, Judicial Watch was in its early years of operation and, due to limited resources, could not address every Clinton outrage. But Hunt having attributed the Hillary case to me was flattering; by this time, I had developed such a reputation as the anti-Clinton advocate that virtually every legal action against them was attributed to Judicial Watch.

Even before Hunt's article, I had begun the process of penetrating the walls of secrecy surrounding the Cheney Energy Task Force. Under the FACA law, I had filed written requests to make all underlying documents publicly available, as well as to allow me to attend any meeting of the task force. When Cheney and company stonewalled, I had no other option but to file suit in the federal court in Washington.

The case was assigned to a Clinton appointee, Judge Emmet Sullivan, which I thought was a stroke of good luck. Sullivan, a liberal African American and a Democrat, would not bend over backward to protect the Bush administration from scrutiny. Indeed, in early hearings, Judge Sullivan took a tough line, and in hearing after hearing he ordered the Cheney Energy Task Force at least to identify those who attended its meetings. But each time Sullivan issued an order, the Bush Justice Department, which represented the Cheney Energy Task Force, filed for reconsideration or used some other delay tactic.

I complained repeatedly to Sullivan that the Bush administration was just trying to run out the clock, and that by the time we got all of the documents, and opened up the task force to public view, it would be long past the next presidential election in 2004. But Sullivan, perhaps fearing retaliation by the Republicans if he were ever nominated to the higher appellate court, where there is a dearth of minority judges, continued to tolerate the delays and frivolous legal arguments by the Bush Justice Department. I reminded the judge that energy policy was tied to the war against terrorism and national security in general, and that the people had a right to know what had gone on behind closed doors, particularly after September 11. But it didn't spur him to more forceful action. While Sullivan was in many ways like Judge Lamberth, he did not have Lamberth's spine and was much more political in his execution of his own orders. As I requested on several occasions, he could have held the energy task force and even Vice President Cheney himself in contempt of court, but he was obviously worried about appearing too aggressive.

The case slogged on for more than three years and finally wound up before the U.S. Supreme Court. In fact, the High Court had no business reviewing Judge Sullivan's orders requiring that at least the names of the lobbyists and others who had been in contact with Cheney and his task force be revealed, since this was purely a discovery issue on which higher courts rarely, if ever, intervene.

Sullivan had not yet ordered that the inner workings and deliberations of the Cheney Energy Task force be revealed, an issue that could, however farfetched under the existing law, raise constitutional "separation of powers" issues potentially suited for the High Court. But similar to when the Supreme Court decided the 2000 Presidential election, its conservative justices, in my view, improperly stepped in to protect their benefactors. (While I was pleased that Bush had been installed as president in 2000, the Supreme Court's ruling did not square with its prior precedent and took jurisdiction away from the Supreme Court of Florida. However flawed the Florida court's decision in favor of Gore, the U.S. Supreme Court had no right to intervene and take the case away from the state judiciary. So strained was the Supreme Court's decision that its written ruling stated that it should not be used as binding precedent for future judicial proceedings.)

This appearance of favoritism became a public spectacle when the media picked up on Vice-President Cheney having secretly taken conservative Justice Antonin Scalia and his son on a duck hunting trip; the outing was paid for in part by the government and took place while the task-force case was before the Supreme Court. When questioned by the press about this inappropriate behavior after giving a college speech, Scalia reacted by shouting "quack, quack, quack!" at the audience, an insulting and unprofessional response for a Supreme Court justice. And when the co-plaintiff in Judicial Watch's case, the environmental group the Sierra Club, moved to have Scalia recuse himself from the Supreme Court's ultimate decision, Scalia, refusing to step aside, wrote how outraged he was that anyone could think that a Supreme Court justice could be bought so cheaply. What a disgrace to the Court, I thought, that a justice would ever write such a thing.

By this time, I myself had stepped down as chairman and general counsel of Judicial Watch to run for the U.S. Senate in Florida. If I had still been with the organization, I too would have moved to have Scalia recuse himself. But Judicial Watch apparently felt that this might anger the justice and turn him against its case. Sure enough, though, when the Supreme Court ultimately ruled and effectively delayed the resolution of the discovery issue until after the 2004 presidential election, Scalia's concurring opinion was the most pro-Cheney of the bunch. So much for discretion, I thought. In my view, it would have been better to put Scalia on the defensive with a challenge from the conservative Judicial Watch, which clearly would have carried much more weight than the weak challenge by the leftist Sierra Club.

In late 2004, the Supreme Court ultimately issued its decision, which effectively gutted the Federal Advisory Committee Act. Perhaps it was influenced by the perceived need for increased presidential power following September 11. Perhaps it was an example of the conservative court protecting the administration it put in power as a result of its flawed 2000 election decision. Whatever the underlying reasons, the Supreme Court found very limited powers by Congress to write laws that allowed scrutiny of the workings of the executive branch. As a result, even though the Court's opinion remanded the case to the appellate court for further consideration, it had undermined Judicial Watch's ability to get meaningful information about the Cheney Energy Task Force out of the White House.

Despite the efforts of the Bush administration to shield itself from scrutiny, I did uncover some documents, however, through Freedom of Information Act requests served on various government agencies that were indirectly part of the Cheney Energy Task Force. This was a clever end run around the legal stalling tactics of the task force itself. What I uncovered, however limited, was startling. For instance, documents showed that our energy companies, long before September 11, were deliberating with the Bush administration to divide up control of the Iraqi oil fields if the United States ever successfully invaded. And Chevron, one of the biggest of the American petroleum concerns, was advocating lifting the sanctions preventing it and other U.S. oil interests from doing business with the terrorist state of Libya and its lunatic leader, Muammar Qaddafi. I became convinced that these documents were just the tip of the iceberg—the real explanation behind Cheney's "principled position" that he should not disclose anything about his communications with his fellow energy industry executives because it would have a chilling effect on the executive getting candid advice. The Clinton administration had simply destroyed or hidden documents to try to avoid scandalous repercussions, but Cheney and company were much more sophisticated. They had learned how to use the politically sensitive Supreme Court and other judicial institutions to successfully maintain their illegal secrecy, obviating the need for outright obstruction of justice à la Nixon and Clinton.

But the Bush administration's incestuous ties with the energy industry would create other problems for the president and his minions. In the spring of 2001, a wave of corporate scandals became public. Companies like Enron were caught inflating profits to try to lure investors. As a result, their stock tanked, destroying the savings of many investors and leading to the collapse of the pension funds and stock options of their own employees. Because of the administration's close ties to energy and big business in general, and because its appointees to the Securities and Exchange Commission seemed too cavalier in policing the accounting industry (we later learned the SEC also failed to police Wall Street, creating the greatest economic collapse since the Great Depression), Bush and Cheney were under a lot of political pressure to do something about the corporate crooks. The Democrats, naturally enough, saw the corporate scandals as a big opening for the congressional elections of 2002 and even the presidential race of 2004.

To contain the damage, Bush hastily called a press conference to announce that his attorney general, John Ashcroft, was commissioning a Justice Department Corporate Fraud Task Force, and that Deputy Attorney General Larry Thompson would head it up. The president added that everyone, and he emphasized everyone, who was involved in the corporate accounting rip-offs should be held accountable.

I'd been studying the corporate scandals from my vantage point at Judicial Watch. What struck me was that several politicians and even some of their wives were involved. For example, Texas Senator Phil Graham's wife, Wendy Graham, the former chairman of the Commodities Futures Trading Commission, had actually sat on the accounting committee of Enron and likely knew, or certainly should have known, of the fraud. That a politician's wife would place herself in such a compromising position was obviously related to financial considerations and the favors a mega-company such as Enron could bestow on the government gentry.

But Phil Graham and his wife were not alone. Prior to joining the Bush Justice Department, Deputy Attorney General Thompson had been the head of the accounting committee for Providian, a San Francisco-based credit card company that also got its hand caught in the corporate cookie jar and was ultimately forced to cough up millions of dollars in settlements. What chutzpah, I thought: The tainted head of the administration's Corporate Fraud Task Force was going to run the investigation himself.

Then there was Vice President Cheney who, when he was CEO of Halliburton, had reportedly allowed the company's outside accountants to inflate profits on cost-plus construction contracts. After investigating the circumstances, I became convinced that Cheney had played a direct role in ordering a change in accounting practices to allow for the overstatement of profits, and that he had not allowed for the disclosure of the change to sufficiently inform the investing public.

Given the involvement of politicians or political appointees, the corporate scandals seemed a perfect opportunity for Judicial Watch to do what it could to protect the integrity of government. So taking the president at his word that everyone should be held accountable, and knowing full well that he would not do so with regard to those in his own administration, I filed suit on behalf of Halliburton shareholders against the vice president on the morning after Bush's press conference announcing the Corporate Fraud Task Force.

The announcement was made at a Miami press conference at the Sheraton Hotel on Brickell Avenue, the place where I had met Stanley Myatt, the Mafioso colleague of Peter Paul. The press reports went national, then global. In suing Dick Cheney along with Halliburton for accounting fraud, I had really hit the mother lode. Many of my conservative friends called me after the event. The messages were similar: You've really done it this time, Larry—meaning that I'd really put my foot in it by taking on perhaps the most powerful conservative in America. But, as always, I was content with my actions, knowing that I had stood up for what I thought was right without regard to political philosophy or party.

In short order, I brought other shareholders' derivative actions against companies such as Larry Thompson's Providian. As with Cheney, Thompson was personally named as a defendant. I had learned over the years that the only way to mete out justice was to hold corporate as well as political malefactors personally accountable. I had no choice but to take action against them individually if Judicial Watch was to enforce its motto that no one is above the law!

The suit against Vice President Cheney was filed in Houston, the home of Halliburton. As with the Cheney Energy Task Force case, it was assigned to an African-American federal judge appointed by Clinton not long before he left office. Another stroke of good luck, I thought. But I was wrong again. The judge, perhaps concerned about hurting his prospects for further judicial promotion, was clearly frightened by the notion of ruling against a patriarch of the Texas energy industry. Instead, he contrived a way to dismiss the case. It was taken up on appeal, but my colleagues at Judicial Watch fouled up the case after I left and no justice was ever done.

⊶18⊷

TERROR WATCH

It was the summer of 2001 and I was summoned to Chicago by David Schippers, the former House impeachment chief counsel I had worked with on my client Dolly Kyle Browning's case. We had become good friends and I admired Dave, not only because he had wanted to enlarge the impeachment proceedings to include Chinagate and other Clinton scandals, but because he, along with Congressman Bob Barr, had been sincere in his desire to bring about justice.

Dave wanted me to meet with his client, FBI Special Agent Robert Wright, in his office. Wright, who had been working out of the Chicago field office, had been the subject of retaliation by the FBI for his insistence that it investigate and prosecute radical Islam's money laundering, used to funnel cash to terrorists. Sham charities in the United States were being used to launder these funds. Higher-ups in the FBI chain of command had essentially ignored his pleas and, as a result, the special agent had taken to writing a book about the dereliction of duty and incompetence of his superiors, along with a detailed chronicling of terrorist activity.

As I listened to Special Agent Wright describe the enormous scope of the illegal use of charities by the terrorists, and warn that an impending disaster in our country was likely, I did not fully appreciate how prescient it was. Sure, Wright revealed that the laundered money was being used by organizations such as the Palestinian terror group Hamas to kill Israeli agents in the United States and elsewhere. But it was hard to believe, even for a cynic like me, that our country had almost totally let its guard down against the invading barbarians of the 21st century.

Dave wanted to bring me into his representation of Wright not only because he needed more fire power to take on the powerful bureaucracy of the FBI, but also because Judicial Watch could help his client get clearance to publish the book, thereby warning the American people of impending disaster. I also could be helpful in forcing the FBI and other antiterror government agencies to finally take action against the growing cancer of Islamic radicalism on American soil.

I agreed to represent Special Agent Wright and developed a strategy, along with Dave, to accomplish our goals. At all times, we made sure to comply with FBI regulations and national security concerns. We wanted to help the country understand quickly the extent of the problem, not reveal sensitive material that could compromise ongoing matters related to antiterrorism activities by the government.

First, we decided to file complaints with the Internal Revenue Service to have the radical Islamic charities audited. It was outrageous that, during the Clinton years, nearly every conservative public interest group, including Judicial Watch, was hit with frivolous and vexatious IRS audits, but the Islamic charities were left alone to carry out their evil deeds. So complaints against such groups as the Holy Land Foundation, a Texas-based charity, and many others were quickly drafted and lodged.

Second, I pressed the FBI to allow Wright to obtain the clearance to publish his book. When no meaningful response was forthcoming from the bureau, I filed suit on Wright's behalf in federal court in Washington to force the matter.

And, third, I assisted Dave in fending off the internal FBI complaints that were generated against Special Agent Wright in retaliation for his "insubordination" and refusal to keep his mouth shut about FBI inaction.

Our legal representation was well underway when the tragic events of September 11 happened. I can remember the exact time of the horrific events. I was just finishing my morning workout at Gold's Gym, a block away from Judicial Watch's D.C. headquarters at 501 School Street, South-west. I was in the locker room looking in the mirror and putting on my necktie when I heard a disc jockey announce on the intercom that one of the towers at New York's World Trade Center had been hit by a plane. She smoothly cut back to the music, a concoction of rap and hip hop. Then, about five minutes later, she broke in again, this time announcing that the second World Trade Center tower had been struck. I had suspected terrorism with the first announcement, but when I heard the latest news, I erupted uncontrollably, screaming, "Those fucking Arab terrorists!" As I hurried to my office about 100 yards away, I thought of what Wright had revealed over the summer. And I reflected on how, with one attack, the dynamic of the government would immediately change. We were at war and I didn't need to hear any confirmation by our newly installed president to drive home the point.

The day's events were a nightmare. When I returned to the office, my staff was transfixed by the television coverage in our press office. Images of a new tragedy were filling the screen: The Pentagon, just a few miles from Judicial Watch's headquarters, was also hit by a plane. Hearing this, I went over to the big bay windows off our conference room and saw the billowing smoke rising beyond the horizon. Washington was under attack as well!

I tried to contact my wife, Stephanie, on her cell phone. She did not answer. So I called the security guards who escorted my children to pre-school. I was able to reach them on the radio function of our cell phones and ordered them to take Isabelle and Lance back to the townhouse in Georgetown. But not knowing why Stephanie was not with the children and fearing that she could not reach them in the pandemonium that was overflowing onto the streets of Washington, I left the office to try to join them. The scene outside was Armageddon. People were on foot, screaming and reacting as if it were every man for himself. The Metro subway system was shut down and even cabs, when they weren't stalled in the middle of the gridlocked traffic, were out of service because their drivers were speeding off to be with their families. So I set out on foot for the six-mile journey to my home in Georgetown, all the while watching the smoke rise over the Pentagon. Little did I or anyone else know at the time that another plane, hijacked by suicide terrorists, was headed for Washington. Its target was later determined to be the Capitol Building, only a few blocks from Judicial Watch's headquarters.

As I was running toward my house, I continued to try to call Stephanie. Thankfully, I finally got through. She had joined up with the children at home. Realizing that it might take hours to reach them, and that the streets would probably later clear, I returned to the office to tend to my staff and get the latest news.

When I got back, all but a few of the staff had fled. I sat in my office thinking about everything from the safety of my family to the well-being of the country. I also thought about Special Agent Wright and how we would need to secure a meeting at the highest level of the Justice Department, of which the FBI is an integral part, to address what had just occurred. Wright, I reasoned, could be instrumental in helping newly installed Attorney General Ashcroft get to the bottom of the Department's obvious failure.

On September 12, I placed a call to John Ashcroft's office and asked to speak with him. He did not take the call, but I was put through to his deputy. Explaining that I represented Special Agent Wright and that he had important information about FBI neglect leading up to yesterday's attacks, I asked for a meeting with the attorney general. The deputy, David Israelite, someone with whom I had dealt during the Peter Paul case, said that he would have someone get back in touch with me quickly.

I did hear back, but not with the response I wanted. Instead, I got a call from Mathew Martins, the counsel to the assistant attorney general for the Criminal Division and thus a top aide to Michael Chertoff, the division head. I explained to Martins the utility of having the attorney general or others at the highest level meet with Wright, since he held the keys to understanding much of what had obviously gone wrong in the government's antiterror activities. But Martins responded nastily: "We've had enough of your conspiracy theories, Klayman!" This was a reference, I assumed, to the Clinton connections in the Peter Paul case. After fruitlessly imploring Martins to reconsider without success, I slammed the phone down in disgust.

The demeanor of Ashcroft's Justice Department was shocking. With people like Martins at the helm, I had to believe the country was in deeper trouble than even the events of September 11 suggested. Talking directly to the FBI leadership, which was responsible in large part for the debacle, would be pointless and futile.

The next step in trying to get an audience for Special Agent Wright was contacting Congress. I had my past difficulties with Senator Arlen Specter over the Judge Keller and Peter Paul matters, but at least he had given me an opportunity to present my case. And he sat on the Senate Intelligence Committee, which conducts oversight of the FBI and other intelligence agencies. Sure enough, he was willing to meet with Wright, but not for a few weeks.

When the meeting eventually took place, Specter sat there looking intently at my client, appearing to digest the seriousness of the FBI's failure. He also seemed to grasp the gravity of the FBI's retaliation against Wright, and he ordered his assistant, who was in attendance, to draft a letter to the new FBI director, Robert Mueller, inquiring about the matter. But as was true with other issues that I had taken to the senator, the letter was never sent and there was virtually no follow-up.

A little while later, another FBI special agent, this time from the Minneapolis field office, blew the whistle on FBI neglect and incompetence with regard to its failure to seek or obtain a search warrant for Zacarias Moussaoui, one of the September 11 would-be hijackers attending flight school in the Midwest. Special Agent Colleen Rowley had written a letter to FBI Director Mueller detailing her agency's incompetence, which had gone unanswered. Her disclosure that a potential September 11 terrorist had not been adequately investigated set off a firestorm in the media. Unlike Wright, who had always played it straight and had not publicly disclosed sensitive information about FBI sources and methods, Rowley revealed in considerable detail how the agency's investigation of Moussaoui had failed. Technically speaking, she could have been criminally indicted for her disclosures on grounds that they compromised FBI investigations. But rather than charging her, Mueller was forced into a defensive crouch by the press and wound up praising and embracing the special agent for her courage.

The warm embrace did not apply to Wright, of course. He had not put the Justice Department on the defensive by going for the jugular, despite documented evidence that the money laundering he was investigating could be linked to al Qaeda's activities in the United States through Saudi businessmen and the royal family. While Special Agent Rowley got a pass, Special Agent Wright continued to be intimidated and threatened by his FBI supervisors and others for his legal and proper criticisms of the department. And rather than profit from meeting with him, the Justice Department removed Wright, one of the foremost experts on antiterrorism in the FBI, from post-9/11 terror investigations. He was eventually allowed to resume his work only as a last resort, when the agency was forced to concede internally that it had no choice; its years of neglect had left a shortage of qualified special agents to pursue terrorism.

The story of Special Agent Robert Wright, like so many others I handled at Judicial Watch, is not finished. But it does serve as an example that nearly anyone who plays it straight and tries to work within the system to make it better usually winds up getting the shaft. The government is not equipped to deal with criticism from inside its own ranks; instead, it instinctively wants to cover up. In the aftermath of September 11, one of the worst tragedies in American history, this now appears truer than ever.

A culture developed in Washington and around the country immediately after September 11 that it was politically incorrect to criticize the government.

It was abetted by the Bush administration, which accused its critics of being unpatriotic as a way to deflect attention from its own shortcomings—not least of which was an inability to connect the dots before the tragedy, dots that included a national security briefing paper on the president's desk that warned of al Qaeda's plans to hijack planes. But there would be time enough for recriminations later. Now, in days after 9/11, I thought that our lack of knowledge about Osama bin Laden's plans and the risks of even bigger attacks using weapons of mass destruction meant there was no time to lose.

And there wasn't: Within two weeks of 9/11, anthrax attacks were in the headlines, with the Florida headquarters of American Media, a tabloid publisher, especially hard hit. Anthrax, a deadly poison, showed up at U.S. Postal Service facilities in Washington and in the Northeast, in Senate Minority Leader Tom Daschle's office at the Capitol and at NBC's offices in New York.

The nation was still in mourning over the victims of 9/11, but the grieving didn't mean paralysis for the Bush administration, which was planning the attack on Afghanistan (and, we would later learn, on Iraq), and I felt it shouldn't paralyze private watchdogs like Judicial Watch and me either. On Judicial Watch's weekly radio and television shows, and in articles I wrote for WorldNetDaily.com, a widely read Internet site, I began to criticize the government for letting down its guard in the face of many signals of what the terrorists intended. I also had our staff begin to prepare a book to alert the country to the obvious fact that the previous administration under Bill Clinton and the current administration under George W. Bush had failed to do their primary job under the United States Constitution—to protect the American people from tyranny at home and abroad. Frankly, I was outraged and determined not to hold back.

It took a little less than a year to write and publish the book, which I titled *Fatal Neglect: The U.S. Government's Continuing Failure to Protect American Citizens from Terrorists*. But it was a job that was worth doing. In it, I detailed the breakdown by one government agency after another. I told the stories of Special Agent Wright and other whistle- blowers and suggested how to shore up the nation's homeland security defenses. Published on the first anniversary of 9/11, *Fatal Neglect* also recommended—years before the slew of reports that began to appear in 2004—that a national security counter-terrorism agency, patterned after Great Britain's MI5, be immediately established to streamline and better organize intelligence efforts. In short, it did not take joint congressional committees and independent commissions, plagued by bipartisan bickering and cover-ups that delayed their work, to brief the American people on the gaps in our homeland security and suggest appropriate changes. With the exception of the whistle-blower information, nearly all of the material in *Fatal Neglect* came from publicly available sources. You didn't need to be a rocket scientist to figure out in general terms what went wrong and what it would take to fix it.

But political foot dragging by Bush and company and their accomplices in both parties in Congress slowed the entire process of reform. Instead, they created a bigger bureaucracy, the Department of Homeland Security (DHS), which simply merged and placed under one roof every incompetent agency that might have anything to do with antiterrorism efforts. It gave new meaning to that old saw about rearranging the deck chairs on the *Titanic*. The new DHS, enacted into law in late 2002, did nothing to immediately solve basic homeland security problems, such as the lack of adequate screening for baggage placed in the cargo holds of airplanes; the failure to screen for chemical, biological or nuclear devices in up to 90% of the containers moving through our porous ports; the shortage of vaccines for any number of potential terrorist-induced plagues, and scores of other threats. To this day, these problems have not been adequately addressed, despite massive government spending that helped usher in huge budget deficits and an increase in the national debt, exceeded only by the corporate and labor bailouts and socialism of the Obama administration. Rather than expenditures on life-and-death homeland security measures, the Bush administration and Congress conspired in social-welfare boondoggles such as the Medicare prescription drug program and doled out so much pork that, in the words of Pat Buchanan, it's a wonder we all don't have trichinosis. Today, with Obama at the helm, the sky is the limit for federal welfare spending, bankrupting the nation even further.

Other than leveling criticism and offering helpful suggestions in *Fatal Neglect*, I felt that Judicial Watch needed to play a proactive role in the fight against terrorism. As a result, we mounted our own antiterrorism effort of sorts and filed lawsuits against Osama bin Laden, the Taliban—the previous government of Afghanistan—Saddam Hussein, the country of Iraq, Fidel Castro and Hugo Chavez on behalf of some of the victims of September 11. Defaults against many of these defendants are pending, with requests to the relevant courts to enter judgment for the damages inflicted on the survivors. One can only hope that the damages will be collected for the victims from frozen assets in the United States. If nothing else, judgments will allow for the conduct discovery to try to find assets from which they can be satisfied. And this will allow public interest groups to track the laundering of money through charities and other front operations to the terrorists, a job the FBI and other government agencies have not completed.

The cases against Saddam Hussein continue, even after his execution, and they concern his involvement in terrorism, including his apparent role in the bombing of the Murrah Federal Building in Oklahoma City in April 1995. Evidence exists, even acknowledged by former Deputy Secretary of Defense Paul Wolfowitz during the period leading up to the 2003 invasion of Iraq, that Saddam Hussein's agents, combined with American neo-Nazis, conspired with Timothy McVeigh and Terry Nichols to perpetrate the Oklahoma City tragedy. And in a deposition taken of the wife of Ramsey Youssef, one of the World Trade Center terrorist bombers in 1993, it was revealed that Youssef had met and worked with Nichols on the Oklahoma City attack. Special Agent Wright did not reveal to me what he knew or did not know about Oklahoma City, but he did tell me during our first meeting that, over the previous decade, there had been numerous terrorist attacks in the United States, which the bureau and other government agencies had covered up. Could this have been the reason that the Bush Justice Department was so hell bent on rushing to execute Timothy McVeigh in June 2001, despite newly discovered evidence that Justice had suppressed a massive amount of trial evidence prior to his conviction?

With regard to Judicial Watch's lawsuit against Hugo Chavez, then pending in federal court in Miami, it was revealed shortly after September 11 by the Venezuelan leader's jet pilot that he had handed over $1 million in cash to the Taliban prior to the date of the attack. Before becoming Venezuela's pro-Castro strongman, Chavez was an avowed terrorist, writing frequently about his activities while in prison. The jet pilot whistle-blower, who fled to Miami, provided me with grounds to file suit for a victim of September 11 against Chavez and the government of Venezuela.

As for Fidel Castro, the godfather of all modern terrorists, it was revealed through leaked U.S. government sources that he had aided Saddam Hussein during the events leading up to the American invasion in the spring of 2003, and is now harboring some of Iraq's pre-war leaders in Havana. Castro is also known to have worked with the Colombian FARC Marxist terrorists, the Basque separatist group ETA in Spain, the Irish Republican Army and a host of other terrorist states and entities. As confirmed by the Bush State Department, he has bio-weapons facilities on the island, and he was one of the first to use chemical weapons during Cuba's involvement in the long-running civil war in Angola. Two years before September 11, while visiting Libya, he vowed, along with fellow dictator Muammar Qaddafi, to bring the United States to its knees.

Many of the cases I brought against Castro while at Judicial Watch were for crimes against humanity, filed for victims of the dictator's terrorism. One such case was lodged for Jose Basulto, the president of Brothers to the Rescue, a nonprofit humanitarian group that saved Cuban rafters fleeing Castro's hell hole. In the late 1990s, four Brothers were shot down by Cuban MiGs over international waters in the Florida Straits. Basulto, who was leading the mission to spot Cuban rafters, miraculously survived. I filed suit for him against Castro for this terrorist act, and ultimately won $2 million in a judgment against Castro and the Cuban Air Force. If relations are ever normalized between the two countries after Castro's death, payment of this judgment should be a precondition, along with other concessions by the Communist state.

And last but hardly least, I filed suit for the U.S. Postal Service workers at the Brentwood Main Post Office in Washington, who did not get antibiotic treatment for days following the post-9/11 anthrax attacks. The victims, mostly African Americans, were neglected while the white guys in the Bush White House and on Capitol Hill received their Cipro—an antibiotic effective in combating inhaled anthrax—and did just fine. Eight postal workers died and many remain sick and infirm from the anthrax contamination that was allowed to fester.

Fatal Neglect notwithstanding, I was a harsh critic of the Bush administration's sometimes indefinite detention of American citizens accused of terrorism without right of legal counsel as well as its decision to wiretap American citizens without first obtaining court-ordered warrants. The detention policy in particular, now overturned by the Supreme Court, arrogantly highlighted its condescension toward the American people and its reckless disregard of the Constitution. It permeated the culture of that presidency and set a bad example for future generations. So, too, has the administration's support for the so-called Patriot Act, which now effectively allows its Justice Department to conduct searches of American citizens and their property virtually unrestrained by judicial supervision or oversight.

Meanwhile, the administration protected its own house and was slow to clean it. Consider the case of George Tenet, former director of Central Intelligence. Rather than removing this Clinton holdover for his breathtaking incompetence leading up to September 11 and the war in Iraq, President Bush presented Tenet with the Medal of Freedom, one of the most coveted honors in Washington. I don't know for sure, but perhaps Bush was rewarding Tenet for remaining silent about the "willing suspension of disbelief" in the White House regarding impending terrorist attacks, which caused the president's national-security staff to do virtually nothing to prepare for or forestall them, despite all the warning signs. If so, the act spoke ill of this president and was yet another nail in his political coffin, culminating in the huge Republican defeat in 2008 and the rise of a socialist administration, packed with resurrected Clinton crooks and cronies.

During his time in office, President Bush and his colleagues did some positive things, although frankly I cannot think of any real achievements other than being a good cheerleader—however distorted his message was—in the war against terrorism. In the 2004 presidential elections, his biggest asset was that he was not John Kerry, his Democrat opponent, an unexciting and intellectually inconsistent liberal who not only failed to galvanize voters but, in fact, turned them off.

At Judicial Watch I tried to "change the world," or at least make the government less dishonest. But the intractability, penchant for secrecy, prevarication, cover-up, corruption and intellectual dishonesty in government created such an endemic gridlock that I came to realize it will take a powerful, irresistible force to set it in motion and aim it in the right direction.

19

FINAL STRAW: THE DECISION TO LEAVE JUDICIAL WATCH

Despite the difficulties inherent in fighting governmental and judicial corruption, Judicial Watch had accomplished a great deal since I founded the organization on July 29, 1994. Our website in the spring of 2003 could boast more than 100 victories, and we were never shy in the area of self-promotion. After all, if the generally liberal elitist media would not give us our due, then we could at least extol our own virtues to further the drive for honest government. In 1999, at the height of the Lewinsky scandal, when the late John Kennedy, Jr. and his *George* magazine poked fun at me as the number-one media hound, among a top 10 list of "winners," I wore this accolade as a badge of honor.

But for me there was always an undercurrent of restlessness, if not insecurity and self-reflection. I was never satisfied. As a child of the 1960s, my goal had always been to live life as someone who would be remembered for changing the world. I had a smug and secret sense that I was destined for greatness—as my grandfather and father would say to me, as if the hand of God were on my shoulder. During the closing years of the Vietnam War, and during my junior year in college studying in France, American foreign policy in Europe was disdained—much in the way it is today. But I would march the streets of Paris singing "Yankee Doodle Dandy," a song my father crooned to me when I was a little boy. Quietly, but with the brashness of a meatpacker's grandson, I honestly believed that someday I could be president of the United States. This thought always stayed with me, even during my years at Judicial Watch, where I painfully learned the limitations of the court system to effect the real change that only the president has the power to implement—if he wants to.

161

Yes, I had been the only Clinton adversary to obtain a legal ruling that Bill Clinton had committed a crime, and I was the one who used the court system to expose Chinagate, one of the biggest scandals in American history. Congressman Bob Barr, my government counterpart during impeachment, had credited me with uncovering about 90% of the corruption during the Clinton years. William Safire and Robert Novak, the premier conservative columnists, as well as Bill Moyers, the liberal king of PBS, had, among many others, also spoken highly of my accomplishments. But I had not scored the knockout punch at Judicial Watch. The Clintons were free on their own recognizance, and neither George W. Bush nor the rest of the Republicans seemed to give a damn. They had accomplished their purpose—removing Democrats from the White House. With their own skeleton-filled closets, it's no wonder there was no real justice for the Bonnie and Clyde of American politics, much less for the current crop of political prostitutes. And without justice and ethical accountability, the country would continue to slip into an abyss of corruption, with all of the attendant consequences foretold by John Adams and other founding fathers. But in the spring of 2003, despite my growing disillusionment, I was still searching for a way to turn the tide of corruption with Judicial Watch.

Over the previous 10 years, I had observed how in case after case at Judicial Watch, I could predict with almost exact certainty how judges would rule. All I had to do was look to their party affiliation and the president who had appointed them to the federal bench. Many judges would dismiss my "too hot to handle" lawsuits—and not just because they were throwing a bone to their political benefactor who might someday appoint them to a higher judicial post. They also did not want to endure the criticism in the press for making hard decisions against the Washington elite, of which the media is an integral part. Indeed, it had become all too commonplace for judges to throw a case out with the cover that if the appeals court reversed it, he or she could not be blamed. I saw this with several of the cases I brought for the women that the Clintons had harassed, intimidated and destroyed, such as Dolly Kyle Browning and Gennifer Flowers. Judge Thomas Penfield Jackson had conceded as much when he tossed out a libel lawsuit I had filed for Paul Weyrich, the religious conservative icon, against the ultra-leftist *New Republic*. The magazine had branded Paul as a paranoid schizophrenic who practically foamed at the mouth. Jackson, a media darling at the time because he was giving Microsoft a hard time, openly said that he would be happy to let the *New Republic* case proceed only if he could be assured the D.C. Circuit would reverse him. And reversed he was years later, as were the Browning and Flowers cases. By then, of course, the impact of any final verdict was diminished because of intervening national crises. What judicial courage and respect for the law!

The one federal judge who on more than one occasion had given me some small degree of confidence in the court system was Royce Lamberth. By luck, and more likely by the grace of God, he was assigned to the first three cases I filed at Judicial Watch, concerning brewing Clinton scandals that later would be come known as "Trustgate," "Chinagate" and "Filegate."

In the first case, I had been forced, through necessity, to use a novel legal theory to attack the Clintons' legal defense fund, a scheme they had set up through lobbyists and other political whores disguised as Democratic and Republican "trustees" to raise money to pay their legal bills. I filed suit to shut it down, claiming that the trustees were, in reality, providing advice on whether the fund was legal and thus comprised a federal advisory committee that either had to make full accountability or cease operations. Otherwise, there was no way that, as a private entity without standing to complain, Judicial Watch could challenge it. When the Clinton trustees refused my request to produce all records and allow me to attend their bogus meetings, I sued them.

Lamberth dismissed the case summarily, but the sinister nature of the fund was ultimately exposed. During campaign finance hearings in early 1997, the Senate Committee on Government Affairs learned that over $300,000 in Communist Chinese cash was illegally laundered into the Clintons' account, and the resulting media frenzy killed the fund. (The principal was returned, but Hillary Clinton refused to give back the interest that had accrued.) But what I remember most about the case was the call that I got from Lamberth after he had thrown it out.

I was sitting in my office opening mail late on a Friday afternoon when my secretary came in and announced that "Royce is on the phone." While I had met Lamberth around Washington on occasion, we had never been on a first name basis, so I did not immediately place the name. Confused, I asked my secretary, "Who is Royce?" She dutifully went back to her phone outside my office and asked for the last name, returned and announced that Judge Lamberth was calling.

I picked up the phone and Lamberth said something that I would never forget. "Larry, I am just calling to let you know that, as an American and a jurist,

I am proud of the way you handled the case. I had to dismiss it based on my reading of the law, but I wanted you to know that I appreciate what you are trying to do in fighting for ethics in government. Keep it up, the country needs you." I was flabbergasted and didn't quite know how to respond. I couldn't discuss the substance of the case, because to do so would be an improper *ex parte* contact if the appellate court later reversed Lamberth's ruling, so I nervously said, "Thanks, I appreciate the kind words," and let it go at that.

It wouldn't be the last time I exchanged a few words with Lamberth. During the Christmas season, I would send him and other judges I admired—a short list, to be sure—nondenominational holiday cards. He called to thank me, and once I said, "You know, judge, the only thing I regret about your being assigned to a number of our cases is that we can't have lunch and compare notes on what has gone on these many years." He chuckled and said with a touch of sadness, if not wry humor, "Yeah, by the time that could happen, we'll be too old to move."

Sometimes during court recesses, Judge Lamberth would talk to the attorneys about the ways of Washington and its lack of respect for the law. I was impressed. In my years of legal practice, I had not found many judges, particularly in the federal system, who were unafraid to do what was right, without regard to the political consequences for their careers. It was a rare and treasured commodity. In many ways, during the Clinton years, Lamberth became my gold-dust twin on the bench; the liberals in the media would frequently claim that I had him in my hip pocket and that we were both right-wing fanatics. They mocked both him and me, but he soldiered on nonetheless, sometimes strongly criticizing my zealous litigation style in court pleadings—perhaps to show them that his rulings against the Clintons and their cronies, like George Stephanopoulos and James Carville, were only to further justice and not meant to help Larry Klayman or some conservative cause.

But over time, even Lamberth proved as vulnerable as anyone when confronted by a group of government thugs. During a deposition of Terry Lenzner, the king of the feared and detested gang of private detectives the Clintonistas sicced on their adversaries to dig up dirt for political smears, I asked if he had been asked by the president's and first lady's attorneys, Williams and Connolly, to gather information on judges in the District of Columbia. This was a frequent Clinton intimidation tactic. Lenzner nervously took the Fifth Amendment and refused to answer. In a contempt motion, I asked Lamberth to order a response to the question, but the judge denied the request, perhaps frightened to confirm that he was one of the judges that Lenzner was assigned to investigate, and thus intimidate.

I had deposed Lenzner in the Filegate case, a lawsuit concerning the misappropriation and misuse by the Clinton White House of more than 900 FBI files on Republicans and others who were real or imagined adversaries. The judge had ruled that evidence showing that privacy rights had been violated by agents of the White House in other contexts could raise an inference that the same thing had happened with the FBI files. This was important, since it was unlikely that the Clintons and those around them would ever admit that the FBI files had been obtained for an illegal purpose—to smear those who challenged their actions.

I filed the case in 1996, shortly after the scandal broke, and I named Hillary Clinton as a defendant. There were public reports that she had hired Craig Livingstone, the former bar bouncer who ordered the FBI to deliver up the files to him at the White House. Later, during discovery, Linda Tripp, who was a secretary in the Office of the White House Counsel when the files appeared, testified that she overheard William Kennedy, then Deputy White House Counsel, admit that Hillary was the one who was responsible for the caper. Kennedy had been Hillary's partner at the Rose Law Firm in Little Rock, and she brought him to Washington with her after Clinton won the presidency. Tripp had also seen Republican FBI files in Kennedy's office and on the desk of another deputy counsel, Vince Foster, the day that he died.

As a defendant in a civil suit, Hillary surely would have to be questioned under oath. In her initial court pleadings, she denied any involvement in Filegate, but this was not enough to remove her from the case and prevent her from being deposed. Indeed, her husband had denied making a pass at Paula Jones and it did not prevent his being questioned under oath and later impeached for his perjury. The Supreme Court, in a historic ruling, found that even a president is not above the law, much less a first lady, who technically is not even a government official.

As a seasoned trial lawyer, I generally liked to depose the ringleader first, before he or she could benefit from hearing the testimony of subordinates. So when I filed the Filegate case, it was natural that I would want to take Hillary's deposition first. But when I sent her lawyer, David Kendall, of Williams and Connolly, the deposition notice, he predictably complained to Lamberth, claiming that it was a Klayman publicity stunt to raise money for Judicial

Watch. Kendall called attention to a Judicial Watch press release that boasted of its desire to depose the first lady in Lamberth's court.

During a hearing in open court, in front of a packed courtroom of the Washington press corps, Lamberth, holding up the press release, grandstanded, bellowing that I would have to wait to depose Mrs. Clinton until other avenues of obtaining testimony were exhausted. And he added that I might never get to depose her. Lamberth cited some precedent, fed to him by Kendall, that high government officials may not have to give testimony if evidence can be obtained through alternative witnesses. But this precedent was inapposite, as lawyers say, because in this case Hillary was a defendant, and in the cases cited by Kendall, the high government official was not. I pointed out to the judge that I had never heard of a civil case in which the lead defendant was not questioned and added that Hillary, as first lady, is not legally even a government official. Lamberth shrugged this off without explanation, his rotund face turning a bright red.

Over the course of the next seven years, Kendall and the so-called Justice Department filed motion after motion seeking to remove Hillary and her White House from the case. As the evidence of Hillary's involvement mounted, the motions were denied, but still Lamberth refused to allow me to depose her. I would bring the subject up at almost every court hearing, and predictably the judge would sidestep the issue—even after the Supreme Court ordered the deposition of the president in the Jones case. By then it was in its seventh year, a testament to the frivolous legal obstacles that Kendall and the Justice Department—under both the Clinton and Bush administrations—were putting up. Indeed, since George W. Bush took office on January 20, 2001, little had changed at the Justice Department. The same lawyers were handling the Clinton lawsuits I had filed, the same bogus legal arguments were being put forth, and there was not one offer, much less discussion, to settle any of them. This was particularly disheartening in the Filegate case.

During the time we were deposing Harold Ickes, former Clinton deputy White House chief of staff, in that case, a red-haired woman walked into Judicial Watch's office. I could see her sitting nervously in the lobby, through the glass partition of the conference room, where I was questioning Ickes. I stopped the deposition and asked Judicial Watch's chief investigator, Chris Farrell, to see what she wanted.

What we learned that day was that the Clinton White House had suppressed hundreds of thousands of e-mails not only to Judicial Watch, but to the various independent counsels investigating the administration's scandals, as well as Congress. Some of these e-mails, according to this woman who worked in the White House computer room, were incriminating and concerned several scandals, including Chinagate and Filegate. The whistle-blower, Sheryl Hall, would later introduce me to another colleague, Betty Lambuth, who confirmed the story.

I immediately filed a motion for criminal contempt with Lamberth, and what followed was a lengthy investigation into this apparent obstruction of justice, with a full-blown evidentiary hearing. In the process, Lamberth ordered the Clinton White House to re-create the missing e-mails, which the administration claimed had been erased as a result of an "innocent computer glitch."

By early 2003, and since the conclusion of the evidentiary hearing at the close of the Clinton administration, for almost two years Lamberth had allowed various motions, including Hillary's latest motion to dismiss, to sit as he awaited the recreation of evidence from the missing e-mails. Nor had he ruled on my motion for criminal contempt for the suppressed e-mails. At a cost of $8 million, the task, which had been assigned to the National Archives, was apparently now complete, and the Justice Department so informed the court. The judge ordered a status conference in his chambers to hear what, if anything, the government had uncovered.

In early March I walked into the small conference room on the fourth floor of D.C.'s famous federal courthouse, where everything from Watergate to Whitewater grand juries had been convened over the years. What I found was David Kendall, Hillary's lawyer, chatting warmly with Jim Gilligan, the Justice Department lawyer who had steadfastly defended the Clintons during my years at Judicial Watch. Gilligan and others in the Federal Programs Branch of Justice's Civil Division had known that their client, the Clinton White House, suppressed the production of the missing e-mails and did nothing about it for years. I had asked the court, during the evidentiary hearing two years earlier, to hold Gilligan and his Justice Department cohorts in criminal contempt as well.

Gilligan and Kendall sat there like partners in crime. Lamberth, as usual, arrived a short while later, jolly and complaining about some new government outrage in another of his pet cases concerning Indian trust funds. The

Interior Department, during both the Clinton and Bush administrations, had cheated Native Americans of their savings to the tune of billions of dollars. Lamberth had just held Bush's interior secretary, Gale Norton, in contempt of court for suppressing evidence, and he was crowing about how the Republicans—and he was one of them—underestimated his conviction to hold them accountable. As he sat down, the judge smiled at me, knowing that I approved of his nonpartisanship. He was aware, particularly given all of the publicity, that my cases against the Cheney Energy Task Force and Halliburton were moving ahead and that even the liberal elitist media was for once giving me my due. Lamberth also yearned to be free of the label "right-wing zealot." Like Gilligan and Kendall, Lamberth and I were birds of a feather, just from a different flock.

As he firmly planted his considerable presence in the armchair at the head of the conference table, the judge turned to Gilligan and asked whether the government had found any relevant documents in its search of the missing e-mails. Gilligan, always sarcastic and partisan, replied that the search had turned up only one document, that it had been produced to Mr. Klayman years earlier, was not incriminating and that it was now time to dismiss the entire case. He grinned with glee and mockingly looked in my direction.

Hardly surprised, given Gilligan's own involvement in the obvious obstruction of justice, I turned to Lamberth. I congratulated Gilligan for at least producing one more document than Saddam Hussein had delivered to the United Nations weapons inspectors. Lamberth and even Kendall chuckled at the line. Gilligan looked like a jilted date. It was still early March, and Bush had not yet ordered the invasion of Iraq.

I pushed further, asking how anyone could expect Gilligan and his crew in the Federal Programs Branch to produce any incriminating documents, since they themselves were part of the cover-up. And I added one more provocative tidbit, just for discussion purposes, of course. I told Lamberth that he could not even consider dismissing the case until Hillary Clinton was deposed and, after seven years, wasn't it long past time to take the testimony of the principal defendant?

The judge tensed up, characteristically turned bright red, gritted his teeth, and shot back at me: "You may never get to depose her, Larry. I told you there is a body of law that says high government officials may not have to testify. And, I haven't seen any hard evidence that she is involved."

Stunned by the use of the same reasoning he had used many years earlier, and finally reaching my breaking point, I decided to drop the atom bomb. "Your honor, you know that I love you. But you have established the principle that there are certain people, like Mrs. Clinton, who are above the law. This is an absolute disgrace! Even her husband was deposed in the Jones case, and Hillary is not a president!" I also wanted to ask him what he was scared of, but I held back. Lamberth had done much for the country before Bush, a fellow Republican and Texan, won the presidency; and he had helped to stem the Clinton scourge. I also knew that Judicial Watch would not have been as successful without him.

But I could not stop there. I lit into all the evidence tying Hillary to Filegate, including Linda Tripp's testimony that William Kennedy had acknowledged her involvement. The judge just stared at me silently, knowing that I was right. "Larry," he said, "I'll reread your pleadings and we'll see."

I had heard this before. Seven years had passed since I had filed the complaint against Hillary. I left the conference room in a daze, shaking my head but not really surprised, given everything I had seen over the years since I founded Judicial Watch. It was now all too clear to me that Lamberth would never allow Hillary's deposition. To do so, particularly years after the Clintons had left the White House, would not only rankle the liberal elitist media, for whom Lamberth was now a darling because of the Indian Trust Fund case, but could awaken the Clinton smear machine. Lamberth must have been thinking whether he needed the aggravation. He had taken enough abuse in making rulings in my favor over the years and he now seemed broken at last.

For me this hearing was the last straw. If Lamberth—the judge I admired above all others—was too scared to take on the likes of Hillary, how could the court system ever be effectively used to reform a corrupt political system? Almost 10 years after I founded Judicial Watch, I needed to find another way.

20

THE DIRTY DOZEN &
THE REVENGE OF THE FELINES

The alternate route I chose for 18 months of my life was a direction I never expected to take: that of a candidate in elective politics. I had put aside any thoughts of entering politics after my experience during Watergate working for Senator Schweiker, and I truly believed I found my calling at Judicial Watch. But now I felt that God wanted me to go in a different direction, and Bob Graham stepping down as senator from Florida was a sign. If I ran for his seat and won, I would have a staff of almost 100 and the increased powers of government to continue the fight against corruption. I could use the bully pulpit of government to teach the American people, as John Adams had tried to do, that ethics, morality and religion are the linchpins of freedom and liberty. I was an antiestablishment public figure, and it would be no small irony that, as a United States senator, I would be a part of the establishment I had fought. But I would have even greater access to the media and perhaps even expanded opportunities to influence the national debate. My entry and time in the Senate could be truly revolutionary. I could give new meaning to my love for Florida and satisfy my desire to reform the country at the same time. Besides, imagine Hillary Clinton's face the day I would be sworn in and take a seat in the Senate chamber alongside her!

But I had to think hard about this. By nature, I am not a politician, nor did I want to become one. The lifestyle would likely be similar to what I'd experienced at Judicial Watch—demanding and stressful. And would the establishment ever allow me to win a seat? What would it do once I were elected? The thought of having a Trojan horse in their midst would be frightening to Democrats and Republicans alike. The *National Journal*, the most prestigious political magazine in the country, had written that the thing the political elite feared most about me was that I couldn't be bought, because I sought no establishment credentials and thus had none to protect.

The Florida Senate race would be critical, perhaps the premier congressional contest in the nation. The state was now the nation's fourth largest—soon to be the third largest—with 27 electoral votes, and its strategic importance to both parties was huge. Florida had not only decided the 2000 presidential election, it was also expected to be pivotal in 2004. The Senate race could have a profound impact on whether the president would be reelected. If I did run, I thought, I might make the straight-talking John McCain look like a Republican warm-up act. The challenge really excited me.

Because I had zero experience running for office and because I would be a threat to the establishment, particularly within my own party, I would need the best and most fearless campaign manager I could find. Scott Reed, an old friend, was my man for guidance. I had met Scott in 1988, shortly before Jack Kemp was confirmed as Housing and Urban Development secretary in the administration of the first President Bush. Scott was Kemp's new chief of staff at HUD, and his office was just a few blocks away from my law firm in Southwest Washington. Later, I did some work for Kemp when he was Bob Dole's running mate against the Clinton-Gore reelection ticket in 1996. Scott had been Dole's campaign manager.

It was early May 2003, when I called Scott and asked him if he was free for lunch. He was, and we met at Morton's steakhouse on Connecticut Avenue. I told Scott the truth. I had grown weary at Judicial Watch seeing people like the Clintons go free while the little guys who were caught making illegal campaign contributions to them were burned at the stake. I explained my plan to run for the U.S. Senate in Florida.

Scott erupted excitedly, "That's a great idea!" He had been looking at recent Republican polling results in Florida. The race was wide open, he insisted. Former Congressman Bill McCollum was running, but he'd lost a Senate bid in 2000 to Democrat Bill Nelson, an ex-astronaut, and he was expected to lose again. Another possible contender, Congressman Mark Foley, supported by Florida Governor Jeb Bush, the president's brother, was about to be outed by a gay newspaper, Scott said. The other two candidates, both state legislators, were lightweights in his view. "You can win this, Larry," Scott said.

Scott had gotten some flak for his handling of the '96 campaign. But I thought he was honest and probably had learned a thing or two since that crushing defeat, so I asked him to be my campaign manager. Scott was flattered but said he would only get involved behind the scenes. His lobbying practice was doing well, and he had several matters that Congressman Mark Foley could influence, so he couldn't afford to alienate him. Besides, he said, Roger Stone was the best guy for the job. Roger was a major-league lobbyist and campaign strategist in Miami whom I'd known since the mid-80s. "He's the smartest guy out there and he's not scared of the Bushes," Scott said. Well, at least I knew what I would be getting. As much as anyone in the Republican Party, Scott and Roger were political heavyweights who would lend my campaign more than an air of seriousness.

I had reservations about Roger—he was then heavily involved as a lobbyist in the gaming and sugar industries—but I thought that Scott could keep him under control. Roger would have to sever his ties to his lobbying clients should we decide to proceed, I said, because I wanted everything done ethically and on the up and up. Scott said that he understood and would talk to Roger about it. Roger's personal and political history posed other potential problems. He had been a Nixon campaign worker at CREEP (the infamous Committee to Reelect the President) and confidant during the Watergate days, and he had been implicated in an alleged sex scandal in the mid-90s. The allegations were never proven, and I helped in getting the media to drop the story, but it might come up again if I hired Roger to run my campaign.

This wasn't going to be easy. I am a Christian and a conservative, and there would be questions about hiring Roger as my campaign manager. But I was about to enter a world I did not really know, and I needed professionals in my camp.

Within an hour of our lunch, Scott called me at my office and, in very enthusiastic terms, said Roger was wild about my possible candidacy and wanted to talk.

A few days later, Roger and I met for dinner in New York City, and he made his pitch. With the large national following I had built at Judicial Watch, we could raise a boatload of money through direct mail to take on the establishment. Roger knew, from public records, that I had raised over $28 million during the last presidential election cycle. He would handle all aspects of the campaign, and he would even bring in his own staff. Since only 15 months remained before the Florida Senate primary on August 31, 2004, we would have to get to work immediately. I made it clear to Roger that he would have to be completely loyal to me, and that he could not do any consulting for another political candidate.

He would also have to cut all ties to his lobbying clients during the period of my campaign. And I stressed the need for ethics; we would not be the masters of dirty tricks, but run the campaign in a straightforward and honest way. No problem, Roger said. I told him to draw up a contract because we needed this in writing to ensure no misunderstandings. My reputation was everything to me, and I was wary of giving Roger and his friends too much of a leash.

Later, in his Miami Beach office overlooking Lincoln Road, Roger laid out a campaign that seemed to make sense. Referring to a Florida map on the wall, he explained that the great majority of voters lived along the I-4 corridor, where Florida's population explosion was greatest. The corridor, a geographic strip between Orlando and Tampa, would be the focus of our media strategy, with lesser amounts of money spent in liberal south Florida and the conservative panhandle, which had a sparser population base. With the exception of the right-wing-oriented Cuban community, which historically tended not to vote in primaries anyway, south Florida would be tough on a conservative like me. And, the media buys there were the most expensive in the state.

Money was crucial. With sufficient money, Roger said, I could be elected sitting in the Bahamas. The nature of politics had changed over the years; personal contact was much less important than television advertising. Roger stressed how the Bushes would try to "screw me," which would make money even more important, and he said he would have to keep a low profile in part because the Bushes weren't terribly fond of him either.

In discussing finances, I told Roger that I could not take Judicial Watch's mailing list, but alternative lists might provide access to some serious fund raising. Based on past experience, my supporters would be kind and we could expect to raise between $500,000 to $1 million per month at the height of any election cycle. Roger's eyes lit up, and I could see that the benefits of my base were not all ideological, to put it mildly.

Roger said that he would begin gathering all the information he could about my public statements, both in print and on radio and television, because anything I'd said in the past could and likely would be used by my adversaries if the campaign turned nasty. He also needed the information to develop position papers on the key issues. Over the years, Roger said, he had followed my work at Judicial Watch and was an admirer. But to flesh out what I stood for, he would have to study Judicial Watch's website. To do all of these things, he would need to begin bringing in staff.

Enter the group I came to call the Dirty Dozen. It included a buxom fund-raiser whose mother was Senator Arlen Specter's chief of staff in Philadelphia, a jukebox of a bodyguard who looked and dressed like the Incredible Hulk, and a frequently well-lubricated press secretary who had once worked for Russian President Boris Yeltsin. And there was Paul Jensen, a lawyer with inherited wealth who had been a campaign manager for Senator Bob Smith of New Hampshire until Smith lost his reelection bid in 2002. I was the one who brought Jensen into our campaign, figuring that his experience and passion for politics would help. Further, he could serve as a check on Roger and his crew, since he had no previous ties to them. Roger, however, welcomed him.

In all, they looked and acted like a bunch of misfits, but then, what did I know about what political staffs looked and acted like? I expressed my reservations to Roger, but he said that I should leave the hiring to him. "This is beneath you," he added. "You're the candidate and you need to keep your mind on the big issues." Roger must be right, I thought. After all, he had helped to elect presidents.

The next big issue was office space, and Roger wanted it to be located on or near Lincoln Road, close to his office. This, too, raised my eyebrows; I didn't think it was a good idea for a conservative to be identified with the fast and loose lifestyle of the swinging set in Miami Beach. If George W. Bush had fashioned himself as "the compassionate conservative," I imagined my opponents would happily label me "the Miami Beach conservative." But Roger again invoked his now all-too-familiar mantra, "It's beneath you," and won the argument, stressing that our official address would soon be in Orlando on the I-4 corridor. Commissioning the husband of his secretary Diane to find space, he leased the entire upper floor of a dilapidated building adjacent to Lincoln Road, right above a dry cleaner. Perhaps I should have taken note of that as an omen. I didn't realize then that Roger and company were taking me to the cleaners.

In mid-August, the Dirty Dozen, Scott Reed and Tony Fabrizio, a pollster Roger hired to do an early survey, all met at Roger's villa in North Miami Beach. As we waited for everyone to arrive, Roger and I sat on the dock overlooking Biscayne Bay. "Isn't this great," Roger chortled. "I feel like Hyman Roth." (Roth was the Meyer Lansky-type character in "The Godfather Part II," played by the actor Lee Strasberg.)

"I'd rather have you be Elliot Ness," I replied.

As everyone arrived, Nydia, Roger's Cuban-American wife, graciously served chicken, rice and black beans to the crowd. We all took seats at the dining room table, and Roger opened up with his analysis of our likely campaign strategy. Subject to Fabrizio's survey analysis, I would have to run in the Republican primary as the most conservative in the race, as the antiestablishment true Republican reformer that I was. Bill McCollum was basically a moderate and a loser, given his prior defeat to Democratic Sena-tor Bill Nelson. But to do an end run around the other two challengers, Dan Webster, a Christian conservative state senator, and Johnnie Byrd, the mild-mannered but unloved speaker of the Florida House of Representatives, I would have to outflank them on the right. For me, this was true to my principles, so I had no problem with it.

Roger proposed that we announce my candidacy right after Labor Day, since we would need a year before the primary to raise money and build a political base. He also wanted to do early advertising, to get out in front of the pack. Roger suggested that we do a rolling announcement—first in Orlando and Tampa, the heart of the I-4 corridor, then in Miami, Jacksonville and the panhandle. We would do all of it in three days, flying around Florida in a chartered plane. The Dirty Dozen liked the plan, and I did not object. But it was clear that we would have to begin fund raising immediately, through direct mail in particular, to afford these luxuries. So Roger and I decided we would go see Richard Viguerie, the dean of conservative direct-mail fund raising.

Viguerie had made many political enemies over the years and had a reputation for double-crossing many of his clients. But to give him credit, the man had invented the use of direct mail fund raising for conservative causes and was instrumental in the election of Ronald Reagan as president in 1980.

After Judicial Watch came to prominence in late 1996, with the burgeoning Chinagate scandal, I enlisted Viguerie's help for my organiza-tion. While he could be difficult, he raised big bucks for us—more than $28 million in 2000 alone. By the time I left Judicial Watch, the nonprofit had over $16 million in liquid and semiliquid assets, thanks to his fund-raising prowess.

Viguerie was enthusiastic about my political plans, realizing the financial potential for his firm, American Target Advertising, and he agreed to take care of the campaign's direct mail. He estimated that he could create a "house file"—the names of donors who would give consistently to the campaign—of about 200,000 nationally and at least 100,000 in Florida alone. This would generate millions of dollars for the campaign, which would be used not just to pay overhead, but for purchasing political advertising, the lifeblood of all big-time political campaigns.

Unfortunately, Viguerie's grandiose commitments did not pan out. But in those days just prior to my announced candidacy, Roger and company were developing a multi-million-dollar budget based on Viguerie's fund-raising plans. Using my personal credit cards, they were buying expensive office equipment, hiring staff and consultants, and renting office space, all with the stated expectation that Viguerie's commitments would come through. I was wary of their actions and made inquiries. But true to form, when I tried to delve into their dealings, Roger would respond, "Larry, trust me. You hired me to run your campaign. I'm the best. You know nothing about political campaigns. To get into these matters is beneath you. You have to be the candidate and stay focused on that." For the first time in my professional life, I let go of the reins and let someone else run the show, assured that Viguerie's efforts would cover the bills Roger was accumulating.

But the truth was, Roger wasn't running the show. When he wasn't holed up in his private office or working out in a sweaty gym on the adjacent Alton Road, or simply sitting in an outdoor café salivating at the cavalcade of bodies, both male and female, marching up and down Lincoln Road, he was in New York, allegedly tending to his sick father. Rarely, if ever, was he seen supervising his staff. When I complained nicely, Roger assured me that he knew what he was doing. Yes, and pigs may one day fly. By the time Roger and I parted company, I had a campaign debt of several hundred thousand dollars, much of it on my own lines of credit.

I also learned that Roger hadn't quite lived up to his pledge not to consult for other candidates. Far from it: Not only was he advising another candidate, he was advising a Democrat—none other than Al Sharpton, who was running a quixotic campaign for president.

September 19, 2003 was a long and profoundly emotional day for me. In formally leaving Judicial Watch, the organization I had conceived and founded, I was sanguine about its future yet buoyed by the prospect of a Senate run in Florida, the state I loved. But the memory of these emotions is dwarfed by the events that unfolded at Dulles Airport later that evening, just four days before the announcement of my candidacy. It was a harbinger of things to come.

When, following our divorce, Stephanie and the kids moved to Cleveland in late August, she presented me with the two cats that I had given her as a gift a few years before we were married. Angel, a white calico, and Munchkin,

Angel's sister, gray and hugely fat, were not destined to take up residence in the Buckeye state. My ex-wife had promised my 5-year-old daughter, Isabelle, that if Angel and Munchkin could be left behind, a new kitten would be added to the family in Ohio. I didn't approve of this plan and thought it set a bad example for Isabelle and my 3-year-old son, Lance; but Stephanie gave me an ultimatum: "Either you take the cats, or I'll give them to the pound." If anyone ever doubted my pro-life credentials, they should know that they extend beyond humans to pets and other critters. Angel and Munchkin were my babies, too, and I was not going to let them go to the pound and likely be euthanized.

After I left Judicial Watch that day, I headed to my apartment in Reston, Virginia, to pick up some of my belongings—suits and other personal effects that I would need for my campaign launch a few days later. It was also an opportunity to bring one of the cats, Angel, down to my Miami condo. Jet Blue, my favorite airline for trips to Florida, only allowed passengers to take one pet at a time.

I packed Angel into her carrier and headed off for Dulles Airport, only a seven-minute drive away. But I was running late, and the airport was jammed. I could not miss my plane, since I needed to be in our campaign offices the next day to prepare for the announcement tour, so I rushed to get my e-ticket and move through security to the shuttle that takes passengers to the boarding gates. Holding Angel's cage in my right hand, I placed the computer case and overnight bag on the conveyor belt to the X-ray machine. The Transportation Security Administration (TSA) agent then asked me to take Angel out of her carrier and place the cage on the conveyor. I obeyed the instruction, but I was tired and worried about missing my plane. There were only 20 minutes left before takeoff.

The TSA agent, a nice, elderly white-haired man, stroked Angel when I removed her from the cage. To move things along, I tried to be funny. "The cat is not a terrorist. The cat does not have a bomb," I joked. I then moved through the screening device as the agent placed Angel back into her cage. As I arrived at the end of the conveyor, where personal property is reclaimed, an African-American woman told me to move over to the adjacent wall. I thought nothing of this at first. Then she added that she was summoning the airport police. I asked her what I had done, unaware that the jokes I had just cracked had provoked her action. "Am I going to miss my plane?"

"Missing your plane is the least of your problems," she said sternly.

Within moments, I was surrounded by two Virginia airport police officers. Without warning, one of them grabbed me and handcuffed me. Shocked, but trying to keep my cool, I asked what I had done. The officer who cuffed me, a sandy-blond middle-aged white man who looked like a cop, asserted his authority: "You've just committed a class five felony. This is a federal airport, and you're going to pay for this. The last person to do what you did, a lawyer, was indicted and he lost his law license. You're in a pack of trouble!"

His companion, a white female police officer, seconded the thought. I asked if I could call my lawyer. "You're not going to be calling anyone," the white male cop snapped.

Within moments, I was led away and herded through Dulles airport by the male cop. People who were standing in line awaiting their turn to move through security turned to look at the spectacle and I wondered if someone would recognize me. Over the years at Judicial Watch, with all of my television appearances, my face had become quite well-known. This would surely wind up in the press, I thought. I had heard one of the TSA security men muse as I was being led away, "Gee, he looks familiar."

I was taken downstairs to the vehicle pick-up zone just outside the airport where a police car was waiting. The cop shoved me into the car, screaming "Turn your head to the left, or I'll break all of your teeth!" Stunned and exhausted, I thought to myself that this must be what it's like to be black and taken into custody by heavy-handed authorities. I realized that I was getting the same treatment that many of my clients had been subjected to. When it happens to you, it not only confirms all of your worst fears about the system, it terrifies you. But I needed to keep calm, something I usually manage reasonably well. I was once trapped with my girlfriend in a burning dormitory at George Washington University in D.C., and I recalled how keeping my wits about me then had been essential to getting us out of that jam. Now, I was in a burning building again, this time with my professional and political career in danger of going up in flames.

As I arrived at the holding area, the officer jerked me out of the car and pushed me into a cell. "Strip down and put on these clothes," he shouted. While obeying the orders, I looked around. The cell had only a toilet and a bench. It was about eight feet by 10 feet in size, and had bars fronting two sides. There was a television camera aimed in my direction. I asked again if

I could call my lawyer. Again, the response was no. "You'll be seeing the FBI, my friend; you've committed a crime at a federal airport," the officer said. I asked to have my Miranda rights read to me, and he ignored me and walked away. I did not want to inflame the situation further, so I called out to him, "I respect you, please respect me," although I knew it must have stemmed from my jokes.

Having been forced to take off my clothes and put on a gray jumpsuit out in the open was humiliating, but not my main concern. Nor was having to explain later how the former head of Judicial Watch had been arrested. What would be embarrassing, I imagined, was having to explain why a crusader against terrorism had been arrested for joking about terrorism inappropriately and to face questions about it at the beginning of my campaign. As I waited in my cell, I only wondered what had happened to Angel and what would become of me. Sitting on the bench with my head in my hands, I prayed.

After my separation from Stephanie, someone I knew, a very Christian woman named Rebecca, said to me, "Larry, there is something missing from your life. You need to talk to God more." I was as religious as my grandfather had been. I didn't need to be in a church or a synagogue to talk to God. And while I had religiously prayed each evening before going to bed since my early childhood days, I had come to pray during the day thanks to Rebecca's advice. Now, I really needed Him. But I am a realist. God does not always do what you think He will. He has His own plans. So I said, "God, I am your servant. Do with me as you will. If a political career is not in my future, so be it."

The wait seemed interminable. But after my prayers, I was calming down. I started to think as a lawyer, and I planned what I would tell the FBI agents when they arrived. I didn't think it a good idea to invoke my Miranda rights and say nothing because I had not really done anything serious. If the jokes were the issue, it would be best to 'fess up, apologize and explain that I respected the TSA, and see what would happen. However, I really didn't know what to expect, especially since the police had been so hostile.

To have credibility with the FBI, I would have to remember what I had said that caused the reaction by the TSA. I sat there and tried to remember my exact words. I had not said that the cat was a terrorist, nor that it had a bomb, so the issue must be the reference to a bomb. That I had said there was no bomb was crucial, I thought. This would underscore that I had only made a lousy joke.

My mind wandered and I thought back to my French literature days at Duke and Albert Camus' novel, *The Stranger*, which had greatly influenced my view not only of the world, but of the justice system. Camus, an existentialist, died in a car accident on the day he had planned to travel by train from Marseille to Nice. He was found dead on the roadside with the train ticket in his pocket, a strangely poetic end for someone who believed that life had no meaning. In his world-famous book, an Algerian man is convicted of a murder he did not commit because of testimony that he did not cry at his own mother's funeral. To the bigoted, anti-Arab French jury, it signaled that death meant very little to him and that he therefore was capable and culpable of murdering a white Frenchman. Would I wind up being charged because of a bad joke having to do with a cat? I needed to get a grip on myself.

Just then, the male cop appeared. He opened the cell, removed my handcuffs and calmly asked me to follow him. I knew then that something had changed, and not just his demeanor; otherwise I would have been led away in the cuffs, and not asked to walk behind him. He led me around a long hallway and I entered a conference room. Coming up to greet me was a handsome young man who introduced himself as a special agent of the FBI.

The FBI agent asked me softly if I would have a seat opposite him. He then said that I did not have to talk with him if I didn't want to—a reference to Miranda and a confirmation that charges were possible. The Virginia officer who had given me a hard time sat on his left. Sizing up the situation, I looked at both of them and knew that the atmosphere was different. It was time simply to explain what had happened and not play hardball with Miranda.

I told them that I was, until earlier that day, the chairman of Judicial Watch, and the FBI agent acknowledged that he had checked me out while I was sitting in the cell. They already knew who I was. He then asked me if I had made certain statements about the cat to the TSA and I gave the responses I had rehearsed earlier in my head. He wrote them down and did not contest what I recounted.

As the FBI agent recorded my "confession," I offered that, as head of Judicial Watch, I had co-authored a book with my colleagues entitled *Fatal Neglect*. I dropped the subtitle—no need to offend unnecessarily. I told him that I respected what the government was trying to do, that I supported the TSA and its efforts, that my jokes were not funny, and at the end of an emotional and tiring day, I had made a mistake. To stress my support for greater security, I talked about how Judicial Watch was representing two FBI agents who had tried to get the attention of higher-ups in the agency to investigate money laundering by radical Islamic groups, but were unsuccessful. I added that their names were Robert Wright and John Vincent, and that their whistle-blowing had resulted in retaliation against them. I also stated, and I meant it, that I supported the frontline agents of the FBI in their efforts to avert September 11.

Appearing to appreciate my sincerity, the FBI agent replied that he knew of Robert Wright and in fact was at the National Press Club a few months ago when Wright gave a press conference criticizing the agency's failure to do more to protect against terrorism.

I did not raise any issues concerning my rough treatment since it was now clear that the previous hostility had evaporated. Besides, I knew that I shouldn't have made the jokes, and I regretted it.

The FBI agent then asked me why I was heading to Miami that evening. When I told him that I was leaving Virginia to run for a U.S. Senate seat in Florida, he looked a little uncomfortable. He said, "You know, I have to file a report about this. It will be forwarded to the U.S. attorney." I said that I understood, and left it at that. But when the FBI agent also asked me if someone could come fetch Angel and me, I breathed a sigh of relief, although at that point I was still too stressed to appreciate that I was being let go. I didn't want to call any of my friends in the area; it had been a long night and, frankly, I just wanted to go back to my Reston apartment, rebook my plane reservation, get a little sleep and prepare to travel to Florida the next morning. I also needed to call my security guard, who had been planning to pick me up in Miami and by now had to be wondering what had happened to me.

The FBI agent and the Virginia cop got up and instructed me on how to find my way back to the main terminal on foot so I could catch a cab to my apartment. I would also need to get my checked bags back. I remember someone handing me a cat carrier with Angel in it, and I left the holding area. As I walked out the door, the Virginia cop put his hand on my shoulder as if to say, let bygones be bygones. That suited me just fine.

When I finally got to Miami the next day, we planned for the big announcement, and the dust-up at Dulles began to recede from my consciousness. But in retrospect, that episode—combining as it did the mindless authority of the state with a tragicomic scene—almost served as a perfect prelude for the campaign that followed.

21

LET THE GAMES BEGIN

After my announcement, I expected the Bushes to launch an attack. Instead, the first assault came from one of my primary opponents, former Congressman Bill McCollum. His media consultant, Harvey Finkelstein, a former mentor of Roger's, issued a press release saying that the people of Florida could never elect as senator someone who had sued his own mother. The press release found its way into several stories that followed the conclusion of my jet-set tour of the state.

I was delighted that McCollum had attacked. It showed that he was scared and took my candidacy seriously. That he would use the shopworn smear line of James Carville from the Clinton years, and later Carville's wife, Mary Matalin, after I sued the Cheney Energy Task Force, not only showed a lack of originality, but also some desperation. In fact, I had planned to talk a lot about the sad saga of my grandmother during the campaign. Florida is a state chock-full of elderly people fearful of being abandoned by their families. If I could stand up for my grandmother when she was abandoned and robbed by her family, then I would stand up for the people of Florida and not abandon them either. I decided to wait for an opening to exploit McCollum's mistake, and it came only a week or so later in Vero Beach.

But first, I had to return to Reston, gather my belongings, pick up Munchkin from her kennel and get back to Florida. My assistant, Lissette, volunteered to help. The next day, packing up some things at Judicial Watch, I reinjured two herniated disks that I thought had healed over the last 10 years. By the time I returned to Miami with Lissette in tow, I was a basket case. Sandy Cobas, my Miami chief of staff and Lissette's mother, rushed me to Cedars Medical Center to see her doctor, who recommended an epidural block. Over the next six months this injury adversely affected the initial phase of my campaign. Three ineffective procedures made it difficult for me to sit or walk straight, and the painkillers sometimes left me foggy-headed and confused. I was in a constant funk. Coupled with my biweekly visits to see my children in Cleveland and the strain of constant travel, it's a miracle I was able to do anything at all. But I was convinced that I was destined to be the next Republican senator from Florida. I had known adversity before and I wasn't about to let mere physical pain stop me.

So a few days after I reinjured my back, I soldiered to Vero Beach. I was accompanied by Sandy, her husband Jose, who had volunteered to help the campaign, and my bodyguard, the Incredible Hulk. The trip by car took about three hours and I could barely move or speak as I squirmed in the front seat of my GMC Envoy, unable to sit straight.

We finally arrived at the country club for the event. It was one of those typical Republican gatherings, filled with blue bloods and well-tanned nouveau riche. As I entered, the proverbial country-club Republicans were in full regalia. I waded into the crowd, introducing myself and shaking hands. I needed something to kill the pain, or at least take the edge off it, so I asked the Incredible Hulk to get me a screwdriver, my favorite drink. As I gulped down my cocktail, I was approached by a middle-aged, handsome woman with dark hair. "I'm Carole Jean Jordan and I'm the party chairman," she said with a pronounced Southern drawl. "I tried contacting you a week ago, before I announced," I replied, trying to look solicitous. I understood that, given her position, I would have to get to know her better, even if I were not an establishment candidate. I had heard that she was not a fan of the Bushes, and Jeb Bush, the governor, was no fan of hers. In fact, he had opposed her candidacy as chairman of the Republican Party of Florida. But Carole Jean was an elected official, not appointed, and Jeb lost. She was independent-minded and something of a renegade. I was pleased that she was direct and sought me out. It was a good sign, I thought.

As I was finishing my initial pleasantries with Carole Jean, I caught a glimpse of Bill McCollum entering the room. Arriving with his wife, Ingrid, he shook hands with a number of guests and made his way to the dining table. It was clear that he knew these people well—not surprising given that he and Ingrid had been campaigning for a Senate seat for almost six years. I thought this would be a good opportunity to size Bill up, and I moved over to his table. I had never met him before, although we had appeared together on television via split screen during the 1999 Clinton impeachment proceedings.

As I approached McCollum from his right, he was standing at his place setting. "Bill," I said in an assertive but friendly tone as I held out my hand, "I just wanted to meet you. We've never met, except through television." In a soft and soothing voice, which is his trademark "honey bear" demeanor, McCollum replied, "I always wanted to meet you, too. I admired your work at Judicial Watch. It's a pleasure."

This was not what I had expected. McCollum was extremely warm and likeable, so I felt a bit guilty about having to dress him down. "Bill, I like you, too," I began. "But the next time your press secretary gets a bright idea to attack me about my grandmother, you should call me first. It's not going to benefit you to discuss this story. The elderly people of Florida will understand that I stood up for my grandmother just like I will stand up for them. If you want to pursue this, bring it on. I welcome discussing it."

McCollum looked at me like a deer in the headlights. He didn't know how to respond, particularly since it was obvious he was not, by nature, an attack dog. So he replied, "Larry, I understand," and awkwardly looked down. I believed from that point on that Bill was essentially a decent guy, but without much backbone. He obviously was controlled by handlers like his press consultant, Harvey Finkelstein, a no-holds-barred media hack. This meant that the race was going to be long and nasty. Bill was the establishment and would not go down easily. It was good that I had confronted him early on.

As I limped around the dining room shaking hands and meeting as many people as I could, for the first time I got a dose of the intoxicating nature of politics. Vero Beach is a bastion of conservatism and many of the attendees were my donors and followers at Judicial Watch. They approached me with groupielike adulation, almost as if I were the political messiah. Florida had not had a Republican senator since Connie Mack had retired four years ago, and they were longing for a conservative "soul brother" to replace Democrat Bob Graham, who they believed had gone off the deep end since he announced his candidacy for the presidency. At one point, Graham had even called for Bush's impeachment over Iraq, which didn't sit well with the Republican faithful. They wanted to have a fighter, and it was clear that at that point in the campaign, I fit the bill.

McCollum and I were the only Senate candidates to appear that evening. In the early days of the campaign, that was routine. State legislators Dan Webster and Johnnie Byrd did not attend many events. It became evident that they were not serious about winning, but ran only to enhance their name recognition, perhaps for future political races. So early on, at least, it came down to Bill and me.

This is the way it must have appeared to the attendees in Vero Beach, and they took advantage of the opportunity to size us up. Neither of us was scheduled to speak, only to mingle during dinner. Then Carole Jean got up, took the microphone and announced that the Senate candidates would briefly address the crowd. This was unexpected, but I was always ready to speak; after all, as a trial lawyer, talking was my trade. But what really surprised me was that Carole Jean asked me to speak first, an obvious slight to Bill, given his seniority as a politician from Florida.

Before a crowd of about 200 die-hard Republicans, I took to the dance floor as Carole Jean handed me a cordless microphone. I felt a bit like a game show host as I slid across the slick, hardwood floor addressing the onlookers. I had only 10 minutes to make my points, so I began with a brief introduction about my background and role at Judicial Watch. I then gave what would essentially become my stump speech, emphasizing how I would provide true conservative Republican leadership as Florida's next U.S. senator. And, to the roars of the crowd, I added for good measure that "Hillary Clinton would never become president on my watch." As I spoke, I glanced at Bill, who was listening intently at the head table right in front of me. He looked concerned, as he undoubtedly began to realize that I would be a more formidable foe than he had thought, given my popularity with conservatives and my ability to communicate. I could not resist addressing the grandmother issue, to rub it in and make sure it did not surface again. "The Clintons and a candidate in this race have criticized me for standing up for my grandmother," I said, explaining the sad story. "These people don't understand family values, and they will cut and run when the going gets tough. You, the people of Florida, are my family and I will never abandon you." Bill almost slid under the table. As he got up to speak, he was visibly shaken. I knew then that he and his campaign would never use the grandmother story again.

Bill launched into what I would come to call his "la-la land speech." Extolling the virtues of President George W. Bush, he toed the line with all of the Republican National Committee's talking points—a strong national defense against terrorism, caps on medical malpractice lawsuits, preserving Social Security, and so on. But the part I really liked was when he made the point, every three minutes or so, that he would vote the way the president wanted, and how voters needed to increase the Republican majority in the U.S. Senate. Bill's platform, crafted by the party hacks in Washington for all congressional candidates willing to parrot this nonsense, was not only unoriginal, it was deathly boring. Indeed, the listeners that evening yawned at his speech. But he gave them a clear choice. Did the people of Florida want a Bush "yes man," or did they want an independent-minded conservative like me? At this point in the campaign, it seemed to me that a vacuous "yes man" was not very appealing, particularly when he had already lost one Senate race once before, to the astronaut Bill Nelson. Incredibly, Bill McCollum even talked about that earlier defeat in his speech, telling the audience that it was good he lost his first Senate race, just as Jeb Bush had lost his first try for governor. I couldn't quite see the logic, but Bill was entitled to say what he wanted, however bizarre.

After he concluded his remarks to polite applause, I got up to mingle more with the crowd. I saw Carole Jean at the other end of the room talking with a few people at her table. She was sipping a glass of wine and, as I came closer, she put her arm around my waist. "Larry," she said, "you know that as party chairman I can't favor any of the candidates. But I want you to know that I think you may be the one for U.S. Senate. We need a Schwarzenegger-type in Florida. You're it." With a Southern twang, she whispered in my ear, "I like Bill, but he ain't gonna cut it. Come up and visit me soon in Tallahassee." In my address, I had alluded to "the Terminator" and compared his no-nonsense approach with my candidacy. Carole Jean obviously got the point. I liked her Southern charm, accent and style. She was direct, no bullshit. And I figured she could become a great ally. This politics game was not so bad, I naively thought. And, Carole Jean had worked a "faith healing." As I walked away from her, I realized that my back pain had miraculously disappeared, at least for the moment. The reality of being Florida's next U.S. Senator was beckoning.

Also speaking that night was a young political and public relations consultant named David Johnson. He was there with his fiancée, Laura Ward. The two of them had started a promotion and marketing firm, operating out of Atlanta and Tallahassee, called Strategic Vision. I was impressed with David's knowledge of Florida politics and I took his and Laura's business card for future reference.

We returned to Miami that evening, since I had to leave the next day for a planned fund-raising trip to California. I was also slated to give a speech at the Reagan Library, a big honor for me. The next morning I was to be picked up at my condo by the Incredible Hulk, but he did not appear. I left on my own and he later joined me in Los Angeles. During the long flight to the west coast my back pain was excruciating, and having a security guard I couldn't count on did not make me feel any better. Even after he caught up to me, a day late, I often felt as if I had to protect him—from himself. But this was how things were going with Roger's band of misfits. I tried to stay positive, particularly after the encounter with Carole Jean the evening before, but it became increasingly difficult as I got reports from Sandy and Lissette of the difficulties that were brewing in the Miami Beach office. While I was away in California trying to raise money for the campaign from wealthy donors I knew through Judicial Watch, my ground crew had fallen into total chaos, thanks in part to Roger's lack of attention. As became routine, Roger was off in New York State somewhere, claiming that his dad needed him. Some months later I learned, thanks to an article in *The Village Voice*, that Roger was not only working for Democrat Al Sharpton, he and his band of misfits were even donating money to Sharpton's presidential campaign. I had no choice but to let Roger go. Fortunately, I remembered David Johnson and Laura Ward and signed them up to join us. I liked my chances.

22

THE EMPIRE STRIKES BACK

During the period leading up to mid-November 2003, I continued to be well-received by the Republican faithful. After each speech, many of the executives of the party would echo Carole Jean's remarks—that Republicans needed their next U.S. senator to be someone who was not part of the Washington establishment, someone who could excite and was independent. It was apparent that, notwithstanding their ingrained loyalty, even the Party functionaries were not happy with Republican senators who busted the budget and failed to push the conservative agenda in any meaningful or effective way. And while they liked President Bush as a person, many conceded privately that he was not doing a particularly good job, and that the country had many problems. The galvanizing force of John Kerry, who would be Bush's opponent in 2004, had not yet entered the political psyche of Florida Republicans.

Word of my criticism of the Washington Republican leadership and my growing popularity among Florida Republicans was moving up the political ladder—from Jeb Bush's office in Tallahassee to the president's people in the nation's capital. I waited for the sparks to start flying, and it didn't take long. Rumor had it that the Bush administration's political machine, with chief strategist Karl Rove at the controls, had picked Cuban-American Mel Martinez, a former commissioner of Orange County in Orlando and then the president's secretary of Housing and Urban Development, to enter the race. His presence on the ticket, Rove seemed to think, would help Bush carry Florida again in November 2004.

This posed a big problem on several fronts. If Mel entered the race, it would force me and the other candidates to criticize the president's policies, since Mel was joined at the hip to the Bush administration. A particularly sensitive matter was the administration's Cuban policy. The president had done little to stop the continued murder, torture and mayhem inflicted by Communist

189

dictator Fidel Castro on political dissidents and ordinary Cubans alike. Miami's Cuban community had grown restless with Bush's chest-thumping and empty promises to remove Castro. Cuban Americans, thanks to Bill Clinton, Janet Reno and the Elian Gonzalez affair, had delivered Florida to Bush in 2000, with over 90% voting Republican; and they now wanted to be paid back.

This was the perfect opportunity to take up Carole Jean's invitation to visit her in Tallahassee, so I set up a lunch in the hope that what I had to tell her would be conveyed to Jeb Bush and then to his brother and Karl Rove—that it was not a good idea to inject Mel into the race. In the light of unfair criticism that Republicans had fixed the 2000 presidential elections in Florida, how would it look if the Bush White House actually *tried* to fix the Republican senatorial primary by greasing the nomination of Mel Martinez? This would give ammunition to Democrats and their comrades in the liberal media and lend substance to the theories about 2000. Furthermore, as someone who would be perceived by "Anglos" in the Bible belt regions of central and northern Florida as the "affirmative action candidate," Mel might even hurt the president's reelection chances in the state.

When I walked into the headquarters of the Republican Party of Florida and greeted Carole Jean and her aides, they were quite friendly. But as I laid out my political analysis during our closed-door meeting, they looked increasingly pained. With a concerned frown, Carole Jean warned me not to do anything that would hurt the president or the party. Even as she assured me that the primary would be open and fair, she made a startling admission: She would have to obey the orders of the Bush White House. The two points were irreconcilable, I said, arguing that I had no problem with Mel in the race so long as the candidates were allowed to compete without interference from the higher-ups in the party. When I saw her grimace, I politely but firmly told her to relay my views to Karl Rove, but my request was greeted with steely silence. Our scheduled lunch never materialized; instead, Carole Jean and her staffers essentially showed me the door.

I was still convinced I could prevail in the primary on the strength of my reputation and independence from the Washington establishment. I had seen indications in my nascent tour around Florida that even the party functionaries, much less the rank-and-file Republican voters, would resent having a Washington establishment figure rammed down their throats. Florida is a new and progressive state, and the party machine was much less formidable there, I thought, than what exists in the Northeast.

As it turned out, the Washington establishment apparently calculated—in much the way I did—that my chances against Mel, given the current dynamics in Florida politics, were reasonably good. First, others were dissuaded from entering the race. Katherine Harris, the popular and bubbly former Florida secretary of state who had certified the 2000 presidential election results, had been elected to Congress in 2002 and was considering a Senate run. She flirted with the idea for a few weeks, but Rove and company had a stern "come-to-Jesus meeting" with her and she backed down. It left her with a bitter taste in her mouth, as I learned from her later on.

Second, after Mel formally announced in early January 2004, he got a rousing endorsement from George Allen, the junior senator from Virginia, who was head of the Republican Senatorial Campaign Committee.

Third, not trusting Mel to his own political devices when his candidacy seemed to flag, Ralph Reed, the Christian Coalition's former executive director and a major figure among religious conservatives, was brought in as campaign manager. Reed, not coincidentally, also was Bush's campaign coordinator for the southern states.

And finally, my old friend Scott Reed told me I didn't have a chance and should withdraw my candidacy. "It's over," Scott said. Later, I learned that Scott was even then quietly working on Mel's behalf. By early February 2004, his role in Mel's campaign was explicit: He co-chaired a $1,000-a-head fund-raiser at the Ronald Reagan Republican Center in Washington, D.C.

One of Scott's co-chairs, incidentally, was the notorious lobbyist Jack Abramoff. The event raised $250,000 for Martinez's campaign, but Mel kept the money even after the Abramoff scandal became public and Abramoff pleaded guilty in January 2006 to various tax and political corruption charges.

I still find Mel's position bizarre. He gave to a charity the $2,500 his campaign received from Ohio Republican Congressman Robert Ney's political action committee in 2004 when Ney became tarred in the Abramoff scandal. One of Martinez's people told *The Miami Herald* that he wasn't interested in "any campaign donations that have even a hint of impropriety..." How's that? The same *Miami Herald* story makes the point that Abramoff had lobbied the Department of Housing and Urban Development during Mel's tenure as HUD secretary on behalf of one of the Native American tribes Abramoff represented at the time. The tribe got about $4 million in HUD funds for various projects. Did that Abramoff-connected $250,000 fund-raiser really pass Martinez's "hint of impropriety" test?

I had placed my trust in Roger Stone and Scott Reed; in the end, neither of them returned the favor. Still, there was no point in going ballistic over any of it. I had fought establishment types from the outside at Judicial Watch, and now I was prepared to fight them from the inside as the future senator from Florida. Scott, Roger, Mel and others like them only increased my resolve to beat the political establishment (power elite?) at its own game, by rising above its political pettiness and refusing to sink into its cesspool. The people of Florida would have the last say.

Bill McCollum, who had viewed himself as the heir to the title of "establishment candidate" and the favorite of the president, reacted quickly to Mel's entry into the race. With his public relations guru Harvey Finkelstein in full battle mode, he immediately attacked Martinez, branding him as a liberal trial lawyer who had supported the candidacies of Democrats like Bob Graham and had worked to defeat now-retired Republican Florida Senator Connie Mack. Indeed, the McCollum campaign had done a good job researching Mel's past. As head of the Florida Trial Lawyers Association, Martinez had taken positions inconsistent with the president's and the party's push for tort reform to put caps on medical malpractice awards. Bill even produced a video commercial to make the point and broadcast it with great fanfare on his website.

While I actually agreed with Mel that placing arbitrary caps on medical malpractice awards was not a good idea since every case should be judged on its own merits, I was glad Bill was cutting him down to size. In response, Mel attacked Bill over his previously failed Senate candidacy.

It was delicious to see the two establishment figures, candidates who were raising big bucks from special interests, begin to shred each other. That's when I named them "the M&M Brothers," coinage that stuck throughout the primary race. But Carole Jean, doubtless on orders from Jeb Bush and the White House, quickly stepped in. Shedding any veneer of neutrality, she sent a letter to each of the candidates, telling us that we would be barred from party events if the "personal attacks" continued. I called Bill, whom I had grown to like personally during our time on the campaign trail, and asked him how he intended to answer Carole Jean. He said that he had already done so, and would e-mail me a copy of his letter. In the response, Bill correctly pointed out that criticisms about a candidate's political philosophy and positions do not amount to personal attacks. The letter I sent to Carole Jean echoed the same thoughts. But for extra spice, and to reinforce my earlier points, I emphasized that her efforts to protect Mel from criticism smacked of party favoritism and were inappropriate.

The first debate, sponsored by the Associated Press and conducted before several dozen reporters and editors in late January in Tallahassee, included Mel, Bill, Dan Webster and, amazingly, former U.S. Senator Bob Smith of New Hampshire. Smith had entered the race in early January, and his candidacy was nothing short of bizarre. Having lost by more than 30 percentage points in his 2002 bid for renomination in his home state, he had since retired and established permanent residency in Sarasota, where he had been vacationing as a "snow bird" for many years. In a press release announcing his candidacy, Smith claimed that he had grown bored of practicing his new trade of commercial real estate and was coming out of retirement to restore real conservative, principled leadership to the U.S. Senate as a representative of Florida. The message sounded a lot like my own, which was no coincidence since Paul Jensen, one of Roger's dirty dozen whom I had let go in late October 2003, had gone to work for Smith, who had been his boss during New Hampshire campaigns. For all I knew, Paul may even have coaxed Smith into the race.

I worried a bit that Jensen might share confidential strategy with Smith, but I also knew that the former senator wasn't the brightest political light bulb. During his Senate career, Smith had espoused conservative principles, although he rarely did anything very effective to advance them. Instead, he would huff and puff and embarrass his Republican Senate colleagues. In a final act of self-destruction, he quit the party, only to beg for reentry just before his failed bid for reelection in New Hampshire. If there were ever anything that Roger said to me that rang true, it was that Smith was dumber than a piece of wood. Indeed, Roger had quipped on several occasions that our campaign slogan should be, "Not as dumb as Bob Smith!"

Still, Smith could create mischief by clouding my message as the only genuine antiestablishment conservative in the race, I thought at first. But my concerns quickly evaporated and I came to view Smith's campaign as a circus act out of Sarasota, where the Ringling Brothers had been based, rather than as a real threat.

At the debate, by luck of the draw, McCollum was picked to make the first opening statement. Predictably, he read from his Republican talking points, emphasizing again that the main reason to elect him to the Senate was to increase the party's majority and support the president's agenda. I was incredulous. Didn't Bill appreciate that he was not speaking to the Republican faithful, but to a liberal press corps whose members generally disliked Bush and would be unimpressed by mindless devotion to him? What added to the la-la-land quality of his presentation was that it was abundantly obvious to anyone living on the planet that the president had stabbed Bill in the back by hand-picking Mel to be his "running mate" in Florida. After the debate, *The Tallahassee Democrat* wrote that McCollum was dead meat. As for myself, I was encouraged that Bill would continue to take this fantasy flight to certain defeat despite his decent polling at the time obviously based on his name recognition.

With one of my principal opponents having just committed political suicide in front of the Florida press corps, I turned my attention to the other half of the M&M Brothers, who was about to speak. Mel's presentation was even more poorly thought out. He began well enough with a combination of humility and flattery—acknowledging that he was not a native-born American, but an immigrant from Cuba who appreciated his welcome into the United States. But within seconds, he could not resist proclaiming himself to be the darling of President Bush and the Senate leadership, one-upping Bill by admitting that he, too, would vote for all of W.'s initiatives and intimating that he had already been promised key positions on Senate committees by the Washington Republican establishment. This, he announced proudly, would be a great benefit for the people of Florida. While it was true that such committee assignments might help the state, Mel also was conceding that the system was corrupt and that he was prepared to profit from it. Watching the reaction of the press corps, I knew Mel was doing himself a great disservice. Like Bill, Mel read from the Republican talking points, except when it came to tort reform. When he finally sat down, his lackluster performance had taken its toll; the media were nearly asleep. I thought, if nothing else, at least I would liven it up.

I opened with a brief introduction about my years at Judicial Watch, and launched into what I believed would truly set apart Larry Klayman as a proud

Republican who could neither be bought nor influenced by the Washington elite and their enablers. "My colleagues all want to be part of the Senate club," I said. "I want to take a club to the Senate." I went through my platform, all the time making sure that, where appropriate, I was critical not only of Democrats, but also of my own party. The message was that Larry Klayman, much like Senator John McCain, was no "yes man." But it was my oratorical skills, honed by 27 years as a trial lawyer, that appeared to catch the attention of the reporters. They were listening intently and seemed to like what I was saying, their leftist tilt notwithstanding. This was particularly evident when, during the question and answer session, I criticized portions of the Patriot Act as an abridgement of civil liberties, and excoriated the Republican Congress and the Bush administration for busting the budget. I also railed against the tax system and was the first to propose in the campaign that we scrap the tax code and move to a flat or national sales tax.

I also called for the immediate removal of Cuba dictator-in-chief Fidel Castro—by force if necessary. When asked his view of my call to arms, Mel backed away, suggesting that Castro wasn't a threat right now. That struck me as a very strange way to appeal to Florida's huge Cuban exile community, whose members wanted Castro gone yesterday, and it caught the attention of reporters. Coming from a Cuban American, who planned to showcase his "American Dream" immigrant past, and who had himself fled the inferno of Castro's Cuba, it demonstrated naiveté in the extreme. Nor was it any way to win over the exiles in Miami and Tampa, who would want to vote on Mel's positions more than his accident of nationality.

When Mel's statement was published in a front-page Metro section story in *The Miami Herald* the next day, alongside a huge photo of me shaking Mel's hand, I knew that strategically I had a great wedge issue down the line. While I am not Cuban, I had done a great deal at Judicial Watch to address Castro's crimes against humanity, and I believed that the vote-rich Cuban-American community would recognize the fact on primary election day. *The Miami Herald* article, written by Leslie Clark, the only unbiased and perhaps only uncompromised *Herald* reporter I would encounter during the race, was the last and single time the newspaper wrote anything substantive about my campaign.

A few weeks later, I would find two other great issues to use against Mel. At the Tiger Bay Club of Tampa, where the second debate was held, the candidates were asked if they would have a litmus test to nominate only pro-life judges who, if given the chance, would rule to reverse Roe v. Wade, the Supreme Court's abortion decision. Mel was handed the microphone just before me. Caught off guard by the question, he was flummoxed at first; then, after a long pause, he dodged the question by meekly whispering that he would nominate judges who obey the law. This, of course, meant that his judges would follow the Supreme Court's decision legalizing abortion. It was clear, once again, that Mel had not thought through his stance. McCollum had characterized Mel as the liberal in the race; even one of Mel's law partners, Scott Maddox, not coincidentally chairman of the Florida Democratic Party, had crowed about Mel's political philosophy as being the most liberal in the GOP primary race.

When Mel finished his pathetic response, I literally grabbed the microphone from his hands and announced that I was not going to give a political answer; I would have a litmus test and no judge would ever be nominated by me unless he or she were prepared to strike down Roe v. Wade. Cheers erupted from the mostly conservative audience.

The second gift from heaven came as a question about the United Nations and its role in Iraq. Seizing the moment, I declared that the international body should have no role in Iraq. In fact, it was a mistake to have gone there asking for approval to invade, since the ensuing nine months of delay only gave Saddam Hussein time to hide what at the time were believed to be his weapons of mass destruction and plan the insurgency that followed the American occupation. In the process, the United States only created ill will with some of our European allies by asking them for permission to invade, then having to go our own way to do what had to be done. I was building to the final and main point: It was time for the United States to get out of the U.N., an organization by and large run by third-world terrorist states and a corrupt secretary general. The crowd erupted and I knew that, at least for the conservative community, which would make up most of my likely voters, I had hit a political motherlode.

The other candidates, who had addressed the U.N. question first, had dodged and wavered; now, after I spoke, someone in the audience followed up and asked the others what they thought about my plan to remove the United States from the U.N. Not realizing the strength of the sovereignty question beyond the conservative confines of the Tiger Bay Club that day, they all responded that they thought withdrawal was a bad idea. That proved to be a great issue for me and, over time, Mel and the others backed away from addressing it again, having already committed to leaving America in the U.N.

The moral to the story of the early debates was simply that my chief opponents, the "M&M Brothers," didn't have a clue why they wanted to be the next U.S. senator from Florida. Indeed, Mel had simply been put up by the Washington Republican establishment in much the same way Texas Governor George W. Bush had been put up for the presidency—as a means to a political end. And McCollum, though not favored by the party elite, knew only that he wanted to be a U.S. senator and thought that he could win solely on his name recognition, hard grassroots work and blind loyalty to the president.

In short, despite all the problems with consultants, my health and the unprecedented financial and political support Mel was getting from the establishment, I still felt in those early days that I had a chance of winning the nomination.

Sandy Cobas, my chief of staff, her husband Jose and I plodded on, driving up and down the Sunshine State in our GMC Envoy, speaking before whatever Republican executive committee and gathering would invite us. Afterwards, many attendees would come up to me and say that they had not known I was running, but that now they would vote for me. Several county chairmen even pledged their active support. But as my popularity grew, so too did the angst in Washington and Tallahassee. Party functionaries, I heard from various sources, were told they could not support me and had to back the president's man. During those early months of the campaign, Bill ran well ahead of Mel in the polls, and I was in third place.

It didn't matter: I still believed in my destiny and, as I always had at Judicial Watch, that justice would prevail.

23

ENTER THE BODY SNATCHERS

In early spring, I attended another of the never-ending series of Lincoln Day dinners—fêtes held to celebrate the famous Republican president by every state party and every county in the nation. The events rarely coincided with Lincoln's birthday of February 12, and Miami was no exception. Sandy and I were anxious to attend this particular event, since it was still unclear to us whether Mel—with his weak stand on Castro—would be a favorite in the Miami Cuban community. Our initial efforts to engage the rank and file of the party had centered not in Miami, but upstate, which was my natural conservative base. So this would be a chance to take the pulse of my hometown.

The headliner for the event, held at the same Ramada Inn where I had announced my candidacy, was none other than Bush henchman Karl Rove himself. Prior to the banquet, Rove was to attend a reception upstairs in the hotel, and I wanted to go—not to see him, but to mingle with the party officials and others who would be there. Still, when I walked into the room and saw Rove surrounded by fawning political groupies, I could not resist going up to him. I had little respect for his political games and cynical approach to governance, much less his role in pushing Mel to run for U.S. Senate, but I wanted to see his reaction to me, perhaps for no other reason than curiosity.

Rove was fully aware that I was more than one of Mel's adversaries, someone who could stand in the way of George W. Bush's reelection in Florida. I also was responsible during my time at Judicial Watch for bringing lawsuits against the administration, particularly the case against the Cheney Energy Task Force, which was scheduled for U.S. Supreme Court argument in just a few weeks. Frankly, I detested nearly everything Rove stood for, and he knew it. I wanted both to see his reaction and convey to him, at the same time, that I was not scared of his machine politics.

I slowly walked in his direction as he was speaking to a rich donor and his wife. During a momentary lull in the conversation, I held out my hand. "Karl," I said softly, "we've never met. I'm Larry Klayman." Rove, not even bothering to be cordial, looked at me with a cold stare and said, "Klayman, why don't you go mingle?"

His reaction didn't surprise me; in fact, it actually warmed my heart because I'd obviously gotten under his skin. My response was instinctive, delivered in the same soft tones as my first overture: "Karl, why don't *you* go mingle?"

I looked him in the eyes, smiling all the time, and went off to shake hands and "mingle" with my fellow Miamians in the room, chuckling under my breath because Karl hadn't disappointed. The solace I took in the encounter was that he viewed me as a threat to his political goals, and this was good news. If I were inconsequential, I would not have gotten that reaction. It strengthened my resolve to take him on. Mel was secondary. I wanted to beat Rove and his boss and win the nomination.

After 45 minutes or so, I grew tired of the handshaking and moved downstairs to attend the main event, the banquet dinner. I was not invited to sit on the dais, despite being the only candidate from Miami at that time, as well as a friend of and legal advocate for the powerful Cuban community. I understood why; Rove had not only dictated that I be excluded as the price for his own attendance, but Miami's two principal members of Congress, Lincoln Diaz-Balart and Ileana Ros-Lehtinen, who sat on the dais with Rove, were supporting their establishment colleagues, Bill and Mel, respectively. As I watched their speeches from my table in the back of the room, I was not only amazed by their meaningless pronouncements that the administration was taking action to remove Castro, but also by their delivery. They seemed like caricatures, marionettes on a Washington string. And, even more unsettling was that few people in the banquet hall seemed to be listening. There was a frigid air of indifference and inattention, something I had not experienced at other Lincoln celebrations throughout the state. I found the Miami Lincoln Day dinner to be strange and deeply troubling. Sandy, a Cuban American, felt the same way, and we left with a better appreciation of the difficulties we would later face.

In late March, David Johnson, the political consultant I hired to replace Roger Stone, started to pick up strong rumors that a Coral Gables computer software multimillionaire, Doug Gallagher, was about to enter the race. I didn't think anything of it at the time, except that I would no longer be able to make the claim that I was the only candidate from south Florida and the Miami area. This, frankly, did not mean much in any event since most of my conservative supporters, save the Cuban community, were upstate. What's more, I thought his candidacy was suspect, a way to keep his surname out there on behalf of his politically ambitious brother, Tom Gallagher, the state finance commissioner. David conceded the point, but he still believed Doug could cause us trouble. For one thing, "Douggie," as I would come to call him, had a campaign manager, Mark Pinsky, who had a reputation for using every dirty trick in the book. David described him as a local version of Roger Stone and, in fact, the two had apparently worked together before and were friends. Equally troubling was that Pinsky had also worked with my former press secretary, Mike Caputo, whom I had let go as part of the Dirty Dozen purge. Finally, Douggie had to be taken seriously because he was boasting around the state that he was prepared to spend $10 million of his own money to win. Even Mel, with the Republican establishment behind him, wasn't raising that kind of dough. All things considered, David warned me to be ready for a rough ride.

The first word of Douggie's "coming out" came from a female Young Republican named Brandy, who was working for David Johnson in his Tallahassee office. Young Republicans are just that, a club of younger diehards who volunteer to work for the party and make up the majority of the worker bees in any election. Brandy had attended a meeting in Palm Beach and heard Gallagher speak. Douggie's core message, she reported, was almost identical to my campaign platform. He was running as an antiestablishment candidate who was critical of the Republican leadership for busting the budget, not confirming conservative judges, failing to reform the tax system, and so forth. But Douggie's mantra had one more element: He was not a lawyer, he said, "and that's a good thing!" That was one way he could separate himself from Mel, Bill and me, all of whom were lawyers. Douggie emphasized that nearly 70% of U.S. senators were lawyers, and "we don't need any more." This fit nicely with the party's push for tort reform, which was necessary, according to the administration, because trial lawyers were abusing the system.

Again, I was not alarmed, despite his effort to morph into Larry Klayman, minus the trial-lawyer label. I thought the voters would be able to recognize the real deal. But David thought otherwise. With $10 million to spend on advertising, Douggie's messge might be difficult to compete with, David said, however politically contrived it may be. And to stay viable as a candidate, we could not let Douggie pass us in the polls.

I first met Douggie at a rally in early April at the Orlando Convention Center, where President Bush was holding his kick-off rally to announce his 2004 candidacy. As I walked up the escalator to the second tier of the building, there was Douggie, greeting Republicans who were filing in for the event. I was struck by his grin, which looked a lot like Robert Kennedy's. But he had a peculiar manner as he smiled and shook the hand of each passerby. He would hunch over, with the palms of his hands flexed toward the ground, looking like an oversized rodent, perched on its hind legs, bearing its big teeth.

As I got to the top of the escalator, he held out his hand to me: "Nice to meet you, Larry. I'm Doug Gallagher." I was not only impressed by his teeth, but also his friendliness, and thought that he might be a natural politician. But as the months wore on, that was virtually all Douggie would say to me or, for that matter, to any of the other Senate candidates that I overheard speaking with him. While appearing warm, Douggie's greetings took on an air of extreme superficiality. Bill McCollum and his wife Ingrid would joke about it. It was clear that, for whatever reason, they detested him.

In mid-April, the Southern Republican Leadership Conference (SRLC) held its annual convention at the Fontainebleau Hilton on Miami Beach. The SRLC is composed of party officials and the rank and file from all regions of the South. Given my hometown-boy status, I figured the event would be a great opportunity for the campaign and for me. Douggie and his campaign manager thought the same thing. But they had the money to make a big splash; I did not.

As I walked into the lobby of the hotel on the first day of the convention, projected onto the walls, through elaborate strobe lighting, was Gallagher's name, with the inscription, "U.S. Senate." David, who was with me at the time, observed that the art was the same as that used by Douggie's brother, Tom, during his state races. Reflecting, I sickly smiled and thought of one of my favorite political comedies, "The Distinguished Gentleman." In this film, a con man from Miami, named Thomas "Jeff" Jefferson, decides, after an incumbent congressman dies making love to his secretary, that he will run for the deceased's seat. Not coincidentally, the con man, played by Eddie Murphy, the black actor-comedian, has the same name as the dead white congressman and obtains the campaign signs of the dead white congressman from the deceased's widow by seducing her. The voters of Miami elect the living black Jeff Jefferson based on name recognition alone, never having seen his face during the campaign. When Jeff Jefferson goes to Washington and gets sworn in, a member of his freshman class comes up to him and asks: "How did you get elected?" Murphy explains the con, and his fellow freshman exclaims, "Fucking brilliant!" Regrettably, even though "The Distinguished Gentleman" is a parody, it's also a dead-on portrayal of our political system. Douggie was simply following the script.

Douggie and his brother Tom used the SRLC to hit it big with the party faithful; each hosted huge and lavish cocktail parties. Given his repetitive, unoriginal message, Douggie appropriately chose Parrot Jungle—now called Jungle Island—a combination zoo and convention center on MacArthur Causeway across from downtown Miam as his venue. I asked David if all of the hoopla would make a difference for the Gallaghers' political aspirations. "Everyone loves free drinks," he sarcastically replied, acknowledging that campaign workers and donors could be bought cheap. In fact, Douggie was no cheapskate. Digging generously into his substantial war chest, he used the event to begin hiring virtually all of the Young Republican leadership in the state, sometimes for as much as $7,000 per month. In principle, they were purchased to spread the word about his emerging candidacy by distributing brochures, stickers, lawn signs and other paraphernalia. They would also help him get out the vote come primary day. And they would later serve the useful purpose of clapping at debates and other public events, particularly when Douggie said something politically stupid, as he did when he got the bright idea to urge the "internationalization of Jerusalem" before an audience of Christian evangelicals and Jews. Douggie may have been out of his political league, and money would have to be his great equalizer.

At the SRLC, however, the Gallaghers were not the only show. Senator George Allen of Virginia, who was heading the Republican senators' campaign committee, was hosting a luncheon for all of the Florida Senate candidates. As I walked into the luncheon with David and one of my volunteers, the senator was standing at the entrance greeting the passersby with his attractive wife. "Senator, how are you?" I asked as I held out my hand. Allen had always been friendly to me, but this time he was not. With a tense stare, he grudgingly put out his hand. Realizing that he was being impolite, his wife intervened and asked me warmly, "Aren't you the Larry Klayman from Judicial Watch? It's nice to meet you." I was impressed and gratified by her Southern charm and hospitality, but knew that something was afoot.

We took our seats at one of the front tables, near the dais where Allen was sitting. Following the benediction and the meal, the senator got up and did a presentation on the party's chances for picking up more seats in the U.S. Senate. He stressed that Florida was crucial to meeting this goal. Projected onto a screen behind the podium was a chart containing the photographs of all of the Florida Senate candidates. While I was faced in the opposite direction of the chart, I listened intently as Allen ticked off the names of the candidates one by one. Of course, he started with Mel, whom he had unofficially endorsed despite party rules to the contrary. Allen singled him out with special praise. Then came Bill, and then Douggie, without much mention of their "virtues." But he failed to mention my name. I wheeled around to see if at least my photograph was being projected on the screen. Nada. No reference was made to my candidacy at all.

This was not the first time that I was snubbed by the National Republican Senatorial Committee. David had told me months earlier that its website listed all of the Florida Senate candidates, except me. Was this because I had filed ethics complaints against its leadership while at Judicial Watch when it was caught, shortly after September 11, selling national security briefings to donors for campaign contributions? Or because the Republican Senate leaders resented my incessant criticism on the stump of their gutless and corrupt rule of the chamber and their abandonment of conservative principles in general? Or was it because they feared my becoming one of them and did not want to give my candidacy any political oxygen? I thought, and still do, that it was a combination of all of the above. In any event, Senator Allen's favoritism and pettiness was par for the course and a major reason why I wanted to take my Trojan horse inside the corrupt and pathetic Capitol Hill compound.

I learned a lot at the SRLC event and left with a better appreciation of the political games that we faced as we approached the backstretch of the campaign. What I did not realize then was that the games would soon turn vicious.

By late April, I was still holding my own in the horse race despite the affirmative action push being applied by the Washington Republican elite for Mel, Bill's continued name recognition and Douggie's money. Bill was still leading the pack in the polls with about 20% of the projected vote, with Mel in second at about 14%. I was polling about 6 to 8%, slightly ahead of

Johnnie Byrd, and Douggie brought up the rear with about 2%. All of us were crisscrossing the state, shaking as many hands and meeting and speaking to as many people as possible. At each debate or public forum where the candidates spoke, Mel, Bill and Douggie would always give their standard speech, without variation. But there was one part of Douggie's diatribe that got under David's skin, and he asked me to deal with it at a donor forum in Palm Beach.

I had previously observed that Douggie's toothy grin made him look like Robert Kennedy. Apparently, the resemblance was not lost on Pinsky either: His candidate would end each speech with the line, "If not we, then who?"—a reference to the need for public service to preserve our nation's great democracy. What Douggie failed to say, however, was that he had stolen the line from Bobby Kennedy. David urged me to call him on the carpet for this plagiarism.

I thought of a polite way to do so, without looking heavy-handed. After all, Douggie's speeches were so uninspiring and dull, why dignify them? So I simply made reference to the quote as belonging to Robert Kennedy, and urged, in front of the audience, that Douggie, as a Republican, should honor the oratory of Ronald Reagan, not that of the late ultraliberal senator from New York. For good measure, having had enough of Douggie's attempt to morph into me, I good-naturedly congratulated him on adopting nearly all of my positions. As I went after Douggie, I glanced at his reaction out of the corner of my eye. He was red and visibly shaken. His Kennedy-like smile had given way to his rodent grin. I knew that I had struck a nerve.

24

THE MIAMI HERALD: UNFAIR, UNBALANCED

Not long afterward, the phone rang in my Miami office around 4:30 in the afternoon. Sandy answered. A Marc Caputo was on the phone. I had a bad feeling, but I didn't know why. I asked Sandy to find out what he wanted. Stating that he was not Mike Caputo, the former press secretary Roger had hired, he identified himself as being from *The Miami Herald*. With the reference to Mike Caputo, I knew that this was not a friendly call. I picked up the phone and heard a whiny and insipid voice. "Larry, I'm not to be confused with Mike Caputo. My name is Marc Caputo and I work for *The Miami Herald*," he said. "What's this about Fabrizio, your pollster, suing you? I want your comments and I'm on deadline."

Tony Fabrizio was one of Roger's Dirty Dozen. Without my authorization, Roger had hired the well-known Republican pollster to conduct a survey during the weeks leading up to my announcement on September 23, 2003. In the survey, Fabrizio asked questions about the concerns of likely voters, a routine polling technique, and their opinion about Judicial Watch and me. From the responses, he concluded that I had an excellent chance of winning the Republican Senate nomination.

But long after I showed Roger and the others the door, a decision that personally had cost me a lot of money, Fabrizio insisted that the campaign pay him $60,000 for his work. This was the fee he claimed to have arranged with Roger. It was eight times the market price for that type of survey, calling into question what kind of deal Roger and his cronies had worked out for themselves. So I tried to negotiate a settlement for a lower amount.

Fabrizio was represented by Mitchell Berger, a sleazy Democrat lawyer and fund-raiser I had investigated at Judicial Watch during the Chinagate scandal.

Berger also was the subject of a related independent counsel probe into an alleged money-laundering scam that involved a Wisconsin Native- American tribe and Clinton administration Interior Secretary Bruce Babbitt. Fabrizio had probably gotten to know Berger, who headed a Fort Lauderdale law firm, through Roger.

In short, Berger was a high-rolling, prominent Democrat, a fund-raiser, lobbyist and political hatchet man, and I was uneasy about negotiating anything, much less speaking to him. He was wary of me, too, and would always have his young associate, Joey, on the phone, whenever we spoke, undoubtedly to make a record of the conversation. During our first talk about his client, Fabrizio, I joked with him about his role in Chinagate, just to put him on the defensive and show him that I had not forgotten. From the silence at the other end of the line, it was clear that Berger hated my guts.

Two days earlier, when I thought that Fabrizio and I had reached a deal, I had gotten a call from the Associated Press, which informed me that he had filed suit. I was surprised, but hardly shocked. The AP reporter, a decent fellow, asked me for a comment and I told him that the matter was just an ordinary commercial disagreement. He correctly published my comment and the abbreviated story that hit the wire that night was no big deal, politically or otherwise.

But Caputo's call was different. His attitude was belligerent, and he said that it would be in my best interest to comment further, but did not say why, only that he had talked with some of my prior staff and landlord. We had recently vacated the old office on Miami Beach for a more economical location in downtown Miami, and were paying off—slowly—the back rent that had accumulated because of the exorbitant price that Roger had arranged through his secretary's husband, a real estate agent. Wanting to get guidance from my advisers before saying anything further to Caputo, I immediately called David, as well as another campaign consultant I had recently hired, Randy Harris from Ocala, Florida. We jointly decided that it would be best if the two of them talked to Caputo.

They did so and called me back immediately. Caputo had asked them about some suppliers to the campaign that had not been paid, and questioned our listing them as disputed debts on the quarterly FEC report. He had commented to David and Randy that this was a novel procedure, suggesting that it was really an excuse not to pay the debts. Fabrizio was included on the disputed

FEC listing. Caputo's gratuitous comment was odd, since the FEC requires that disputed debts be set forth, for full disclosure purposes.

David and Randy, not knowing where Caputo was going with his inquiry, had thought it best not to make matters worse by anticipating the story, so they simply told him, correctly, that disputed debts, by law, must be listed. They also commented, again appropriately, that the debts were run up by our campaign manager at the time without authorization, and that he and his staff had been let go. Caputo inquired no further, telling my advisers that he had to go, since he had yet to write his story for publication the next morning.

Since Caputo had added only one more wrinkle to the brief story of the Associated Press, David, Randy and I had wanted to respond narrowly to him and felt that we had handled the inquiry correctly. But I also knew that Caputo's tone suggested something more. *The Miami Herald* had been no friend during the campaign. With the exception of the story about Cuban policy after the first debate in Tallahassee, it had ignored my candidacy, despite my hometown status. So, there was nothing more to do than wait for the next morning's paper.

I had gotten into the habit, because of my back injury, to walk early in the morning around the island where I then lived in Miami. This loosened me up and allowed me to think through the day that lay ahead. I usually stopped at the Mandarin Oriental Hotel, located on the walking path, to get a cup of coffee and to take a look at the complimentary copies of the morning papers. I opened *The Miami Herald* with some trepidation. In the metro section, above the fold, was a huge story with the headline, "U.S. Senate Candidate Fails to Pay Debts." The headline was bad enough, but further on in the long story was a chart listing the debts. As I read on, I was shocked. Quoting Fabrizio, Caputo had written that I stiffed him because I was mad that he had predicted my easy defeat. That wasn't all. The other Caputo, Mike Caputo, was claiming that I had also failed to pay him, a single parent who moved to Miami with his infant child to work on my campaign. In fact, Mike Caputo, who was paid handsomely thanks to Roger, rarely showed up to work on time or for that matter much at all, and he still owed me money I had loaned to him when he claimed to be short for payments to his estranged wife, whom he was divorcing.

There were other comments from members of the Dirty Dozen, including an advance man who messed up during the announcement tour but charged my campaign dearly anyway, then walked off with my laptop computer. Cleverly, Roger refused to comment. Why should he? His misfits were doing his dirty work. The reporter, Marc Caputo, even mocked the lawsuit concerning my mother and, toward the end of his long piece, claimed to quote the old landlord, who said that I'd left cat droppings on the floor of the suite when we left. The metaphor was obvious: I had even shat on the landlord. And for added good measure, Caputo revealed yet another cat story, the one involving Angel at Dulles airport—making Angel and Munchkin the two most famous cats since Cleopatra's felines hit the world stage. That confirmed Roger's involvement, since he was the only one except Sandy who knew about the incident from me. But the thrust of Caputo's story was that the litigious former chairman and general counsel of Judicial Watch had been sued himself. His political point was that lawyers—and certainly Larry Klayman—could not be trusted. This fit nicely with the theme of Douggie's campaign—"I'm not a lawyer and that's a good thing"—and I instantly thought that he and his campaign manager Pinsky must be behind it in some way.

I immediately called David and Randy on my cell phone and asked their opinion on how to handle the *Herald*. Clearly, at a minimum, I wanted a retraction of the false and misleading statements in Caputo's article, particularly a statement that I had refused to comment. This was a blatant lie! Rather than threatening the *Herald*, at my suggestion we decided to ask for a meeting with its then-editor-in-chief, Tom Fiedler. I had first met Fiedler, whom I sized up as a prissy, self-styled intellectual, during my days at Judicial Watch. At the time he had seemed to be a decent enough fellow, however leftist his tilt. At the outset of my Senate campaign, I had met with him again to explain the rationale for my candidacy. Despite not having covered my campaign, I felt Fiedler might give us a fair hearing. So rather than threatening a libel suit, I decided to use diplomacy first.

I called his office to arrange for a meeting, but it took three weeks to get one, despite the urgency with which I conveyed the request. In fact, it is likely that a meeting would have never occurred had it not been for the intervention of the *Herald's* publisher, Alberto Ibarguen, a Cuban American whose secretary I contacted when Fiedler did not respond to my oral and written requests.

In the interim, David, who had cultivated a number of friends in the Florida media, confirmed that Douggie's campaign had peddled the story to every political reporter in the state. Only Caputo of the *Herald* bought it. The rest thought it either mundane or the political crap that it was. During this interim period, I also pondered the motivation for Fabrizio and Roger to have placed

210

the story, particularly on the same day that I thought the dispute had been settled. Like Afghan warlord mercenaries who follow the money, they must now be working for Douggie's campaign or getting paid by the campaign to do this specific dirty work.

As we waited for the meeting with Fiedler, a virtually identical story appeared in another south Florida newspaper, *The Palm Beach Post*. Lastly, the conservative website Newsmax.com, founded and run by my "friend," Christopher Ruddy, published a compilation of the *Herald* and *Post* stories, without even calling me for a comment.

During my days at Judicial Watch, I had come to know Ruddy well. He and I were like two sons to Dick Scaife, a philanthropist who had funded Ruddy's investigation into the death of Clinton's Deputy White House Counsel Vince Foster and had helped my organization financially. When I called Ruddy and informed him that the republished stories were libelous and that he should take his cannibalized story down, he at first agreed but then failed to do so for several days, despite my incessant follow-up calls. I later found out the likely reason why. Ruddy, who by then lived in Florida and ran Newsmax from its headquarters in Palm Beach, was supporting Mel, and the bad publicity obviously would not hurt his efforts to ingratiate himself with the person whom conventional wisdom predicted would be the state's next U.S. senator. At that point in the campaign, I was running only about six percentage points behind Martinez. The stories in south Florida, my home base, and in the conservative media, my life's blood, were particularly harmful to my campaign and my personal reputation.

When I finally got to meet with Fiedler, I brought along David and Randy, not only as a show of strength, but as witnesses. Having dealt with the press over a number of years, I knew that Fiedler would not readily agree to do anything. The arrogance of the media frequently holds sway, and they do the right thing unfortunately only at gunpoint. But I hoped things would be different this time, since the last thing I wanted to do as a candidate for U.S. Senate was to file suit. That would be seen as proving the point—that Larry Klayman would sue anyone, even his own mother. So I tried to keep an optimistic attitude about the meeting.

We were greeted by Fiedler's secretary, who took us to a conference room where Fiedler and his metro editor, Manny Garcia, were waiting. I greeted Fiedler warmly, but he responded by muttering hello under his breath. He looked worried.

David, Randy and I sat down on the same side of the large conference table, facing out toward Biscayne Bay. Fiedler sat at my right, at the head of the table, and Garcia was just opposite me. I began by explaining that we were there not as adversaries, but to provide facts from which the *Herald* could do its own internal investigation, reach its own conclusions, and then, if necessary, correct the errors contained in Caputo's article. Garcia quickly shot back: "If you're going to talk about Marc, then we want to get him on the phone." I had requested that the meeting not include Caputo since we did not trust him. His presence would also raise tension, I had thought. But Garcia's demand, which I rejected, immediately set the tone for the rest of the meeting.

I then proceeded to lay out the false and misleading statements, backing them up with proof, including a signed letter from the Miami Beach landlord, clearly spelling out that he had never said the things Caputo attributed to him, including the remarks about cat droppings. The landlord, Danny Dominguez, called Caputo's actions unethical, and we sat there as Fiedler read the letter, grimacing the whole time. When he finished, he looked up and injected his analysis. "I don't see anything wrong with Marc's article; you have a reputation for suing people and all my reporter is saying is that you got sued. This is fair game, you are a political candidate." I was stunned. The editor of a major newspaper was playing games and insulting my intelligence. Again restraining myself, I reemphasized that the article contained false and misleading statements that harmed my campaign and reputation. I turned to David and asked him to "enlighten" Fiedler and company on the involvement of Douggie's campaign. Their response was a cold stare.

It was quickly becoming apparent that we were accomplishing nothing at the meeting. So I ended it with a subtle but stern warning: "We came here as friends, to give the *Herald* the opportunity to correct the false and misleading statements. We hope that you will now conduct an internal investigation and do what is right and journalistically required. The next step is yours,." I politely and calmly shook both Fiedler's and his colleague's hands, and we left with an air of confidence and the strength of our convictions.

I later arranged for a meeting with the *Herald*'s publisher, Alberto Ibaurgen, who claimed to have an interest, but no action was ever taken by the paper. Instead, shortly before the primary, the *Herald* wrote that Mel was the best of the Republican primary candidates, in part because he had supported Democrats like Bob Graham in the past. In its "review" of all the candidates, *The Herald* failed even to mention me. In fact, it referred to Douggie as the only candidate from south Florida. Essentially, it was the *Herald*'s response to my meeting with Fiedler. Now, to paraphrase George W. Bush after the September 11 attacks: Caputo, Fiedler, the *Herald*, Roger, Berger and the Gallagher gang will all hear back from me at the "time and place of my choosing." As for Fabrizio, I countersued him for defamation.

In late July, 2005, almost a year and a half later, Tom Fiedler fired Jim DeFede, one of his top writers. DeFede got canned because he had tape-recorded a telephone conversation with Arthur Teele, a former Miami commissioner who was under federal and state investigation for alleged bribery and extortion, at Miami International Airport. Shortly after DeFede, who in general terms was favorably disposed to Teele's situation, taped the call, Teele entered the lobby of *The Miami Herald*, put a gun to his head and committed suicide. The *Herald*'s reporting had likely driven Teele to this final act.

Teele, a Reagan Republican and an African American, was deeply loved in Miami's black community. Obviously fearing a backlash against the *Herald*, Fiedler immediately fired DeFede for taping Teele's last conversation, despite the likely fact that the reporter was merely making a record of a suicide-in-the-making, and thus preserving evidence. DeFede had revealed the taping, which was technically wrong under Florida law, to Fiedler and offered to take a suspension and reprimand should the *Herald* deem such punishment appropriate.

Instead, justifying the firing, Fiedler wrote in an editorial on Sunday, July 31, 2005, that "when it comes to maintaining our integrity, we must be absolutists. There can be no parsing of ethics. We cannot be a little bit unethical." For Fiedler, now a visiting lecturer of Press and Public Policy at Harvard University, and the *Herald*, ethics are in the eye of the beholder, much as any whore justifies her craft. Just ask Jim DeFede, the paper's own muckraking political journalist.

25

MY BAY OF PIGS

By mid-May, the primary campaign was heading into the final stages. But because of my campaign's many distractions and tribulations, it had been tough to get traction, especially since we did not have the resources for paid publicity. To compensate, at least in part, I attempted to do as many Florida and national radio shows as possible on whatever topic was hot at any particular time, and I stepped up my fund-raising efforts by phone.

I had been pushing Sandy Cobas to find volunteers in the Cuban community to help us in the office, since we could not afford a lot of paid staff. Sandy, who had been head of Judicial Watch's Miami office, was my best friend and campaign chief of staff. I had filed lawsuits on behalf of many people in the Cuban community while I was at Judicial Watch, particularly related to the government's raid to seize Elian Gonzalez. Now, most of them offered to help only if they got paid, which we couldn't do. I thought my being the only U.S. Senate candidate advocating the immediate removal of Castro might move them, but I could only conclude that they had lost all hope that Castro would ever be booted out.

To try to generate excitement and draw the flock to my side, I decided to challenge Mel to a debate on Cuba policy. Perhaps this would rally the Cubans, I thought, even though Martinez's ancestry clearly worked in his favor. Sandy and I contacted Jaime Suchlicki, the head of the Cuban Studies Center at the University of Miami. I had gotten to know Jaime well over the years, and we liked each other. The Cuban Studies Center would be the ideal sponsor for the debate, which would perform a real service for the Cuban community since, amazingly, there had been little discussion about Cuba during the campaign. Jaime jumped at the idea. He readily admitted to being a friend of Mel, hardly

215

a surprise given the large photo of Martinez adorning his office wall, but he assured me that he could stay neutral. Sandy, Jaime and I came up with a number of dates for the event, which we hoped would be broadcast on Anglo and Hispanic television and radio.

A debate would be very timely. The Bush White House had put Mel in charge of the Cuba Commission, a sham task force contrived mainly to relieve political pressure from the Miami Cuban community, which had grown restless over the president's empty promises to remove Castro. The commission had just released its recommendations and one of them was particularly controversial. It entailed a ban on travel to Cuba for American relatives of Cuban nationals. If implemented, and the Bush administration said that it was prepared to take action, the ban would prevent relatives in the United States from traveling to Cuba to see their loved ones, except once every three years. This pointless gesture would not remove Fidel Castro, but it would impose an inhumane hardship on Cuban families. If the goal was to oust Castro and introduce democracy to the island, then the cancer itself had to be cut out. Mel was vulnerable on this and other Cuba issues and a debate would put him in his place. He had been basing his campaigning in the community only on the fact that he was Cuban.

At first, I didn't hear back from Jaime with confirmation of a date. Only after I inundated him with calls and e-mails did he respond, sheepishly admitting that Mel's people never got back to him. Their strategy was simply to campaign on Mel's heritage, believing that the Cuban community would vote for him over an activist Anglo regardless of his relative stand on the issues. I also proposed to several Spanish-language television and radio networks that they sponsor debates of all the candidates, to no avail. Mel never got back to them, and without the Cuban candidate, the networks had no interest in sponsoring a debate only among the "gringos."

Despite my unsuccessful efforts to engage Mel in a debate, I had other ideas. With the few resources we had, I had prepared a brochure in Spanish, along with bumper stickers, which we planned to distribute in the Cuban community. The brochure, which also was printed as a poster, had Castro and me facing off like prize fighters, with the slogan: "Quitemos a Castro Ahora!"—"Let's Remove Castro Now!" On the back of the brochure, I listed my Cuba policy differences with Mel, quoting his early statement to the media at the debate in Tallahassee that he did not consider Fidel to be much of a threat. We also prepared road signs for use during the final days of the campaign, when we would have some radio and television advertising.

During Sandy's and my time at Judicial Watch, Castro had attacked us personally in the media for our strong legal actions against him. *Granma*, Fidel's press organ, had even labeled me one of the top two enemies of the Cuban people, along with my client Jose Basulto, the leader of Brothers to the Rescue, a group that patrolled the skies to find and rescue rafters fleeing the island nightmare. It had lost four pilots when Castro's air force shot them down over international waters while they were on a mission. I had brought a lawsuit for Basulto, who miraculously escaped the attack.

Again, with the goal of rallying the Cubans to my side, I got the bright idea of e-mailing the brochure to *Granma* and the Cuban Interests Section in Washington, which in effect serves as the Cuban Embassy since the island has no diplomatic status in the United States. In this way, I hoped that Castro would again attack me in the media, underscoring for Cuban exiles the old adage, "The enemy of my enemy is my friend."

Unfortunately, my strategy worked better than expected. In the early morning after the e-mails were sent, I received an urgent phone message from David Johnson's fiancé, Laura Ward, who was in charge of running the campaign's Internet site. She was frantic. Posted on the front page of our website late the night before was a large Cuban flag, with a direction in Spanish to vote for Mel. When Laura checked with the Internet provider, she learned that our site had been hacked from outside the country, probably from Cuba. Castro had retaliated, all right, by effectively endorsing Mel—in the dictator's view, the lesser of two evils.

We couldn't use the incident in our advertising since we couldn't prove absolutely that Castro's minions had done the hacking, but it did find its way into a favorable article written about me in the prestigious *Diario Las Americas,* which is very much like a Latino *Wall Street Journal*. Still, I felt like a spurned child: No matter what I did or said, I couldn't get the attention, let alone the support, of Miami's Cuban community. It told me that most of the people I had tried to help were no longer that serious about removing Castro, since they had lost hope after more than 40 years of broken promises by politicians, even by their own Miami-based Cuban-American leaders. It was enough for them that Mel was Cuban, and they would surely vote for him in droves on election day. Despite my deep affection for the Cuban community, I would be less than honest if I did not admit to feeling abandoned and even betrayed, left on the beaches of Florida politics by a community I had given so much to. This felt like my Bay of Pigs.

Instead, I would have to rely on the conservative religious community if I were to have any chance of winning. Indeed, this was the principal reason why I had hired Randy Harris. Randy not only lived in Ocala, the buckle of Florida's bible belt, but he had previously worked for the Christian Coalition and he was county chairman of the Republican Party of Marion County. For many reasons, Judicial Watch and I were well-liked in this central Florida community. Shortly after I announced my candidacy, Randy offered his help. I eventually took him up on it.

I even thought about moving our campaign headquarters to Ocala. From a base in central Florida, we could rally support in the Christian and religious communities. But for reasons I did not realize then, Randy never devoted the necessary time or moved quickly enough in the community to shore up support. We parted ways as friends. Randy is a good, decent person who probably would have played a significant role if he could have. After the primary, I learned that he was battling thyroid cancer, an illness he bravely kept to himself.

If my campaign were struggling in the conservative Christian community, Mel's was not. With Ralph Reed's help, Mel was busy recasting himself as a religious conservative, despite the ambivalence toward pro-life issues he had demonstrated in a debate months earlier. To pull off this last-minute conversion, Ralph gathered up all of the conservative religious leaders and promised them the world if Mel were elected. Mel got endorsements from the National Right to Life Foundation and other groups. But he was still trailing Bill McCollum in the polls and, with the clock ticking, stronger medicine was needed. To erase Bill's lead, Ralph and Mel set out to show religious conservatives that Bill could not be trusted on social issues; after all, he had previously backed hate crimes legislation, a favorite issue on the gay agenda, and stem-cell research, anathema to pro-lifers. Initially, Mel's campaign against Bill was conducted quietly, but it would later break out into the open just days before the election at a pivotal televised debate. Meanwhile, I was under the gun from Douggie. With his attacks on me, the disinterest of the Cuban community and Mel's miraculous conversion to born-again Christianity sucking the air out of my base of support, I was sinking fast in the polls—from a high of 8% to 2%—with just a short time before primary day.

I wasn't without support among prominent religious conservatives. A few, like Paul Weyrich, stepped forward and proudly endorsed my candidacy. But some real heavyweights, with national followings that could have made a difference, played a little fast and loose with their sincerity. Early on, after I announced my candidacy, Jerry Falwell, Mr. Moral Majority, privately said he'd support me, but I couldn't even get him on the phone when his public endorsement would have helped. I asked James Dobson of Focus on the Family for his support, too. He was sympathetic but said he never endorsed candidates in primaries. Later on, I learned that he did support primary candidates—when the spirit moved him.

With what I thought to be my advantage as a public speaker, as well as my television presence, the only thing that could boost my candidacy, I believed, were the upcoming statewide televised debates. I was excluded from the first of these because my numbers in what I regarded as a suspect poll did not meet the prescribed threshold. However, I would participate in the second and last televised debate, sponsored by PBS in Tampa. It was the best debate of the election season, because it would be aired on multiple occasions the weekend before the primary on August 31, 2004. This was my last chance, I thought. I would have to outperform my opponents, and do so in convincing fashion.

The PBS debate opened on my terms. I had drawn to go first and was asked about my positions on issues such as abortion, judges and stem cell research. These questions were a chip shot for me, and I used the occasion to point out how the "MGM Brothers"—I had sandwiched Gallagher between the M&M Brothers—would talk a good game, but not deliver for conservatives. But by the time the questions reached Bill, the battle began in earnest—McCollum vs. Martinez. Pulling a flyer out of the inside pocket of his suit, Bill revealed that Mel had been sending it around the state, and that it contained "despicable" attacks accusing him of being pro-homosexual and weak on pro-life issues. Bill called Mel unfit for office, turning a bright red in front of the television cameras. It was the press highlight of the debate and drowned out the rest. Despite this, I was able to re-connect with the crowd during my closing when I stressed that "Senator Klayman would never allow Hillary Clinton to become president." The staffs of all of the candidates sitting in the television audience erupted in applause.

Bill captured the headlines at the debate, but his campaign was in serious trouble. As I suggested to him in private on several occasions, Mel was destined to overtake him with a vengeance at the end. Not only were Mel's attacks against him working, but Mel's organization, which was President Bush's as well, would be able to road test its machinery and get out the vote for Mel during the primary. In effect, it would be a dry run for President Bush leading up to the general election on November 2, 2004.

On August 31, 2004, the staff and I "celebrated" our year-long efforts, watching the primary returns in a Cuban restaurant on Calle Ocho in Little Havana. As I downed screwdrivers and ate paella, my predictions were coming true. Despite a lead in the polls of five to ten percentage points in the last days before the primary, Bill was being blown out by the Martinez organization's prowess at getting out the vote. When it was over, Bill lost to Mel by more than 15 percentage points, a huge swing in so short a period of time. The president had gotten his wish: a nominee for the U.S. Senate who, while he stood for little other than undying loyalty to the administration, would certainly help him during the general election in the Hispanic community. The Cubans had voted for Mel overwhelmingly, apparently trading their dream of a "Cuba Libre" for something more pragmatic—a senator from the island with an Hispanic last name.

By then I was prepared for the outcome and took it in stride, however disgusted I became once again with politics.

On September 1, the morning after the primary, I flew up to New York for the Republican National Convention. I wasn't afraid to show my face. To the contrary: By all accounts, I had acquitted myself well in the party. Realizing months earlier that my candidacy was a long shot, especially given the president's support for Martinez, I had made a special effort to keep my campaign positive. My presence at the convention, particularly among the Florida delegates, would help cement the foundation I had hoped to build for the future.

Indeed, at the convention I was complimented profusely. Carole Jean Jordan, the party's elected chairman in Florida, made a special point of getting me delegate tickets for the convention floor, and I was treated like royalty. But what really took me by surprise was Mel's attitude toward me at a post-convention party put on by the Republican Party of Florida. In one of the ballrooms in the Hilton Hotel on Sixth Avenue, where the Florida delegation was staying, Mel made a special point of introducing me before he spoke, praising my campaign and me. This was very gracious, I thought at the time. To show my appreciation, I walked over to Mel afterward and offered my support during the upcoming general election. Mel responded favorably and we parted ways that evening on friendly terms.

Following the convention, I phoned and e-mailed Mel on several occasions, again offering a formal endorsement and support. Neither he nor Carole Jean ever took me up on my offer. From their viewpoint, that probably was wise. The liberal press in Florida had turned on Mel, following his apparent conversion to conservative orthodoxy, and he had to tack to the left, where he probably felt more comfortable anyway. Being seen with true, rock-ribbed conservatives was no longer part of his program. Instead, Rudy Giuliani, a pro-choice liberal Republican whose leadership after 9/11 had established him as a national figure, was called upon to campaign with Mel during the closing days. It dawned on me then that the attention I had received at the convention from Mel and Carole Jean probably was intended to hold me at bay more than anything else.

Mel went on to win the general election, just barely. His half-point margin of victory over liberal lightweight Betty Castor fell a full four points short of the president's winning margin. In fact, it was Bush who pulled Mel across the finish line, not vice versa. But the White House had brought their man home, and now Mel would be expected to perform on cue for the president in the Senate. This was not my idea of what being a senator was all about.

Predictably, on August 7, 2009, a full 17 months before his term was to end, Mel quit as U.S. Senator from Florida, confirming that his heart was never in the post, but that he was simply serving as a Latino shill for W. and his henchman, Karl Rove, for vote getting purposes.

Bill McCollum ran for attorney general of Florida two years later and, against a hapless opponent, won his first state-wide office. The same year, Charlie Crist, a moderate-to-liberal Republican, succeeded Jeb Bush as governor of Florida.

In the spring of 2009, both Crist and McCollum declared that they would run for the U.S. Senate and the Florida governorship respectively, in 2010. The National Republican Senatorial committee immediately endorsed Crist, and the new Florida Republican party chairman immediately endorsed both contenders, attempting to eliminate all competition and trying "to put the fix" into the election for establishment candidates, as had occurred in my campaign. It is amazing, given the disastrous results of the 2008 election, that the Republican party refuses to turn over a new leaf. As the French say, "The more things change, the more things remain the same."

——26——

LIVE OR MAKE DIE

During the fall of 2004, following my U.S. Senate race, I reentered private legal practice to continue my work as an advocate on cases that could make a difference and to remain active politically.

At that time, and through the early spring of 2005, the Terri Schiavo controversy represented just such a case. The story was huge—and compelling. Here was a young woman who, during a period of marital strife, had collapsed and fallen into a severely debilitated state and whose husband, seven years after her collapse, had conveniently "revealed" her alleged secret desire to die—while he was living and siring children with another woman.

The Terri Schiavo case also was tearing apart the body politic of the nation as courts kept upholding the wishes of the husband, Michael Schiavo, to remove her feeding tube and essentially starve her to death. Who were the courts to judge, based on the hearsay "evidence" of Michael Schiavo, what Terri would have wanted, or the satisfaction and comfort she derived daily from being with her loved ones at bedside? Indeed, following the tragedy of September 11 three years earlier, it was the first real story that had the force to overshadow the continuing terrorist threat.

It was no wonder that the situation touched the passions of the country. According to many recognized medical experts, Terri was *not* in a persistent vegetative state. For those who believed that parents should be able to care for their sick children without interference by the courts, much less an estranged husband, Terri's case became not only a crusade for the reform of the family law system, but also a testament to pro-life issues. On the other side of the political spectrum, many liberals and feminists took a special interest in having Terri put to death because, as I analyzed it, allowing her to live might set a bad legal precedent for the pro-choice agenda.

223

But from my vantage point, I saw the Schindler family going through anguish and despair that surpassed even the emotional trauma visited upon me years earlier when I had tried to save my grandmother. I identified with Bob and Mary Schindler and their efforts to rescue their daughter from judicially assisted murder. Everything that was wrong with the political and legal systems seemed to be wrapped up in this ongoing tragedy in the making.

Not surprisingly, then, I jumped at the chance to help the Schindler family when asked to do so in late March 2005. By that time, virtually all appeals had been exhausted and, on March 18, Terri's feeding tubes had been removed for the third time. According to medical experts, the young woman, then 41 years old, had only two weeks to live, at a maximum.

My role, given the failure of the court and political systems to stop the barbaric and morally reprehensible act of starving an innocent woman to death, was to lobby Governor Jeb Bush of Florida to himself save Terri's life.

I had known Jeb for some time. While his father, George Sr., was president, Amando Candina, a high-rolling Cuban and Republican real estate agency owner, installed Jeb as president of his firm, Candina Real Estate, for obvious reasons. When I returned to Miami in 1994, after Jeb had lost his first race for governor, I went to visit him and offered my help in promoting international trade in Miami. During our conversation I mentioned that I was looking for office space, and Jeb quickly offered his firm's services. Now that he was governor, I wanted to remind him of his legal responsibilities.

Under the Florida Constitution, Article I, the governor has a duty to protect the lives of Floridians. My friend, Alan Keyes, the highly intelligent and articulate African-American conservative and one-time presidential candidate, and I thought Jeb should step in and perform his legal duty. The Florida Supreme Court had failed to do so—in effect, the moral equivalent of refusing to prevent a lynching in front of the Capitol Building in Tallahassee. Under such circumstances, the governor, as head of the executive branch of the state and co-equal to the legislature and the state Supreme Court, has the duty and ability to act on his own to preserve a life. Governor Bush would be bound to obey the Florida Constitution by stepping in to prevent that hypothetical lynching, Alan and I reasoned. So, too, would he have to act in the real-world case of Terri Schiavo.

Within hours of the removal of Terri's feeding tubes, Alan and I flew to Tallahassee to present legal analysis to the governor in the hope of moving him to action. As we entered the Capitol Building that day, where the governor's office is also situated, we could see hordes of supporters praying for Terri's life. They had come from all over America to do what they could. Many had severe disabilities themselves; one had even been comatose for years before awakening and ultimately being rehabilitated to lead a normal life. I was touched, and their warmth toward us made me feel that surely we must be doing God's work.

Alan and I had hoped to meet with the governor; instead, we were shunted off to his general counsel and chief of staff as Jeb remained closeted inside his office, supposedly dealing with the crisis. Rather than make any real effort to listen to our legal analysis, the governor's functionaries simply and abruptly gave us short shrift, informing Alan and me that the governor would not step in because "he could not go against the courts." It was apparent to us that Jeb wanted to have it both ways. He professed his support for the Schindler family and took baby steps in announcing that the Department of Children and Families would be investigating new allegations of abuse by the husband, Michael Schiavo. But he was also exiting stage left, undoubtedly to avoid appearing too pro-life, lest he ever decide to run for president of the United States. In effect, if he appeared to be taking steps to save Terri's life but really did nothing of substance, he could please both sides of the debate. *C'est la politique*, if not vintage Bush family values. (Indeed, while professing his strong support for life issues, W. has always tried to play it both ways with his mother, Barbara, and wife, Laura, making it known from time to time that they are pro-choice.)

Under the circumstances, our only real recourse was to pump up the decibel level and blanket the airwaves, explaining the governor's duty to act and trying to shame him into doing so. Having exhausted the press corps in Tallahassee, I flew on to Pinellas Park, a suburb of Tampa, where Terri was being starved to death in a hospice managed and directed by Michael Schiavo's lawyer, George Felos—Florida's angel-of-death version of Dr. Jack Kevorkian. That it was Easter Sunday, March 27, 2005, was not lost on me.

I had the taxi drop me off a short distance away from the hospice and walked toward the building. The atmosphere seemed thick, and not just because it was an extremely hot day, even by Florida standards. Thousands of onlookers and well-wishers, many carrying signs and praying, were crowded along the street leading to the hospice entrance as television trucks and satellite dishes jockeyed for space. There was a surreal quality about it: On the day that Jesus had ascended to heaven, the scene was reminiscent of the Elian Gonzalez spectacle, the surrealism of the film "Apocalypse Now," and a religious vigil preceding an execution, all rolled into one.

My role that day was to participate in a press conference, called by the Schindler family, to report on the status of our last-ditch legal effort and other attempts to save Terri. Leading the press conference, which was to be held at two in the afternoon, was Randall Terri, the anti-abortion activist, founder of Operation Rescue and the Schindler family spokesman.

The conference took place right in front of the entry to the hospice, and it began on time. After a brief update of events, Randall handed the microphone to me. Jammed in front of me were television cameras of all of the major and non-major networks, as well as members of the print press. I did not realize at the time that, except for the Terri Schiavo nightmare, it was a very slow news day—the press conference was being carried live by most of the big cable news networks.

I began by explaining the law that required Governor Bush to act. Then, speaking straight from the heart, I gave my own testimony about my beloved grandmother and what it meant to me to watch her die without court intervention. I ended the speech, which lasted about 10 minutes, by asking the rhetorical question: If the governor does not exercise his constitutional duty to save the life of a fellow Floridian, then isn't it time for him to return to his prior calling, which was a Miami commercial real estate agent?

I had not intended to get this personal with Jeb, but the flow of my testimony and the emotion of the moment led me to it. The more I spoke, the more incensed I got. Sure enough, the crack about his true calling was the sound bite most of the media carried. Over the next full-day news cycle, it was broadcast nearly every half hour on the cable networks. Coupled with my and others' appearances on a variety of television shows being transmitted live from the hospice area, the media lobbying on our part was intense.

But even the bad publicity did not force Jeb Bush to act. Instead, he stood by disingenuously—and conveniently—whining about how he could not, in his opinion, intervene in the legal court process.

I had intended to return to Miami following the first day's efforts to continue to use the media to push Jeb to act. But as I spent more and more time with the Schindler family, I could not leave. There was a strong and in some ways metaphysical need to being with them to the end. The plight of the parents,

Bob and Mary, and Terri's brother and sister, Bobby and Suzanne—all of them emotionally spent, yet holding up with grace and dignity—more than touched me. This was a family that had no political agenda, only a desire to be with and love Terri to the very end. I had bonded with them; and in a real sense, they became my family, too. We spent much time talking in the building that a convenience-store owner had made available to them right across from the entrance to the hospice. The television reporters who were camped outside joked with me about wearing the same suit each day, as I had come to Pinellas Park with only the clothes on my back that Easter Sunday when I arrived.

At this point, Terri's time was running out. On Easter, it had been nine days since the feeding tube had been ordered removed by the court. Nearly all hope was lost. Then, as I was standing next to Bob Schindler in the adjacent building, he received a call on his cell phone. It was the Reverend Jesse Jackson! Since Jackson was speaking loudly, I could hear both ends of the conversation. Jackson told Bob that he wanted to come and help, but that if he did, the Schindlers would have to tell the press that it was their idea, not his. He represented the liberal end of the political spectrum, and liberals in general endorsed putting Terri to death, in part to preserve their pro-choice agenda. But that was precisely why Jackson's intervention could be a great asset for us, even if his principal motive, as some suspected, was to generate publicity for himself. The Schindlers readily accepted and "invited" Jackson. What did they have to lose? He came at once, arriving the next morning on his own chartered jet. His limousine pulled up to the hospice, and with great fanfare, given the media crush, he joined us in the adjacent building. He was, as ever, cordial and charming to one and all.

But as I introduced myself, he looked at me a little askance. Perhaps he remembered an incident from my days as chairman of Judicial Watch. A conservative black activist, the Reverend Jesse Lee Peterson, had billed himself as the anti-Jesse Jackson in his efforts to promote self-help in the black community, rather than lobbying for government handouts. That rankled Jesse Jackson. At a town hall meeting that both preachers attended, Peterson said that Jackson and his son had threatened, pushed and shoved him. I filed suit on Peterson's behalf, alleging assault. The case was still proceeding in Los Angeles Superior Court, Jackson unsuccessfully having moved to dismiss it.

Asking for a cup of coffee, Jackson sat on a couch as the Schindler family, their clergy and other inner-circle supporters, including me, looked on.

The scene was a little reminiscent of a football huddle, with Jackson as the quarterback.

He began by talking about his belief in God and how perhaps Terri's death, like Martin Luther King Jr.'s, would serve a useful purpose and thus was meant to be. He referred to how King's father could never really come to grips with his son's death, save for how it had served the civil rights movement. In Terri's case, the purpose he cited was a reform of the family law system, and I could not disagree. But despite his consoling tone, and his apparent heartfelt kindness toward the Schindler family, he seemed to be writing Terri off, without any strong personal intervention. I found that offensive, particularly in light of his planned media blitz, so I interjected as politely as I could. "We also need your help to try to head off this legally assisted killing," I told him—and to his credit, Jackson agreed and asked what he could do.

Janet Folger, a Florida lawyer and activist who also had been helping the Schindler family, proposed that a last-ditch effort be made before the Florida legislature to save Terri's life. Weeks earlier, an attempt to have the legislature step in had failed. The votes of some key black representatives and senators could have made the difference, so we asked Jackson to travel to Tallahassee that day to lobby them. Following a number of media interviews outside the building, Jackson complied, but his efforts failed; the black legislators, it turned out, resented his intervention. Indeed, all that Jackson accomplished in Tallahassee was to get a meeting with Jeb Bush, who came out of hiding to greet the civil rights activist.

What hypocrisy! The governor would not meet with Alan Keyes and me, two conservative Republicans, but he could find time to rub shoulders with Jesse Jackson, a liberal Democrat, who could attract the media spotlight in a big way.

In short, despite Jackson's efforts, everything remained at the status quo and the death watch at the hospice continued, with nothing left to do but wait for the end. The governor still refused to do anything. Except for granting a few television interviews in which he lamely claimed that he was powerless to act, he went into hiding. In the final days, Mary Schindler appealed to Michael Schiavo for mercy, and the family attempted to be at Terri's side at all times, despite Michael's interference. We all continued to pray for her salvation.

The end came on March 31, 2005. To characterize the mood of that moment as profoundly sad would be, if anything, an understatement. At a memorial service held in a Catholic church in Pinellas Park, thousands of Terri's supporters and all of those who tried to help her sat and worshipped and hoped that, as Jesse Jackson had forecast, there would be a brighter day.

The final chapter has not been written for the Terri Schiavo story. In my opinion, it will go down as one of the darker periods in American history, but good will indeed come of it. All interests have been forced to concede that the family law system is broken and needs to be fixed. And most people can now understand that the courts serving it are intellectually flawed, if not bankrupt. Following Terri's death, many other people have contacted me and sought my legal assistance with similar tales of horror in the family law and judicial system, and I have represented some of them since.

27

JUDICIAL WATCH:
A NEAR-DEATH EXPERIENCE

I returned to the law firm of Walter & Haverfield in Cleveland in the late spring of 2005 deeply troubled. The death of Terri Schiavo and the way it had occurred by legal fiat left me shaken in my faith about this country. It seemed to me that the principles of freedom and justice on which our founding fathers had built the Constitution were being ignored and perverted by rampant self-interest, unchecked desire for personal and corporate enrichment and mean-spirited discourse.

During my tenure in Cleveland, I underwent a period of self-examination and rediscovery that continues to this day. And I became as determined as ever to find a way to make an impact that would better our judicial and political system. Each of the three lawsuits I brought then was a reflection of that process—at once consistent with my professional history and what I hope is an evolving maturity of mind on the complex issues our country faces.

The case against the government on behalf of Scott Tooley, involving illegal wiretaps of American citizens during the Bush administration, for example, plays out across a much-altered national-security landscape, but it is ahead at full steam. The issue is whether federal officials, up to and including the president of the United States, can use their tremendous powers to break laws they have pledged to uphold, even when they do so believing such actions are necessary to protect American citizens. That's what the National Security Agency wiretapping controversy is all about: whether the government can wiretap an American citizen without a warrant.

Some of my conservative friends who defended President Bush and this program really ought to look themselves in the mirror and think again. Under a law enacted in 1978, federal agents can wiretap without a warrant for 72 hours

231

before they are required to seek legal authorization from a secret court—the Federal Intelligence Surveillance Court—that has denied such requests only on very rare occasions. If the law needed updating to reflect the realities of modern terrorism, the administration could have asked Congress for new legislation. Instead, it chose to ignore Congress and pursue this NSA program on its own. Talk about an imperial presidency: What happened there was worse than what Richard Nixon did. By deed if not word, the Bush people sent a clear signal that they did not believe the people have the right to any information that might make for more transparent government.

In a way, my representation of Alice Alyse in her lawsuit against the people behind the "Movin' Out" stage musical was the flip side of the Tooley case—this time, legal proceedings against vast private-sector power. The people and institutions who committed unfair and allegedly illegal action against Alice include Liberty Mutual Insurance Co., the choreographer Twyla Tharp and members of the Nederlander family—a major force in the American theater. Taking them on was very much like taking on powerful political figures: the same establishment, different branch. I simply could not stomach when those in power use their considerable resources to abuse innocent ordinary people. Because of my friendship with Alice and empathy for her plight, as well as my direct involvement in her attempts to settle the case, I became a witness to her extreme emotional distress and pain caused by the attempts to destroy her professional life and personal well-being. Legally it's difficult to be both lawyer and witness, and I had to turn the representation over to other counsel. Nonetheless, I firmly believe in this case, which is ongoing.

My attempted legal rescue of Judicial Watch, of course, is a labor of love compounded by outrage over how this national treasure has been tarnished by the people charged with its safekeeping. Their disparagement of me and their violations of our severance agreement are the least of it. They also have debased what made Judicial Watch special—"a true independent counsel" for the people, beholden to no party or special interest. Tom Fitton, the president I mistakenly hired, isn't a lawyer, and had passed himself off as a graduate of George Washington University when in fact he had no undergraduate college degree at the time. He has never done what he promised to do, which was to hire a distinguished lawyer to serve as chairman and general counsel—the positions I held in the organization. He has closed Judicial Watch branch offices and diminished its profile as a watchdog on the public's behalf. Judicial Watch, in short, is a pale shadow of its former self.

Worst of all, I maintain that Fitton defrauded as many as 3,687 Judicial Watch donors, including Louise Benson, a large financial sponsor who also is a plaintiff in the lawsuit. Back in November 2002, when I was still chairman and general counsel of Judicial Watch, we started a campaign to raise money from our supporters. The donations were not intended for our general fund. In fact, we intended to use the money solely to buy the building housing our headquarters office—and said precisely that in our fund-raising appeal to potential donors. Benson, for one, pledged $50,000 based on our representation that the money would be used as we said it would.

But after I left Judicial Watch, "Fitton caused Judicial Watch to cease actively pursuing the purchase of the building," as we maintain in the lawsuit, "but concealed that fact from Benson and other similarly situated donors and supporters of Judicial Watch." Indeed, a Judicial Watch newsletter published in February 2005 led Benson and other donors to believe the organization was still undertaking the building's purchase and was keeping donations in a separate, interest-bearing account. That was an outright lie, we insist in the lawsuit. Instead, at Fitton's direction, Judicial Watch commingled with operating funds or misused in other ways the $1.4 million raised from donors. And the fraud continued: Another Judicial Watch newsletter, this one dated September 2005, falsely states that "this fund has been one of the most comprehensive fund-raising efforts in Judicial Watch history. The long-term goal of the fund is to provide financial stability for Judicial Watch through the ownership of an office building." There's more, but you get the general idea.

I put everything into Judicial Watch, conceived in my mind as a truly independent attorney general. The choice of a motto for this unofficial Justice Department was not made casually: "Because no one is above the law" was the entire point. What Fitton and his crowd have done makes a mockery of what we pledged. Judicial Watch is now an organization as corrupt and morally bankrupt as the targets of its legal challenges during its heyday. That irony just breaks my heart.

But it's crucial to be clear about one thing: My crusade to regain control of Judicial Watch is no exercise in vanity. To the contrary, I would have been happy if my baby had continued to grow from its birth and early years into a productive and responsible adulthood.

It's been said in the new age of terrorism that the U.S. Constitution is not a suicide pact, that significantly altered circumstances require adjustments to ensure a democratic government's first duty—to do its best to protect its citizens and keep them safe.

But we compromise our fundamental rights at our own peril; if some of those rights disappear, it won't be easy to restore them when the crisis has passed. My legal career has evolved over three decades. With Judicial Watch during its heyday and with my steps to rescue it, with my lawsuits on behalf of Scott Tooley, Alice Alyse and others, I have tried to fight—and continue to fight—against the abuses of big government and of large private-sector institutions.

In fact, in the post-9/11 era, when people feel an unfamiliar and troubling sense of vulnerability, the average Joe and Jane need strong and principled representation more than ever. I want to be there for them. If there is a more noble goal for a servant of the law and for me, I don't know what it is.

So in the last few years, as I've fought to retake Judicial Watch, I formed a new group and named it Freedom Watch—after the organization represented by Harry Claypool on "The West Wing." The regional directors of Judicial Watch joined me during this interim period, and our new "Dream Team" took up the cause of freedom.

28

"Humility, Humility, Humility" & the Return of the Clintons

I was at LaGuardia airport on my way back to Miami after filming an interview in Manhattan with ABC's Charles Gibson. It involved a lawsuit Freedom Watch had filed against OPEC for price fixing and artificially raising the price of gasoline. As I approached the gate, I noticed former Florida Governor Jeb Bush sitting in the waiting area. Seeing Jeb couched there like any other traveler, working on his Apple laptop, it hit me how pathetic he looked. Hunched over his computer—Jeb is at least six foot three—he looked more like a beaten honey bear than the former chief executive of my home state.

As I approached him, he looked at me and with some shock of recognition said, "Larry, how are you doing? Are you still in Miami?" "Yes," I replied, and added jokingly, "but I am also living in Los Angeles promoting films about a lawyer, not coincidentally, me, who fights for the people against a dishonest government." I then continued, somewhat sarcastically, "How are we going to save our party, Jeb?" With a sheepish grin, the brother of the fallen, if not disgraced, president, George W. Bush, surprisingly said, "Humility, humility and humility!" I took this to mean, in common terms, "My brother really fucked up and now we must endure the pain of exile."

Not much of an endorsement for his kinsman or the Republican Party, I thought. Indeed, this was one of the things I always liked about Jeb. Although he was scared of me, he always was candid when I had him one on one. And, even if he did not want to get too close to Judicial Watch and now Freedom Watch, for fear that we might someday investigate his conduct, he had respect and admiration for what we did, to the point that he will engage me on issues of national importance—so long as the discourse is between "friends." There is

235

no question in my mind that Jeb would have made a fine president, far different from his brother or father. He not only has the brains for it, but the resolve and character, the Terri Schiavo case notwithstanding. And, he has "humility" without the insipid apologetic anti-American leftist rhetoric of our new commander-in-chief, Barack Obama.

I further thought what a shame that W. had ruined the Bush name for Jeb, in all likelihood, forever. After all, what can one say about W. after his total neglect and incompetence concerning the economy, and the huge international crises he left in North Korea, Iran, Pakistan, Afghanistan and Iraq (once we leave, it will likely be another Vietnam, only worse, with Arabs killing other Arabs, as they still have little concept of democracy). Having violated every known concept of civil rights for American citizens, he created a nervous reaction to what the public came to wrongly view as "conservatism." W. did more for this country's move to socialism than Marx or Mao could have ever done, by force or otherwise. After Bush, Happy the Clown could have been elected president, and he at least would have provided some humor to the current state of domestic and international meltdown. This helps explain why an ultraleftist president like Obama has been given so much slack in the early days of his administration, while a politically moderate and equally personable Democratic president, Bill Clinton, was immediately, out of the gate, attacked and vilified for his hypocrisy and ethical transgressions.

So Jeb had it right; it was time for soul searching in the nominal political base of conservatism—the Republican Party. If Newt Gingrich, Karl Rove, Sean Hannity and Rush Limbaugh are now its leaders—"robotic Republican yes men," if not opportunists, which Roger Ailes and Fox News have been showcasing as respected "political consultants"—then the Republican Party will find itself wandering the political wilderness longer than Moses wandered the desert seeking the promised land.

The obvious being said, after a month or so of watching President Obama, postelection, bring a flock of Clinton officials into his administration, it became clear that the return of corruption was in full swing. To get elected, Obama had to cut a deal with the Clintonesque devils, and Obama himself was no saint.

To be fair, Obama inherited a difficult mess left behind by George Bush and his cronies, including the beginnings of the massive corporate bailout, and it would take a special leader to clean it up using sound conservative principles. Obama also has considerable skills as a politician and leader. He understands the new realities created by the Internet better than anyone in office, and he knows how to use the media to further his image and agenda—however socialist it may be—better than anyone since Ronald Reagan. I also am fine with Obama's selection of Sonia Sotomayor for the Supreme Court—she is not as far left as some conservatives try to paint her and I consider her a reasonably good choice. Bearing in mind some of the far-left alternatives, I consider her a reasonably good pick, and the president does get to choose his own jurists.

But, that selection has been a rare exception in a rogue's gallery of corrupt Clintonistas. First, Rahm Emanuel, the former Clinton White House official who helped cover up Clinton scandals, was named Obama's chief of staff. Later, Gregory Craig, the outside greaser lawyer of Williams & Connolly, became White House counsel. He had not only helped stave off impeachment and conviction for Bill Clinton, but also, on behalf of the ultra-left National Council of Churches, orchestrated the return of Elian Gonzalez to the hellhole of Castro's Cuba. Incredibly, Eric Holder, the former corrupt deputy attorney general in Janet Reno's Justice Department, who had had Nolanda Hill indicted for spilling the beans about the Clinton Commerce Department's illegal sale of seats on Ron Brown trade missions, was named attorney general. And Leon Panetta, the former White House chief of staff who obstructed Judicial Watch's Chinagate case by telling his staff to "slow pedal" document production (resulting in an order issued by Judge Lambreth to show cause for contempt), was put in charge of the Central Intelligence Agency. Given the fact that the CIA did its best to obstruct the Commerce Department case and the resulting Chinagate Congressional investigation, he should feel right at home. I could go on and on, but there is not enough space in this chapter to list all of the Clinton cronies who have now infested the Obama administration.

Last but not least, there is Hillary Clinton herself, now the czarina of foreign affairs and secretary of state. I don't think it was accidental that her early focus was on China—her and her husband's illegal foreign donor to Bill Clinton's reelecction bid in 1996.

Unlike George W. Bush and his band of ethically compromised Republican hacks who, feeling a kinship with the Clintons let them go free after they left office, the Democrats were not quite so docile and forgiving with the entry of the Obama-Clinton regime into the White House in early 2009. Threatening Bush officials with prosecution for war crimes resulting from illegal detentions in the fight against terrorism, the approval of torture, and other crimes against humanity, Obama's henchmen were decidedly going for the jugular. Although after a few months the Democrats' push for neutering of the Republican Party and the Bushies seemed to subside somewhat, it's still "out there," hanging over the private parts of the Republican elephant like a Sword of Damocles—ready to castrate the pachyderm if it tries to get out of the rut it put itself into.

The result: Two compromised political parties—Democrat and Republican—reintroducing corruption into the body politic or lost in the wilderness of doing penance for past crimes, respectively; and a nation moving far left, with the specter of nearly total government control of our lives looming large. It was time for Freedom Watch to shift into even higher gear.

Along with my advisers, I decided to dedicate Freedom Watch to five basic objectives for the near future. We would: (1) Monitor the massive government bailout pushed through by the Obama regime to try to limit what obviously would become a "grab bag" of fraud, waste and corruption; (2) Take on the oil-producing nations to attempt to keep the price of gasoline from going through the roof during this time of economic recession, if not depression; (3) Pick up the legal fight against terrorism sponsored by nation states in the Middle East and Venezuela at a time when the Obama crowd was cozying up to these terrorist states and giving an impression of a lack of American resolve; (4) Bring about justice vis-à-vis the Clintons, who had been rehabilitated and reinstalled in power thanks to the disastrous mess the Republicans had left behind and the people's understandable overreaction, and (5) Pursue reform in our legal and judicial systems, and change the way we choose and police lawyers and judges.

So in the early months of the Obama administration, Freedom Watch, through its national headquarters in Washington, D.C., its western regional office in Beverly Hills, California, and its southern regional and Latin American office in Miami, Florida, sprang into action. We filed a bevy of Freedom of Information Act requests and lawsuits to do for the conservative, libertarian and nonpartisan American people what our government could not and would not do—police itself in the name of individual freedom.

We began by filing FOIA document requests with the Department of the Treasury, Federal Reserve Board and other federal agencies to obtain documents showing how taxpayer dollars were being doled out in a supposed effort to stimulate the economy. What did we find? Sure enough, nearly every left-leaning public and nonpublic interest group attempting to pick the pockets of the government's "bailout," with pet projects ranging from funding abortions, to anti-gun legislation and regulations, to support for foreign leftist dictatorships. Only a handful of nonleftist groups were seeking government money; either a shocking display of principle or a further example of incompetence from the right.

But this was not enough! With revelations that the insurance giant AIG was doling out huge million-dollar bonuses to the same corporate executives who had ponied up phony derivatives to the investing public, sending the economy into a massive tailspin, Freedom Watch dared to tread where the government would not. We brought a huge federal class action suit in Los Angeles (later transferred to New York City) to recoup these monies for AIG's shareholders, which now included average Americans, thanks to the Obama administration buying shares in the company on our behalf. We also sued to remove the directors of AIG and make them personally pay back the losses to the company for their felonious actions. The case was widely reported on television and radio, and set a precedent for yet more shareholder suits against AIG and other Wall Street crooks. Once again, the government had failed to act, so "We the People" had to step into the breach, in effect waging a second American revolution to protect our hard-earned dollars.

Meanwhile, the Obama White House was holding nearly nightly parties with entertainers like Stevie Wonder. In fact, the partying became so frequent that Freedom Watch also requested from the General Services Administration and Government Accounting Office expense reports on the money spent on these events, as we saw this as inappropriate behavior during these troubled times. It was as if the Beverly Hillbillies had just discovered the perks of office at 1600 Pennsylvania Avenue; only these interlopers were not hillbillies, but hard-core leftists bent on elevating government control to Orwellian proportions by pushing their social, economic and international agenda off on the American people while they were too distracted and hurting to pay attention. How ironic that the portraits of Washington, Adams, Jefferson and other early presidents, which hang in the White House quarters, must bear witness to the Obama crowd celebrating the dismantling of the very individual freedoms that the founders had embodied in the Declaration of Independence, Constitution and Bill of Rights.

During the presidential campaign, then-candidate Obama played down his Muslim roots for obvious reasons, given his close association with Black

Muslim leaders in Chicago, including the anti-Semite leader of the Nation of Islam, Louis Farrakhan. But upon his election to the presidency, Obama showed his true colors. He dressed down newly elected conservative Israeli Prime Minister Benjamin Netanyahu, demanding a Palestinian state on the West Bank right in the heart of the Jewish nation, an end to settlements on the West Bank, and called for "even-handedness" in U.S. relations among Jews, Christians and Islamic interests in the Middle East generally. Later, in a speech given at Cairo University, Obama extolled his own Muslim heritage, praised his association with Black Muslim leaders in the United States and made a point of crediting Arabic culture for the rise of European civilization.

In the days that followed, even leftist Jews who had supported Obama during the campaign and voted for him in the election expressed bewilderment, if not dismay, over the betrayal by the one they had "loved." I conducted an informal poll among my Jewish friends in Los Angeles and found a sense of consternation. They understood the implications of Obama's highly personal embrace of the Arab world and its meaning for Israel, peace and freedom—not only in the Middle East, but throughout the world.

Israel is the only democracy in the Middle East. Indeed, it is telling that a revolutionary uprising by the people, such that we have seen in Iran in recent months, has never taken place in an Arab country. Iranians are Persians, not Arabs, and ironically, Obama's push for greater relations with Iran makes sense given their desire to be free. But Arabs in the Middle East do not know, nor do they want, freedom; what they do want is the destruction of the Jewish state, no matter how they try to sugarcoat their current "intentions" to get a foothold on the West Bank. And, if they cannot achieve this, they will go on fighting turf wars among themselves for control of the Middle East. However weak his support for Iranian freedom fighters, Obama's got Iran right, but his Muslim roots have blinded him to the importance of security for Israel and the West at the expense of his Arab friends.

To counter Obama's tilt toward the Palestinian cause at the expense of Israel, and to offset the emergence of Al Jazeera as a news source in the United States, Freedom Watch and its public relations expert, Tom Madden of TransMedia Group, are joint venturing to form an "Israel News Network" or "INN." The Israelis, never adept at promoting themselves in the media, being too involved with fighting terrorism and securing their nation, need all the help they can get in the face of an American president who woke up after the election only to find himself "wearing a sheet and riding a camel," to put it most diplomatically.

But what gives Arab and other terrorist states like Hugo Chavez's Venezuela the power to destabilize and threaten Israeli and world security interests? The answer is oil revenues. So Freedom Watch's lawsuit against OPEC for price fixing takes on greater importance under Obama, as artificial limits on production drive oil prices higher and retard American and world economic recovery. Prolonged high oil prices can destroy American and western economies forever.

Incredibly, after I traveled to Vienna, Austria, in late 2008 to serve our antitrust complaint against OPEC on oil ministers meeting at the organization's headquarters there, an American federal court in Miami ruled that Austrian law effectively prevented us from suing OPEC. The absurd claim that our case negated service of process in Austria, which gives Austrian law precedence over American law, is being appealed all the way to the U.S. Supreme Court. So what made the Democrat-nominated federal judge, Alan Gold, who is Jewish, take such a stand? The likely answer is that he did not want to put President Obama or any president in a difficult position by having the courts enforce the anticompetition laws which our government in Washington never has had the guts to do with the oil-producing states. And why would this be? Because our politicians have been in bed with the key players in the oil-producing world. Why else would W. have flown the Saudi royal family out of the country immediately after September 11, despite 17 of the 19 terrorists being of Saudi origin? And why else would President Obama, shortly after he took office, warmly embrace Hugo Chavez at the Summit of the Americas in Trinidad Tobago? The stark reality is that our politicians, through surrogates like the Carlyle Group, an investment house for the elite in America, do business with these oil producers, reaping large profits above and under the table. Michael Moore's leftist film "Fahrenheit 911," which exposed Bush Sr.'s involvement and profiteering with the Carlyle Group, was not entirely wrong, much of its material having been taken from investigations and reports I had ordered while chairman of Judicial Watch.

So Freedom Watch's case against OPEC is hugely important to preserve our freedom from control by Arab and Venezuelan terrorist states that seek to choke off our economy's recovery by keeping the price of oil high.

Furthermore, the large oil revenues are used by terrorist dictators like Hugo Chavez to advance terrorism and other crimes against humanity. Chavez, the president of one of the biggest petroleum-producing states and the owner of Citgo, is a self-proclaimed communist and, in his former life, an avowed terrorist, Castro style. Indeed, the oil revenues of Venezuela have sustained Cuba since it was abandoned by Russia following the fall of the Soviet Union.

Chavez oppresses his own people if they criticize him and does not hesitate to use torture as a means of exerting his control. He has seized foreign holdings in Venezuela contrary to international law and thrown political adversaries in prison to silence them. Even worse, he uses the oil revenues of Citgo to support Middle Eastern terrorism through groups like Hamas and Hezbollah, both serious threats to Israel and the Western alliance. While at Judicial Watch, I sued Chavez for giving over $1 million to the Taliban leading up to September 11.

But the situation has grown even worse in the years since I left Judicial Watch. Chavez has consolidated his power in Venezuela and is now a major player, using the oil revenues to foment communism, big time, in South and Latin America. Brazil, Bolivia, Argentina, Paraguay and other Latin states are now run by socialists, if not by ultraleftist Communists.

So in the spring of 2009, in the days just preceding the Summit of the Americas, when it was apparent that President Obama was going to embrace Hugo Chavez at the international gathering of American leaders, I decided to take a stand. Thanks to a distinguished exiled Venezuelan journalist, Ricardo Guanipa, who had been threatened with death for revealing Chavez's involvement in the Colombian drug trade and with FARC, the Colombian Marxist-Leninist terrorists, Freedom Watch was able to file suit under the Alien Tort Claims Act. This law allows for civil prosecution for human rights violations and terrorist acts in U.S. courts. To be inclusive, the case was filed as a class action, to unite all of Chavez's victims, in the federal court in Miami, where many Venezuelan exiles live. It is likely that the lawsuit, once it goes to trial, will have a favorable jury to judge the crimes of Chavez and the Venezuelan government ministers we joined as defendants along with him.

After we filed suit, the American and foreign press gave it large play. But before boarding his presidential plane on a visit to Bolivia, Chavez commented to the media that he found Freedom Watch's case "funny." Then he joked that at least he would have to come to Miami for trial with his "friends," meaning the Venezuelan government officials and Citgo also sued by Freedom Watch for human rights violations.

Chavez's comment about Freedom Watch and me personally reminded me of when then-President Clinton had exploded before the press after I blocked his purchase of a house in Chappaqua, New York. It was a mistake on Clinton's part and just as big a mistake by Chavez to take me on personally, as these attacks underscore and ironically further legitimize the importance of our endeavors in the eyes of ordinary citizens. I have no doubt that a Miami jury will find Chavez liable for human rights violations. By so doing, we will not only collect large damages for the victims of his barbarous oppression, but also set an example for President Obama and the world that there is only one way to deal with terrorists like Chavez—not through appeasement and weakness, but strength. They must be held accountable for their insidious efforts to stifle freedom for their own people and the world! Freedom Watch may not have the reach of a government, but we can be "The Mouse that Roared." In that movie, Peter Sellers plays the head of a small, imaginary European nation state that brings other countries to their knees after obtaining an atomic weapon by accident. Our nuclear weapon is persistence, the support of the American people and other like-minded individuals around the globe, and the rule of law.

But Hugo Chavez, Arab terrorist states and others notwithstanding, there remains unfinished business over the abuse of human rights during the George W. Bush years. Freedom Watch and I do not advocate emasculating our national security by closing Guantanamo, eliminating all forms of torture, and sending terrorists to American prisons on the continent, which will make American cities the targets for retaliation by al Qaeda and other terrorists. But the illegal wiretapping of American citizens (not terrorists) by Bush and Cheney was simply not acceptable. To combat this we had brought a case on behalf of a Christian conservative Republican, Scott Tooley, who had been wiretapped, without a warrant, after he stressed the importance of checking baggage for terrorist bombs on Southwest Airlines.

I have discussed the essence of the case in the previous chapter already. When we filed it several years ago in the federal court in Washington, D.C., it was randomly assigned to Judge Colleen Kollar-Kotelly, not coincidentally the chief judge of the so-called national security court, or "FISA court." At the time, Freedom Watch and I believed this to be a "good draw," as President Bush and Vice President Cheney had circumvented the FISA court in not obtaining warrants to conduct wiretapping of American citizens, warrants that would help insure that the wiretaps were not used for illegal purposes.

But Judge Kollar-Kotelly, ironically a Clinton appointee, cut a deal on behalf of the FISA court that henceforth Bush and Cheney would abide by the law, and likely as a quid pro quo with the Republican administration, dismissed the case under the contrived and procedurally illegal premise that press reports showed our client could not have been wiretapped. However, the federal appeals court recently reversed the decision, ruling that Judge Kollar-Kotelly could not look to press reports to make this decision, but that discovery in the case would have to proceed to get to the facts.

While President Obama and his Clinton cronies may want to hang Bush and Cheney from the nearest tree to keep the Republican Party from regaining its footing while the administration attempts to push through its socialist agenda, our case is not designed for retribution. We want to preserve the civil liberties of Americans who are subjected to the heavy-handedness of the government. For if Scott Tooley, or even an Arab American, can be wiretapped illegally, no one's freedoms are safe, and we will be living in an Orwellian world of total government control and intimidation.

There is also the unfinished business of bringing about justice concerning the Clintons. We will not turn our backs on their rampant crimes, which were never prosecuted thanks to the politically attuned Ken Starr and later, Robert Ray—independent counsels who were either too inept or, for political reasons, acted that way so as not to offend the establishment in Washington, D.C. should they later seek nomination to a higher post. We will send a message to any administration that it is not above the law and will be held accountable.

In this regard, the Filegate case I instituted in 1996 continues to this day. Hillary Clinton, through her legal counsel David Kendall, recently asked Judge Lamberth to dismiss her from the case—for the third time—despite the fact that it would be unprecedented to not have the principal defendant put under oath. Yet on July 16, 2009, the judge ruled that Hillary Clinton could not be deposed because she is now a cabinet secretary. This decision flies in the face of the Supreme Court verdict in Jones v. Clinton that even a sitting president could be put under oath. Indeed, Lamberth had previously held Department of Interior Secretary Gail Norton in contempt for refusing to testify in the Indian trust fund case. But in this matter, he has acted more like a groundhog afraid of the long shadow of the Clintons. On the other hand, his opinion is crafted in a way that makes reversal by the appellate court likely. Perhaps he was simply "passing the buck" to the higher court, having been criticized in the past for being too anti-Clinton.

Then there is the case of Jared Stern, a freelance journalist who wrote unflattering articles about Bill and Hillary Clinton for the famous Page Six of the *New York Post*, the most widely read gossip column in the world. Jared was set up by Ron Burkle, a Clinton friend and major financial backer, who likes to pal around with Bill picking up underage and highly attractive girls for fun. Burkle is a billionaire supermarket tycoon from Los Angeles and the owner of Yucaipa, an investment company. Not coincidentally, he paid Bill Clinton over $15 million per year after the president's term in office ended, just to travel the world glad-handing for his company.

Jared was invited to Burkle's apartment in Manhattan and offered $250,000 to write positive stories about the Clintons and Burkle, obviously as a prelude to Hillary's presidential bid in 2008. Regrettably, Jared listened, not knowing that the meeting was being secretly videotaped by Clinton private investigators, who also worked for Burkle. Jared made the mistake of not saying no, but he never said yes either. The videotapes were then edited by the Burkle henchmen and given to the *New York Daily News*, the *Post's* fierce competitor. The *Daily News* published front page stories that Jared had tried to blackmail and extort money from Burkle, obviously in an attempt to harm the *Post* and put its owner, Rupert Murdoch of Newscorp and its subsidiary, the Republican-leaning Fox News, on the defensive. The publicity, along with a likely push from then-Senator Hillary Clinton, caused the federal prosecutor in New York City to open a criminal grand jury investigation.

Panicking, the *Post* then laid off Jared, claiming that he did not meet the "high ethical standards" of Page Six—a joke given the column's dicey public image. Jared's career was ruined, and he retired to upstate New York to await the results of the grand jury probe.

Indeed, the Clinton-Burkle hit on Jared and the *Post* accomplished its purpose. Faster than a whore removing her panties, Murdoch caved in to the Clintons, hired Howard Wolfson, Hillary's public relations guru, and began throwing fund-raisers and donating money to her presidential campaign himself.

When Jared was eventually exonerated of any wrongdoing by the federal prosecutor, the *Post* refused to take him back as its premier freelance journalist. It was at this point that Jared contacted me. He wanted to file a civil lawsuit against Burkle, the Clintons and the *Daily News* for ruining his life by defaming him. He also wanted his job back at the *Post*. While he had used Joe Tacopina, a renowned criminal defense lawyer during the federal prosecutor's probe, Jared knew that I was the only lawyer who would take on the Clintons and Burkle, given their history for vindictive retribution.

So Freedom Watch crafted a complaint and filed it in the lower court in New York City—curiously called the New York Supreme Court—where the offenses had occurred. The case was assigned to Judge Walter Tolub, a card-carrying member of the New York Liberal Party and an ultraleftist jurist. Shortly after the complaint was served, my old adversary David Kendall of Williams & Connolly entered the case on behalf of Bill and Hillary Clinton. Since I am not a member of the New York legal bar, I had applied to enter the case *pro hac vice*, meaning that I could appear as counsel for Jared on this particular case. Unsurprisingly, as he had tried before, but failed, Kendall opposed my entry on grounds that I had tangled with other judges in the past, notably Judge Chin and Judge Keller.

Our local counsel, Michael Dowd, who has significant litigation experience in controversial cases such as this—he recently won an $11 million judgment against the Catholic Church over pedophilia committed by its New York priests—advised me not to worry about the motion, as in New York, a client has an absolute right to choose his lawyer. And, I have been a member of three states' bars in absolute good standing for over 30 years, with no reprimands or censures of any kind.

Nevertheless, without holding any hearing, Judge Tolub issued an order barring me from representing Jared, quoting from the orders of Chin and Keller and a few other judges I had taken on. The order, which is under appeal, was an obvious attempt to sandbag me in order to protect the Clintons. Indeed, it is quite likely that the judge, thinking that Senator Clinton would win the Democratic nomination for president and then the presidency, thought he might get some bigger job as a result. Later, the politics of the decision became apparent when the judge accidentally came upon an associate of Mike Dowd in the filing clerk's office and, New York-style, foolishly shot his mouth off in front of him, opining that "it's too bad this case was not filed after the election." An ethics judicial grievance is pending against Judge Tolub before New York legal authorities, and it is likely that he will be sanctioned for his misconduct.

After denying my entry into the case, Judge Tolub, right before the Democratic presidential primary in New York, dismissed Jared's case, claiming that he had not pled appropriate causes of action. The dismissal was as politically contrived as Judge Kollar-Kotelly's in the wiretapping case, and it is likely to be reversed on appeal. Freedom Watch, Jared and I will not rest until justice is done not only to Burkle, the Clintons and the *Daily News*, but also to this corrupt judge.

But now that Jared's case was on appeal, at least I could focus on Murdoch and Newscorp, which had put Jared on leave of absence pending the results of the federal investigation, but then refused to hire him back when exonerated. At the time, the excuse that Jared did not meet the "high ethical standards" of Page Six was an actionable defamatory statement in and of itself, and we had grounds to sue if this proved necessary.

I therefore contacted the owner of Newscorp, Murdoch himself, to try to negotiate an amicable settlement. I was then told to contact Genie Gavenchak, the head lawyer of the company and Murdoch's "right-hand man." When I explained to Genie that Jared would file suit if he were not taken back or properly compensated, she dug in her heals and refused to budge, disparaging Jared in the process.

Around this time, Jared put me in contact with another former reporter of Page Six, Ian Spiegelman, who offered to prepare a sworn statement on behalf of my client. In his affidavit, Spiegelman detailed how the editor, the infamous Richard Johnson, and others of the *Post's* Page Six, had taken bribes and other perks, such as gaining free admission to strip clubs. In return, they wrote complimentary stories, and killed or modified stories under the heavy hand of Murdoch himself when he deemed a piece contrary to his business interests in China and elsewhere.

Thus, Jared certainly met the "high ethical standards" of the *Post*; indeed, his standards were higher than the other miscreants on the staff. Spiegelman attested to this fact as well, stating that Jared was the most honest reporter on Page Six. Therefore there was no legal reason to deny Jared his return and the statement was actionable defamation.

Of particular interest to me was that, according to Spiegelman's testimony, Murdoch had killed books scheduled to be published by HarperCollins, the tycoon's venerable book publishing company. One of these books was an exposé written by the former governor of Hong Kong, Chris Patten, who had excoriated the Communist Chinese leadership. Murdoch, married to a woman from China, and having significant business interests in China, did not want to offend his benefactors and killed Patten's book.

The book you are reading was scheduled to be published by HarperCollins, and it too had been put in the tank after Murdoch fired Judith Regan over the O.J. Simpson memoir *If I Did It*. Although supported by Murdoch at the time—indeed, it looked like a big moneymaker and Murdoch, like all businessmen, loves money—it became the subject of intense public controversy and Murdoch disclaimed ownership. Instead, he had his henchmen blame Judith's firing on anti-Semitic comments she supposedly made to the managing editor of HarperCollins, a death sentence in Hollywood, where Judith had relocated to promote her books for feature films. Judith, whom I consider a friend, by the way, is no anti-Semite, and she reportedly later collected $8 million in a settlement with Murdoch to make the point.

So Spiegelman's sworn statement rang true to me, as I was the victim of the same Murdoch despotism—in all likelihood because *Whores* was critical of his propaganda-ridden Fox News network, and I was about to sue him over Jared Stern. I also learned that Fox News had a major case at the time before Judge Denny Chin, the Chinese-American judge I had locked horns with over John Huang, who had recommended him to the bench. My criticism of Chin in the book could, if noticed in a Murdoch-owned HarperCollins publication, damage Fox's chances before this compromised jurist. As all of the elements of Murdoch's and Newscorp's slimy deceit were coming into clear focus for me, I had more than a mere professional stake in Jared's fight against Murdoch as a matter of justice for all.

Nevertheless, I had a client to represent, so I gave Genie Gavenchak the affidavit of Spiegelman and told her we would use it if Jared had to file suit, although we were still seeking a settlement for his claims.

We did not hear back from Murdoch's lawyer. But the next day, the sleazy mogul had large portions of the affidavit published on Page Six of the *Post* in an obvious attempt to blunt the fallout if we did file suit. This self-flagellation, it turns out, was the "brilliant" idea of Howard Rubenstein of the William Morris Public Relations agency. Rubenstein, a PR icon, felt it was better to do a Clinton-style mea culpa than to let Freedom Watch and me publicize the likely civil complaint we would have to file.

The publication of the Spiegelman affidavit caused a firestorm in the media, and Rubenstein, it appeared to all, was finally "over the hill," his age probably blurring his formerly keen PR prowess. ABC's "Nightline" and a host of other television, radio and print media ran stories about the sleaziness of Newscorp. For nearly a year this negative publicity stalled Murdoch's hoped-for acquisition of *The Wall Street Journal*, whose then-owners were already nervous that Murdoch would turn a great newspaper into another version of Fox News and the *Post*.

Ultimately, Freedom Watch and Jared had no choice but to sue Murdoch and Newscorp, and the case remains pending, awaiting discovery and trial. Ironically, it was assigned to another ultraleftist jurist in New York City, U.S. District Judge Deborah Batts, known as an African-American leader in the transgender/gay/lesbian civil rights community. While I don't harbor any ill feelings toward gay judges, I have often found that they assume I am prejudiced against them because I am a Christian and a conservative, and rule accordingly. Sure enough, even before I applied for entry into the case, the Clinton-appointed judge, who had been mentioned as a candidate for the U.S. Supreme Court by Obama, excluded me from the case, citing the Tolub order, which is on appeal. A judicial grievance has been filed against this latest hack jurist, as well as an appeal.

The moral to the story: Keep punching until justice is done. Justice does not come easily in our courts, particularly when political issues are involved. I have always been known as a fighter, and the Jared Stern case will be no exception. Freedom Watch and I will continue to fight whores wherever we find them. The nation cannot afford more!

In the early summer of 2009, as the Islamic Republic of Iran engaged in what anyone with a brain could see was a fraudulent presidential election, leading to a new Iranian revolution, this time for freedom, I was contacted by Nasrin Mohammadi, a young, articulate and beautiful Iranian woman whose brother, Akbar (meaning "great" in Farsi), was murdered in an Iranian prison for protesting against the radical regime.

At a very young age, Akbar had become a legend in the Iranian freedom movement, a Persian Nelson Mandela so to speak. Having been imprisoned for his freedom advocacy by the supreme leader, he spent nine years in confinement before being brutally murdered by the government.

Nasrin, a loving sister and activist herself, now lives in Los Angeles, where the total population of exiled Iranians exeeds one million, giving rise to the name "Tehrangeles." Hard-working and self-made people much like the Miami Cubans, only with a more determined edge, Nasrin and her band of followers asked me to file a lawsuit against the ruling despots in Iran for torture, terrorism and other human rights violations of international law under the Alien Tort Claims Act, the same vehicle I had used to sue another dictator, Hugo Chavez of Venezuela.

I gladly did so, not only because I identify with the plight of the Iranian people, but because Nasrin and her uncle, also an activist, touched my heart. Representative of Iranians yearning to be free in their country and around the world, they explained to me how freedom for Iran could be the cornerstone for eventual peace in the Middle East, and justice for Akbar. Filed as a class action in federal court in Washington, D.C., this case will have far-reaching implications, and seeks justice not only by claiming large damages in excess of ten trillion dollars for all of the Iranians who have been brutally tortured, maimed and killed, but by setting an example for the Obama administration, which has abdicated the moral high ground by putting its head in the sand regarding these atrocities. Obama apparently thinks that by coddling these dictators he can, à la Jimmy Carter, negotiate a "nuclear solution". But appeasement is not the answer; and Iranian and all free people must now act on their own. To this end, Freedom Watch also intends to file a criminal complaint against the Iranian leadership in Spain, before the same judge who indicted, convicted and extradicted former President Pinochet of Chile, for crimes against humanity. Let justice be done and let freedom ring!

But one organization can only do so much; and the need for judicial reform is as evident to me as ever. Without a major overhaul of the system, we are doomed to endure political appointees to the bench who occupy their positions for life, meting out injustice at every turn.

— EPILOGUE —

SOME CONSTRUCTIVE (AND RADICAL) SOLUTIONS

The founding fathers, icons like John Adams, Thomas Jefferson and Benjamin Franklin, were certainly enlightened. I believe that God instilled in them the wisdom to craft a great nation. But they were not God, they were not infallible and they made some mistakes.

One of their biggest errors, underscored by my years leading up to and during my time at Judicial Watch, was the decision to give federal judges lifetime tenure. At the time the Constitution was written, it may have seemed like a good idea to insulate the judiciary from the outside influences of political society. But in practice over nearly 220 years, it has not worked out that way. Because prospective judges are sent up for presidential nomination by politicians, usually the U.S. senator or senators from the president's party in each state, what the nation gets are politicians in black robes. And these politicians in robes know, instinctively, how to rule to feather the nest of their benefactors—the politicians who hold the keys to a higher court appointment or other perks. In many ways, they are more political than the politicians themselves.

In the average commercial case or other reasonably routine legal procedure, it may not matter as much that judges arrive on the federal bench through political patronage rather than on the basis of their intellectual acumen and independence. But when a politically sensitive case comes before them, as I saw many times at Judicial Watch and now at Freedom Watch, they have more than a tendency to cut and run and not want to make the hard decisions to enforce the law against the establishment. And who gets hurt in the process? The little guy, who frequently cannot afford even to take an appeal to a higher court, and the nation as a whole.

Over the decades, lifetime tenure as a practical matter has meant that federal judges can only be impeached and removed if they are caught red-handed accepting a bribe. It's happened only once in recent years, when U.S. District Court Judge Alcee Hastings of Miami was removed by Congress, only to run for office later and become a congressman himself. The Justice Department and the FBI are loath to investigate federal judges for corruption, since they depend on them for convictions and other matters. As a result, the corruption on the federal bench goes unaddressed, particularly since ethics committees currently set up to review judicial misconduct are staffed by fellow judges, who are not inclined to rule against their peers. That was one of the reasons I established Judicial Watch, to monitor and take action against judges who did not fulfill their oath of office. But Judicial Watch, even if restored to its original focus, and Freedom Watch, are not enough.

Judges are our most important public servants. They protect us from the tyranny of the other two branches of government and are an integral part of the checks and balances put in place by our founding fathers. They were to be free from the influences of politics. To insure that we get the best and the brightest, and that they are held accountable for their misdeeds, I propose a five-part plan to reform the federal judiciary:

ONE: Federal judges should be nominated on the basis of their legal and intellectual ability, not politics. To accomplish this, merit panels, not U.S. senators, should have the power to review candidates and send them to the president. Of course, how these merit panels are constituted is crucial, and the selection process must be as free of politics as possible. They should be staffed with experienced trial and appellate lawyers, law professors and others who will decide on the best candidate on the basis of merit.

TWO: Prospective federal judges should be required to go to "judge school" before they are even eligible for nomination. In effect, judge school would be the prerequisite for serving on the federal bench. A tax lawyer generally must get a master's degree in taxation before he or she can effectively take up the trade. Judges should have to attend an accredited law school program in judicial studies, where not only the art of legal decision-making is taught, but also how to treat parties and litigants. What is important is not only that justice be done; it's also critical that the people believe that the court has been fair—in essence, the appearance of justice as well as justice itself. This obviously was not the case when I encountered judges like William Keller and Denny Chin in private practice and at Judicial Watch. Both acted like lunatics on the bench. For a justice system to survive, and for the nation to prosper, it needs judges who are not only fair, but appear fair. In this way, society can feel confident that it has recourse for the misdeeds of its countrymen and government. At the extreme, such confidence can stave off insurrection and civil war.

THREE: Federal judges should be term-limited. In my view, two terms of five years each seem appropriate. After five years, the merit panels should undertake a judicial evaluation, and, if the judge has behaved properly and been a credit to the bench, he or she can be renominated for a second term. But to leave jurists in power forever gives current federal judges the license to act as if they are above the law—a phenomenon I saw many times both before and during my days at Judicial Watch. Federal judges must know that one day they will again be held accountable by society.

FOUR: Like private lawyers, federal judges should have to obtain professional liability insurance to cover losses arising from intentionally wrong or reckless decisions. On many occasions during my years in private practice, working for the government and at Judicial Watch and now Freedom Watch, I saw judges making decisions that they knew were wrong, but since there was no accountability, they couldn't have cared less. The individual or small company caught in the crossfire of politics or other outside judicial influences, for instance, frequently cannot afford to appeal an adverse ruling, which can cost hundreds of thousands of dollars in some cases and take years to resolve. As a partial remedy, arbitration panels, which would decide on the level of compensation and other relief for victims of judicial misconduct, should be put in place and the damage awards paid for through professional liability insurance. The government can underwrite the cost of this insurance.

FIVE: Federal judges should be psychologically tested before they take the bench, and periodically after they are on the bench. Some judges, like Keller, are just plain crazy and cannot be left to their own devices. Drug and alcohol testing should also be implemented. We cannot take any chances with jurists who, in so many ways, have such a great impact on the lives of Americans.

In addition to this five-part plan, we should also seriously consider whether federal judges should be paid better. This might help eliminate the temptation to take bribes or other perks, and allow government to recruit the best and brightest to the bench. Currently, federal judges make a lot less money than do most private practitioners, a fact that also creates resentment among some on the bench toward the attorneys who appear before them. Thus, paying federal judges more may foster better relations with the private lawyers in their courtrooms, furthering the interests of justice.

My proposals, particularly with respect to term limits, would require a constitutional amendment to implement. But if we can propose to amend the Constitution for issues such as gay marriage, we certainly can consider doing so for the crucial federal judiciary. After all, it was this judiciary that has created law where none exists, establishing in some jurisdictions the right of gay marriage—an example, in my view, of the judiciary gone haywire.

As for state judges, while they are generally elected, and can be removed by the people, that system is flawed, too. Since judges must run, in effect, as political candidates to gain office, they are heavily dependent on campaign contributions from large law firms and other vested interests, and their decisions on the bench frequently reflect the fact. This process also needs serious study, with an eye on reform that would result in getting better and less-political judges.

I founded Judicial Watch and now Freedom Watch not only because of what I perceived to be injustice in our court system, but because of the corrosive effect that lining politicians' pockets had on the decision-making of government agencies in general. Obviously, when a vested interest or anyone, for that matter, makes a contribution or delivers some other perk, and the politician or government person knows who and where it came from, there is more than a tendency to return the favor. It's human nature.

I therefore propose that the idea of establishing "campaign finance banks" be studied, perfected and implemented. My idea is to allow for contributions to candidates by depositing them, anonymously, into a government-monitored banking repository that does not reveal the name of the donor. In this way, candidates could receive contributions from supporters without knowing specifically where they came from. It would satisfy First Amendment concerns that the right of political free speech, which extends to campaign contributions, not to be arbitrarily curtailed, while at the same time eliminating back-scratching by politicians, judges and others. If the donor reveals to the recipient the source of his campaign contribution, he would be subject to criminal penalties. As an analogue, consider the "insider trading" laws in the securities industry that prohibit corporate officials from revealing inside information to one or more than one investor, who can then profit from that information by buying or selling the company's stock.

Finally, my most radical, and in many ways most important, proposal is to establish an independent Justice Department, free from the political vagaries of the executive branch—that is, the White House and the various departments under its control. In effect, the Justice Department would become a fourth branch of government that would add to the checks and balances envisioned by the founding fathers. Because it would be independent, it could prosecute crimes against politicians, judges and others without concerns about the kind of political retribution that now undermines the system. As I saw many times both before and during my time at Judicial Watch, crimes went unpunished simply because the politics of prosecuting those crimes proved an unwise career choice for the functionary assigned to the case.

An independent public prosecutor at the federal level also would eliminate the need for independent counsels, such as Ken Starr and others who became the whipping boys of their political adversaries. Indeed, both Democrats and Republicans, toward the end of the Clinton administration, gleefully did away with the statute that allowed for their appointment. With an independent Justice Department, the concept of account-ability among the political, judicial and other vested interest classes could be reestablished.

The idea of an independent prosecutor is not unique. Many countries, such as Israel, have one. And in the United States, the attorneys general of many of our states are independently elected by the people and are therefore free to act on behalf of their interests. Just look at what former and now disgraced New York State Attorney General Eliot Spitzer was able to accomplish in prosecuting and reforming the securities and insurance industries, before he was caught soliciting and paying prostitutes—an ironic twist to his long career in battling crime on Wall Street.

But placing all of the prosecutorial power in the hands of a government official is not the answer either. While Spitzer did a lot with his considerable powers, he also left his post to run for governor of New York. When he announced his plans to enter the race, he turned over many of his ongoing investigations and prosecutions to federal regulators such as the Securities and Exchange Commission. Why? The obvious reason is that he no longer wanted to investigate and prosecute industries that ultimately donated heavily to his campaign for governor. And, indeed, he won the governorship hands down before he himself got caught with his hands, or perhaps other body parts, in the proverbial "cookie jar."

As a result, we need to devise a way that private interests, and even ordinary citizens can empanel grand juries to hear complaints about criminal conduct. At Judicial Watch and now at Freedom Watch, I used the civil court system to seek and obtain justice as best I could. But I do not have the powers to indict someone or some government, labor union or corporate interest for criminal acts.

Some states already allow private interests to present evidence to a sitting grand jury. This should be extended to all of the states, since state prosecutors, even Attorney General Eliot Spitzer of New York, eventually succumb to political pressures or aspirations and cease doing their jobs effectively.

I experienced much as a young and idealistic private attorney in Miami, as a prosecutor for the Justice Department, as founder, chairman and general counsel of Judicial Watch and now Freedom Watch, as a U.S. Senate candidate from Florida and, of course, as a lawyer again in private practice, over the five or so years since that eye-opening adventure in Sunshine State politics. Along the way, I learned many lessons about the lack of integrity and honesty in our legal, governmental and political establishment. While I have at times felt as if I were bullied and bloodied, I always picked myself up off the mat and never gave up. In the words of our greatest founding father, John Adams, a member of the nation's first Continental Congress, the advocate who sold the Declaration of Independence to his peers in my birthplace of Philadelphia, a Revolutionary War hero and the second president of the United States: Without ethics, morality and religion there will be no lasting liberty. In these trying times, 230 years after the country declared its independence from the British Commonwealth to set sail on its own journey of freedom, Adams' words ring even truer today.

As I've said, at Freedom Watch I continue to take high-profile cases that serve the public interest, and I am now more motivated than ever to have an even greater impact. A major effort beyond being a citizen advocate is necessary to preserve the Republic and further the cause of liberty and freedom around the world. As foretold in Isaiah, the tarnished city must be turned into the shining city. If we are all to survive, the body politic of this nation cannot remain a whore to special interests, the establishment and power elites, and its counselors and judges must be restored. Not only do the American people depend on this for their survival in these dangerous and trying times, but so too does the entire world.

INDEX

Larry Klayman, Esq., founder and former chairman of the successful non-profit foundation Judicial Watch, has dedicated his career to fighting against injustice and restoring ethics to the legal profession and government. He was born and raised in Philadelphia, graduated with honors in political science and French literature from Duke University, and later received a law degree from Emory University. He is the only lawyer ever to have obtained a court ruling that a U.S. president committed a crime, which occurred during his tenure at Judicial Watch. He became so well known that NBC's hit drama series "The West Wing" created a character inspired by him, named Harry Klaypool of Freedom Watch. In 2003, Mr. Klayman left Judicial Watch to run for the U.S. Senate. After his Senate race, he established Freedom Watch. As head of that organization, he now divides his time between Miami, Los Angeles and Washington, DC.